Brothers Gonna Work It Out

Brothers Gonna Work It Out

Sexual Politics in the
Golden Age of Rap Nationalism

Charise L. Cheney

NEW YORK UNIVERSITY PRESS
New York and London

NEW YORK UNIVERSITY PRESS
New York and London
www.nyupress.org

Library of Congress Cataloging-in-Publication Data
Cheney, Charise L.
Brothers gonna work it out : sexual politics in the
golden age of rap nationalism / Charise L. Cheney.
p. cm.
Includes bibliographical references (p.   ), discography
(p.   ), and index.
ISBN 0–8147–1612–1 (cloth : alk. paper) —
ISBN 0–8147–1613–X (pbk. : alk. paper)
1. Rap (Music)—Political aspects—United States.
2. African American men—Attitudes.   3. Masculinity—
United States.   4. Sex role—United States.   5. Black nationalism—
United States—History.   I. Title.
ML3918.R37.C54   2005
306.4'84249'08996073—dc22   2005001778

New York University Press books are printed on acid-free paper,
and their binding materials are chosen for strength and durability.

Manufactured in the United States of America

c 10 9 8 7 6 5 4 3 2 1
p 10 9 8 7 6 5 4 3 2 1

To Constance "Tootie" Mann.
No matter how high I get,
I'll still be looking up to you.

Contents

Acknowledgments

I am a product of the golden age of rap nationalism. Throughout my college years the artists featured in this book—especially Chuck D, KRS-One, Ice Cube, Paris, X-Clan, and Poor Righteous Teachers—sparked my curiosity for learning more about American history and shaped my burgeoning consciousness about the history of African America. For that, I am eternally grateful.

This project began during my senior year at Northwestern University as a series of discussions I shared with a group of brothers who loved debating, among other things, the virtues of hip-hop culture and the Nation of Islam. Much respect to Kevin Whitmore, David Muhammad, Greg Smith, and the rest of the crew for their instigation. Sterling Stuckey and Lawrence Levine were also sources of inspiration. Their body of work opened up a world of possibility for me and encouraged my research into the political discourse of rap nationalism.

Brothers Gonna Work It Out is the culmination of many conversations and much meditation. The first version of this book was honed as a dissertation at the University of Illinois at Urbana-Champaign under the mentorship of James Anderson, Vincent Wimbush, Daniel Littlefield, and Mark Leff. Thankfully, Niko Pfund at New York University Press recognized its potential and passed it along to my editor, Jennifer Hammer, who had patience and a never-ending belief in and enthusiasm for the manuscript. Financial support for further development of this project was afforded by a Ford Foundation postdoctoral fellowship, as well as by grants and release time provided through the resourcefulness of Susan Opava, dean of Research and Graduate Programs at California Polytechnic State University. It has been my great fortune to have colleagues, friends, and mentors at Cal Poly—particularly Colleen O'Neill, Yolanda Tiscareño, Debra Valencia-Laver, and Harry Hellenbrand—who, in various ways, valued and evaluated my work. I am especially appreciative of the generosity of Mark Fabionar, who, among other things, came to my rescue at the eleventh hour with a last-minute reading of the manuscript. I also need to thank Derek Sanders, aka Dante Jenkins, for keeping his post-youth professor up to date on what's hot and what's not in hip-hop culture.

This book came to life through interviews with hip-hop practitioners. I am truly thankful to those artists and activists who took time out of their busy schedules to share their ideas and experiences: Baye Adofo, principal organizer of the Black August Hip-Hop Collective and co-organizer of the first National Hip-Hop Political Convention; Ras Baraka, deputy mayor of Newark, New Jersey, and another co-organizer of the first National Hip-Hop Political Convention; Ulises Bella of Ozomatli; Chuck D of Public Enemy; Rosa Clemente, hip-hop activist extraordinaire and manager of dead prez; Fred Hampton, Jr., chairman of the Prisoners of Conscious Committee; Talib Kweli, hip-hop artist and member of the Black August Hip-Hop Collective; M-1 of dead prez and the Black August Hip-Hop Collective; Kevin Powell of HipHop Speaks; Bill Stephney, cofounder of Public Enemy and president of StepSun Music; and Wise Intelligent of Poor Righteous Teachers.

On a personal note, much love goes to my girls. Jane Rhodes and Lynn Hudson were my "secret weapons." They not only provided guidance and support, but they also showed me that there is light at the end of the seemingly never-ending tunnel. Words cannot express my love and appreciation for my sister-girls Marshailena Butler, Melina Pappademos, Joy Williamson, Stephanie Wright, and Alicia Young, who gave me undying support in graduate school and beyond, and for my partner-in-crime Alesha Doan, whose friendship is nothing short of true sisterhood.

Last, but not least, the women in my family led by example and raised me to believe that life is boundless. I'll always love my mamma, Angela Davis, who instilled in me the spirit of defiance, and my aunts Valerie Napue and Cheryl McIntosh, whose unconditional love and support never faltered. A final special thank you goes to Fannie and Vernon Whitmore, who cherish and encourage me as their "daughter."

1

From the Revolutionary War to the "Revolutionary Generation"

Some Introductory Thoughts on Rap Music, Black Nationalism, and the Golden Age of Rap Nationalism

While in Europe for a recent academic conference, I walked the streets of the Marais district in Paris in search of a restaurant an epicurean friend promised would be both trendy and tasty. However, after thirty minutes of wandering aimlessly, I found myself quickly losing affection for the "City of Love." I had spent forty-eight hours navigating a foreign terrain alone, and I was frustrated, hungry, and longing for home. Just when I was about to surrender to hopelessness, I saw something strangely familiar out of the corner of my eye. Retracing my steps, I came face to face with Bobby Seale and Kathleen Cleaver. More accurately, I was in front of a retail store and its window displayed a t-shirt that featured a reprint of a Black Panther Party flier. The flier announced a March 5, 1971, event to celebrate the birthday of party founder Huey P. Newton and to publicize the cases of political prisoners Bobby Seale, Ericka Huggins, Angela Davis, and Ruchell Magee. I was intrigued: Why would a merchandiser in Paris, France, be selling *this* t-shirt, a throwback to the American Black Power movement? Who was the intended market? It seemed so random. I decided: I need that shirt.

Unbeknownst to me, I had stumbled upon a hip-hop specialty shop, and the t-shirt served as advertisement for a local hip-hop group. When I marveled to the young white Parisian assisting me, "It just seems so strange to find a Black Panther Party t-shirt in Paris," he answered with righteous indignation, "Why? We get American pop culture here. We listen to rap music."

It was a response that seemed so wrong, and yet so right. Who could argue with the fact that the commodification of rap music has both introduced and popularized the African American freedom struggle to a generation of youth regardless of race, gender, and—in this case—nationality? As the young man in the Parisian hip-hop shop suggested, I should not underestimate the power of popular culture or its proven ability to both transcend boundaries and articulate political discontent. But at what cost? Style over substance? Revision beyond recognition? What are the (dis)advantages to having politics mediated through popular culture?

Brothers Gonna Work It Out: Sexual Politics in the Golden Age of Rap Nationalism is my attempt to answer those questions and more. This book is a study of rap, race, and resistance. Specifically, it is an examination of black neonationalist rap music. For it wasn't just rap music, but a specific type of rap music, that demonstrated the potential of hip-hop culture to be a voice for disenfranchised and disillusioned youth all over the world. What this book is not is the definitive history of hip-hop culture or a survey of the historical development of rap music. In fact, it is not even about rap music as much as it is about how rap music functioned as a vehicle for disseminating political discourse. This book is my attempt to capture the dynamics of the politics of black nationalism as it has evolved and been expressed in post–Civil Rights African America. In particular I focus on the golden age of rap nationalism, a period in rap music history marked by the release of two hip-hop classics: Public Enemy's *It Takes a Nation of Millions to Hold Us Back* in 1988, which staged the debut of the "Prophets of Rage," and Ice Cube's *Lethal Injection* in 1993, which bid adieu to the profits of rage.[1]

This book situates the political expression of a select group of rap artists within the historical tradition of black nationalist-masculinist discourse. I explore the development of rap nationalism, both outlining and explicating the politicization of rap music that occurred during the late 1980's/early 1990's. I investigate the ideological and political influences of rap nationalism and show how this popular/political culture figures as the legitimate postmodern heir to a tradition of black nationalism that reaches back to the early nineteenth century. By using lyrics as texts and interweaving personal interviews with hip-hop artists and activists, I examine the ways in which "raptivists," as I shall call them, fused music and politics, providing significance and urgency to a struggle for black empowerment and inspiring young African Americans to revolutionize their minds, move their bodies, and ultimately, as Chuck D (Carlton Riden-hour) of Public Enemy articulated, to "Bring the Noise."[2]

While that historicizing is important, this project is first and foremost an exploration of the ways in which these rap artists have embraced the tradition of race *and* gender politicking so central to the theory and practice of black nationalism in the United States. American black nationalism was, and is, configured by the social construction and material realities of race and gender. Since the early nineteenth century, U.S. black nationalism has been profoundly influenced by hegemonic masculinity. In fact, black nationalist ideologues and activists, male and female, have been engaged in a centuries-old struggle for the reclamation of black manhood; the cry for "manhood rights," or patriarchal privilege in the public and private spheres, has proven itself to be as prominent as the demand for civil rights in the oral and literary texts of black nationalists. Therefore the primary objective of this book is to explicate black nationalism as an embodied-social politics, or a politics that is determined by race and gender discourses, and to analyze the way that race/gender politicking is manifest within the Hip-Hop Nation.[3] Through an analysis of both oral and literary texts, I trace the unique—and ironic—survival and transformation of U.S. black nationalism from a literary political tradition initiated by an early-nineteenth-century urban black male petit bourgeoisie into an oral/aural tradition politicized by a late-twentieth-century urban black male "underclass."

Defining the "Prophets of Rage": The Historiography of Hip-Hop and the Politics of Rap

This book locates "raptivism" within black popular *and* political culture. Like scholar Jeffrey Louis Decker, I make the case that "[h]ip hop nationalists are the most recent in a long line of organic cultural workers who are situated between the intellectual activist and the commercialized entertainer."[4] While academic inquiries into the sites and sounds of hip-hop culture are constantly expanding, the discussion concerning rap nationalism both within hip-hop culture and in post–Civil Rights black politics has been quite limited. Most importantly, among those scholars who profess to take rap music seriously, few take it seriously enough. Many academic observers do not hold rap music and/or hip-hop culture to the same kind of analytic standards or scholarly gaze as they would, say, the literary prose of Langston Hughes or a historical study by Darlene Clark Hine, primarily because much of the literature produced on rap music is written in response to public indictments that brand hip-hop culture misogynistic or the hip-hop generation nihilistic.

Take, for example, two articles on rap music published by Henry Louis Gates in 1990. Gates's work as a literary critic is highly respected, yet his writings on rap music demonstrate a tendency among scholars to over-analyze the lyrics of rap artists in an effort to defend them from an overzealous mainstream media. Gates pled the case of rap group 2 Live Crew during the censorship controversy over the sexually explicit lyrics of their 1989 release *As Nasty As They Wanna Be*. Gates argued in a *New York Times* op-ed piece and again in the *New York Herald Tribune* that the group's antiwoman lyrics were not, in fact, misogyny, but a post-modern manifestation of signifying, an African American vernacular tradition in which word play is used to subvert dominant culture. Therefore, according to Gates, interpretation of 2 Live Crew's narratives should be contextual, not literal. There may be some validity to this argument; nonetheless, Gates's failure to directly address the issue of sexism and misogyny in 2 Live Crew's lyrics was extremely problematic.[5] And yet, Gates was not alone. Religious studies scholar Jon Michael Spencer took this line of defense a step further. Not only did Spencer fail to take a critical position on the degradation of women in rap music; he also adopted the artists' sexualized language and, at times, defiantly championed their masculinist and misogynist sexual politics. In a special issue of *Black Sacred Music: A Journal of Theomusicology*, Spencer glibly calls the sexually exploitative lyrics of notorious groups like 2 Live Crew and Niggaz With Attitude (N.W.A.) "an insurrection of subjugated sexualities." He argues that these groups play upon white men's historical fear of the black male rapist and suggests that the lyrics of 2 Live Crew provide evidence of a movement toward black male empowerment: "For oppressed black males aware of this white terror of black male sexuality, *it is gratifying to wield such power*."[6]

Like scholars Jeffrey Louis Decker (1993), Clarence Lusane (1993), Tricia Rose (1994), and Robin D. G. Kelley (1994), I look beyond uncritical, superficial, and apologist scholarship to place rap music in its proper historical context, addressing it as both a black American and a diasporic cultural and political phenomenon. At its inception, "hip-hop" was reflective of the ethos of a post–Civil Rights generation of black and Latino youth, while "rap," a musical expression of "hip-hop" culture, like DJ-ing, graffiti art, breakdancing, language, and styles of dress, is the cultural production of the hip-hop community.[7] As such, rap music is a valuable tool that enables the scholar of African American popular/political culture to observe and assess some of the beliefs, values, worldviews, and aspirations of post–Civil Rights black youth. This is especially true for the golden age of rap nationalism, a period in hip-hop history that preceded the mass commodification of rap music.

When the music industry ventured into the genre during the early 1990's, profits began to outweigh creative expression as a prime motivator for many rap artists, and rap music became less and less of a barometer of the culture of young black Americans. "Artists today record and they try to be similar for the sake of keeping their contracts," Chuck D explained. "Because if they're different and it [fails], then they're gone. Capitalism says that people are judged by their quantity instead of their quality. The business is about moving units." At the risk of romanticizing the early years (after all, the success of the Sugarhill Gang's "Rapper's Delight" introduced a commercial incentive in 1979), the ever increasing commodification of hip-hop culture occurred because major record companies—recognizing the investment potential of rap music—had the capital to contract new acts and buy out independent labels. The impact was profound. Chuck D contends that the moment corporations became involved in the production of rap music, hip-hop culture became divorced from black culture. "The nerve center of the expression of black people is now controlled in the boardroom," he asserted. "Whereas in the '80s and early '90s, what started on the street then was reflected by these corporations. After a while, that reflection turned into a dictation."[8]

It is important, therefore, not to overstate the case for the existence of seditious thinking within hip-hop culture. While the power of rap music lies in its ability to articulate the hidden transcript of black cultural expression, not all rap music is counterdiscourse. There is much within hip-hop culture in general, and rap music specifically, that supports mainstream American social, political, economic, and cultural values. The widespread endorsement of conventional gender roles, the rampant heterosexism and homophobia, and the romanticization of capitalist pursuit and conspicuous consumption are all, in fact, conservative elements of hip-hop culture. The most sensational aspects of rap music that reflect cultural hegemony, however, are sexism and misogyny; and the rap music genre most known for these social offenses is "gangsta rap."

Gangsta rap, also referred to as "reality rap" by hip-hop aficionados, exploded in popularity during the late 1980's and early 1990's with the groundbreaking West Coast group Niggaz With Attitude, its breakouts rapper Ice Cube (O'Shea Jackson) and rapper/producer Dr. Dre (Andre Young), as well as Dr. Dre's protégé Snoop Doggy Dogg (Calvin Broadus). Since its emergence, gangsta rap has gained a lot of media and scholarly attention—so much so, in fact, that many observers mistakenly assume this genre represents all rap music. Much of its critical acclaim (and censure) was due to the subject matter. As a form of creative expression, gangsta rap spotlighted the socioeconomic conditions facing many young black men in urban America—black-on-black crime, drug trafficking, police harassment and brutality—at the same time that it tapped into fantasies that culturally resonated with many young heterosexual men regardless of race: rebelliousness, irreverence, fierce aggression, and the sexual exploitation of women. Gangsta rappers claimed to represent an alternative news media (most often when criticized for their violent and misogynist lyrics): "We call ourselves underground street reporters," rationalized Ice Cube. "We just tell it how we see it, nothing more, nothing less."[9] However, what began as a playful celebration and/or dramatic critique of black life in America's inner cities quickly devolved into contemporary minstrelsy. The descriptive, anthropological narratives that characterized gangsta rap in the early years challenged misrepresentations of black men as pathological (violent, hypersexual, criminal) by providing a sociological context for understanding the psychology of some young black men living in postindustrial urban America. Once the genre became lucrative, though, the dialogic between reality and fantasy was reconfigured: gangsta rap was no longer oppositional as caricatures became the norm and stereotypes the rule. "If you ain't got control over your reality, the fantasy can be replaced," explained Chuck D, lamenting the corporate takeover of rap music. "And when you have that situation, not only does art imitate life, but life can imitate art. [Now] there is a blur between fantasy in reality."[10]

Unlike some highly noted scholars who have studied rap music as a form of social commentary—Jon Michael Spencer (1991), Michael Eric Dyson (1995), and Russell A. Potter (1995)—I contend that not all rap music can be categorized as political expression. Nor do I attempt to find a politics in rap lyrics where it clearly does not exist. I understand the impulse to legitimate an art form that is consistently under attack, particularly when those attacks convey a thinly veiled racism. However, the kind of inclusiveness exhibited in, for example, Tricia Rose's argument that the definition of "political" should be expanded to include all of hip-hop culture both dilutes rap music's significance as a mode of black cultural expression and misrepresents its origins by reducing it to a subculture that evolved exclusively as a response to white domination. Furthermore, at the same time that this positivism overestimates hip-hop's cultural politics, the argument that *all* rap music is political or subversive undermines the social authority of those artists whose lyrics explicitly and mindfully engage the issue of black liberation. To be fair, Rose made the above argument before the rampant commodification of hip-hop culture. However, it is important to resist "the populist optimism of cultural studies"[11] or the tendency to overdetermine the politics in rap music and attempt to discover an alternative, more accurate assessment of how rap music informs and influences the race, class, and gender consciousness of white, black, Latino, Asian, and Native American youth—whether the music is constructive or not.

I define hip-hop as a total culture, as opposed to a subculture, in order to fully appreciate its dynamics: its distinctions, contradictions, and diverse genres. Rap music has undergone a number of different manifestations, and what is now deemed "old school" hip-hop provides a good example of its various trends. The nascent years of hip-hop music during the mid- to late 1970's were heavily influenced by DJs like Kool Herc, Grandmaster Flash, and Afrika Bambaataa, pioneers who elevated traditional "disc-jockeying" into an art form by using two turntables (as opposed to one), and innovative techniques like cutting, mixing, and scratching to transform and transcend musical recordings. But in the 1980's, the emcee transitioned from sidekick to star as improvisational rhyming to "move the crowd" evolved and put the "rap" in rap music, and the American public was introduced to "disco rappers" like the Sugarhill Gang and the message raps of Kurtis Blow, and Grandmaster Flash and the Furious Five. There were classic emcee battles between UTFO and Roxanne Shante, LL Cool J and Kool Mo Dee, and KRS-One and MC Shan, and styles varied from those of comedic rappers like the Fat Boys, Biz Markie, and the Fresh Prince to the storytelling of Dana Dane and Slick Rick to the rock-inspired rap of Run-DMC and the Beastie Boys and to the lyrical genius of rappers like Big Daddy Kane and Kool G Rap. All of these developments in hip-hop culture predated raptivism and gangsta rap, rivalries between East Coast and West Coast artists like Notorious B.I.G. and Tupac Shakur, the mainstream invasion of "Dirty South" rap entrepreneurs Master P and the Cash Money Millionaires, and the shift in marketing female artists from androgynous (MC Lyte and Boss) to pornographic (Lil Kim, Foxy Brown, and Trina).

It is important to recognize diversity among rap artists and to acknowledge historical trends in rap music; otherwise, lines of demarcation are blurred, obscuring knowledge production about hip-hop culture as a form of artistic and commercial expression. Therefore, as an explication of the politicization of rap music during the late 1980's/early 1990's, this book only analyzes the lyrics of those artists who are deliberately political in their work. These rap artists, like Public Enemy, KRS-One (Lawrence Kris Parker) and Boogie Down Productions, X-Clan, Poor Righteous Teachers, Ice Cube, and Paris (Oscar Jackson, Jr.), explicitly critique historical and contemporary power relations and the way those relationships manifest in social, political, and economic institutions.

From "The Message" to the Messenger: The Historical Origins and Identity Politics of Rap Music

> Don't push me 'cause I'm close to the edge
> I'm trying not to lose my head
> It's like a jungle sometimes it makes me wonder
> How I keep from going under.
> —Melle Mel, "The Message"

Grandmaster Flash and the Furious Five's 1982 rap classic "The Message"—overwhelmingly referred to by artists and academics alike as one of the most important songs in hip-hop history—is a lyrical picture of the urban crisis that produced hip-hop culture during the early to mid-1970's. The song, which made Grandmaster Flash and the Furious Five one of rap music's first successful groups, is historically significant because it provides the student of urban histories a view into the kind of devastation and depression experienced by many people of color during the 1970's and '80s as an increasingly global economy moved stable employment opportunities out of American inner cities and overseas. In "The Message" rap artist Melle Mel takes the listener on a journey, narrating the story of a black male "born with no state of mind / blind to the ways of mankind" whose life chances were nevertheless shaped by the destabilizing social violence that accompanied the economic policies of the Reagan administration. Melle Mel describes the urban landscape ("the places you play and where you stay / look like one great big alley-way"), the frustration it engenders ("now you grow up in the ghetto livin' second rate / and your eyes will sing a song of deep hate"), the underground economy it inspires ("turn stick up kid / look what you done did / got sent up for an eight-year bid") and the often dangerous, sometimes deadly effects of choices born out of desperation: "Now your manhood is took and you're a name tag / Spent the next few years as an undercover fag / Being used and abused to serve like hell / Till one day you were found hung dead in a cell." Nevertheless, in the end, it is the song's hook that provided one of the most memorable—and poignant—moments in the history of rap music; it is a line that, for many, captured the spirit (or lack thereof) of life in the ghettos of late-twentieth-century America: "Don't push me 'cause I'm close to the edge / I'm trying not to lose my head / It's like a jungle sometimes it makes me wonder / How I keep from going under."

The exact origins of rap music are difficult to determine. According to old-school hip-hop artists Afrika Bambaataa, Grandmaster Flash, and Kool Herc, rap music appeared around 1974 in the streets of the South Bronx, an area of the New York City borough that was a model for postindustrial urban blight: it was plagued by poverty, unemployment and underemployment, limited affordable/substandard housing, declining social services, and an increase in violent crime. To make matters worse, the New York City government subjected the South Bronx to an urban renewal project that encouraged the out-migration of white and middle-class residents and a welfare department that encouraged the in-migration and relocation of poor blacks and Latinos.[12] The situation in the South Bronx was so desperate that in 1977 after a visit from then-president Jimmy Carter, the *New York Times* reported that the area was "as crucial to an understanding of American urban life as a visit to Auschwitz is crucial to an understanding of Nazism."[13] And yet the South Bronx was not exceptional. Urban areas across the United States were experiencing similar processes of disruption and deterioration as first stagflation and then Reaganomics ushered in an era of economic devastation in poor communities of color. "I think we could say that the Bronx, more than any part of the city and the nation, represents the total pathology of what has been happening to major cities—except that it has suffered from it on a grander scale," announced Victor Marrero, then chairman of New York's City Planning Commission.[14] The most important youth culture of the late twentieth century emerged in spite of local and federal governments' criminal neglect of poor and working-class communities during the 1970's and '80s. "This is the world hip-hop would come to 'represent,'" writes religious studies scholar Michael Eric Dyson.[15] And rap artists are its "cultural griots" he explains, "privileged persons speaking for less visible or vocal peers."[16]

Born in the school of hard knocks at the crossroads of black Atlantic migrations, rap music is a form of black and urban expression that was forged as a truly New World, or diasporic, music. Writer Russell A. Potter describes it as a "cultural recycling center," a postmodern "social heterolect"[17] that receives its power from an ability to "'turn the tables' of previous black traditions, making a future out of fragments from the archive of the past."[18] By appropriating and signifying upon beats, melodies, and any number of other recorded sounds, DJs and producers can assume the role of historians, using those sonic files as primary sources to create a historical narrative and to introduce audiences to political figures of the past and present; or, they can assume the role of cultural critic, using music as a method to construct and deconstruct historical narratives. Sampling, therefore, "is another potential guerrilla tactic," for as Potter writes, "it takes words literally out of the mouths of politicians and media personalities and remixes them in ways that highlight their absurdity."[19]

While cultural critics applaud the innovative techniques of sampling, those whose voices and/or music are subjected to sampling are not always so appreciative. Some musicians have argued that it is downright theft. Others, like Abiodun Oyewole of the pioneering spoken word ensemble the Last Poets, object to its signifying capabilities. In the *New York Times* Oyewole protested the use of his poetry by gangsta rap group N.W.A. because he felt its original meaning was distorted. "It really hurt me when N.W.A. sampled us on 'Real Niggers Don't Die,'" he stated, because "they missed the most important part." The Last Poets' "Die Nigger" is a consciousness-raising track that uses the term "nigger" in reference to passive, long-suffering African Americans. Oyewole maintains that the song's message is to "[g]et rid of the nigger, you get rid of the bitch, so that the beauty of your folks will emerge."[20] N.W.A., however, altered the denotative meaning of the song: the group sampled "Die Nigger" to punctuate their violent, largely apolitical narrative describing black-on-black crime.

Although controversial, the historiography of rap music is rich with examples and explication of the cultural forebears of a music that appropriates—or "samples"—sonic (re)sources and combines, as Cornel West articulates, "the two major organic artistic traditions in black America— black rhetoric and black music."[21] Yet while rap music clearly has roots in black American orality (folktales, preaching, signifying) and aurality (blues, soul, funk), it is also grounded in Afro-Caribbean oral/aural traditions, particularly Jamaican ska, reggae, and dancehall.[22] Many influential hip-hop artists—both DJs and lyricists—are first- or second-generation West Indian immigrants, the most highly cited being hip-hop pioneer Clive Campbell, aka DJ Kool Herc, who relocated from the concrete jungle of Kingston, Jamaica, to that of the Bronx in 1967. While Herc claims that rap music has its origins in Jamaica, the intercultural exchange between the United States and the Caribbean was more complicated than he suggests. Jamaican ska and reggae of the 1960's and '70s, two of the oral and musical forerunners of rap, were influenced by African American radio DJs as well as by the rhythm & blues music of the 1940's and '50s.[23] Therefore, the syncretization process that characterizes the ever evolving expressions of rap music is a truly pan-American phenomenon, a postmodern example of the type of cultural traffic that has been occurring in the black Atlantic since Africans were first brought to the New World. The evolution of rap music provides an opportunity to examine cross-cultural community formations and an occasion to study the political economies that influence the development of innovations in cultural production. Popular culture scholar George Lipsitz, for example, explains the cultural impact of globalization on postcolonial communities in a manner that is particularly germane for rap music: "The accelerated flow of commerce, commodities, and people across national boundaries creates new social and political realities that enable some people in colonized countries to create new opportunities and alliances."[24]

While the origins of rap music are transnational, its perspective is deliberately national and urban. Even with the global expansion of rap music, it continues to be identified with America's metropolitan areas, an imaging propagated by rap artists themselves. As hip-hop culture evolved and attained phenomenal commercial success, rap artists' legitimacy, or "authenticity," became more and more dependent on their so-called street credentials, delimiting the boundaries of "true" hip-hop culture to America's inner city. This constructed identity, a phenomenon Nelson

George labeled "ghettocentricity,"[25] is a race/class/gender identity that—unlike Molefi Asante's "Afrocentrism"—places the ghetto at the center of black life, defining itself not only against white Americans but against middle-class (and middle-aged) blacks as well.

Rap music's "ghettocentrists," or self-proclaimed "niggas,"[26] claim they bear witness to the struggles of the black urban poor, the devalued and disempowered black masses, who have been exploited by whites and abandoned and/or betrayed by bourgeois blacks. This argument—represented by Chuck D's oft-quoted and now historic statement that rap music is black America's CNN[27]—has led some observers to believe that its "potential for maintaining group solidarity . . . and evoking social change in a particular African-American experience is therefore immense."[28] Yet this community—this "ghetto"—of working-class or poor blacks is a construction in and of itself. It is an "imagined community" that is at times portrayed as hard working and virtuous, but is most often characterized as lawless, violent, and hypersexual. This imag(in)ing ironically taps into racist stereotypes at the same time that it validates the anger and frustration manifest in many rap lyrics. Nevertheless, the lure of ghettocentricity remains particularly attractive to young black men. "Male rap artists romanticize the ghetto as the fertile root of cultural identity and racial authenticity, asserting that knowledge of ghetto styles and sensibilities provides a Rorschach test of legitimate masculinity," writes Michael Eric Dyson.[29] These "ghetto styles and sensibilities" have reinscribed the cultural nationalist Afrocentric idea in rap music, signifying power in "authenticity" and posing as counterdiscourse. Ghettocentrism is not only decidedly vernacular, but it is also purposefully masculine; and in spite of itself, it is strangely bourgeois, a trait that is most evident in the race/gender politicking of rap nationalists.

Ghettocentrism may be the most recognizable and enduring identity politics of the hip-hop generation, but it is not the only one. Much like their nineteenth- and twentieth-century black nationalist forefathers, raptivists during the golden age of rap nationalism imagined a community based on both race and gender rationales. Yet few journalists, academicians, or political observers have attempted to thoroughly explicate the phenomenon of rap nationalism. They proceeded in their debates, discourse, and discussions as though the political positioning of rap artists is a given and in no need of explanation. As a hip-hop fan, I realize the transformative potential of politicized rap music; as a historian I recognize both the preservation and the revision of the black nationalist tradition in the lyrics of raptivists. Understanding and appreciating these (dis)continuities requires defining the political phenomenon of black nationalism and surveying its historical development.

Fight the Power: The Political Philosophy of Black Nationalism (Re)defined

In the song "Fire and Earth (100% Natural)," Brother J of the black neonationalist group X-Clan outlines his political standpoint by rejecting bourgeois humanism. He exposes the hypocrisy of American democracy and refutes white claims to moral superiority:

> Revolution, evolution the solution
> No amendments so burn the Constitution
> You check the authors a bunch of old Whiggers
> who strategized extinction of the pro-black niggas
> Know why?
> 'Cause I'm that nigga that they can't stand
> Teach the African how to say "Black Man"
> And I'm that nigga they can plainly see
> with the nationalist colors of the red, black, green.

According to Brother J, black nationalism is the culmination of a collectivist ethic that is both the legacy of a cultural tradition defined by Africans and a byproduct of the oppressive conditions that defined African America. It is the latter determinant that fuels his black nationalist politicking. Racial terrorism is at the center of X-Clan's historical memory and at the core of their contemporary social critique. Brother J highlights the political struggles for, social violence against, and cultural degradation of black people in the United States:

> Point blank livin'-ism is a check
> 'cause there's just some things that I'll never forget
> I remember green suits on a black mayor
> I remember nine-millimeter child-slayers
> I remember all the times that you called me an animal
> but in Milwaukee there's a cannibal.[30]

As Brother J passes the mike to his partner in rhyme Professor X (son of Brooklyn nationalist-activist Sonny Carson), the group unveils their antidote to centuries of antiblack discrimination and exploitation. Their revelation: "pro-black dedication." Their strategy: armed rebellion. "The solution, revolution / evolution, the conclusion / the trigger."

This song is a tribute to revolutionary nationalism during which the "ever-nappy crew set[s] the mood" by claiming an inalienable right to self-determination and warning those who attempt to transgress that right: "Our nation is protected by some pro-black niggas."[31] While it is tempting to presume that this lyrical composition is a manifestation of postmodern, postindustrial, post–Civil Rights black nationalism, it is important to interrogate the parameters of its political content. Is it legitimate to categorize X-Clan as black nationalists? Is "Fire and Earth" a black nationalist manifesto because of its call for racial solidarity and/or its militant demand for self-determination? Does the song's attempt to authenticate the African roots of black America qualify it as a primary source for the study of contemporary black nationalism in the United States? How do scholars determine which oral and/or literary works are representative of the American black nationalist tradition? What are the criteria for determining whether an individual or a group is black nationalist?

Any academic research on the history or significance of a political theory or practice is well advised to begin with its definition. However, as political scientist Benedict Anderson notes in his groundbreaking study *Imagined Communities: Reflections on the Origin and Spread of Nationalism* (1983), the attempt to define "nationalism" has eluded, and continues to elude, scholars and social scientists: "Nation, nationality, nationalism—all have proved notoriously difficult to define, let alone to analyze."[32] These difficulties emerge within social science scholarship because, as a political ideology, nationalism has developed in multiple locations across space and time; the shape that it assumes is dependent on the historical moment during which it surfaces, and its content is contingent on the political entities by which it is governed. The imperial nationalism of the British was different from the colonial nationalism of Anglo-Americans, for instance, both of which were different from that of African Americans—nevertheless, they are all examples of the varying (and somewhat akin) politics of nationalism. Therefore, any attempt to define "nationalism" must encompass its diverse manifestations, variations that are the products of site, subject, and circumstance.

Scholars of various disciplines have failed at this task because they tend to simplify a political concept that demands a complex, interdisciplinary reading. The study of all nationalisms requires a historical and sociological approach that is able to account for appeals to group identity based in perceived differences of race/ethnicity/culture, gender and sexuality, and class, as well as for the mutability of this politicking. Significant contributions to the study of nationalism must adopt a both/and orientation toward its seductive qualities and resist the temptation to over/under-rationalize a political standpoint with which rhetoricians are able to evoke great enthusiasm by embracing both the cerebral and the sentimental. Therefore, what follows is a brief assessment of the scholarship on U.S. black nationalism and a description of its history as an ideology and a politics.

In 1969 researcher Theodore Draper reviewed the historiography of black nationalism and concluded, "As matters stand, it is much easier to be a black nationalist than to know what black nationalism is."[33] Things have not changed a great deal since then. In fact, almost thirty years later, historian of African America William L. Van Deburg wittily remarked that trying to encapsulate American black nationalism "is a bit like trying to eat Jell-O with chopsticks."[34] Much of the controversy and confusion that characterizes the academic literature on U.S. black nationalism is a product of varying interpretations by both scholars and practitioners and can be reduced to an inability to reach a consensus around the question, What is nationalism? Yet, as previously mentioned, this variance is not exclusive to discussions of black nationalism. While scholars the world over struggle to devise a definition of nationalism that can account for its adaptations across space and time, observers of U.S. black nationalism must first deal with an obvious theoretical dilemma: African Americans who consider themselves "nationalists" are a nation within a nation or, more accurately, a nation without a nation. In this instance, the intercourse on the definition of nationalism is centered around a dispute over whether or not the configuration of the nation-state should figure prominently within—or is fundamental to—black nationalism in the United States.

A number of scholars put geopolitical concerns at the center of their definition of black nationalism. Their perspective concurs with that of Malcolm X, who in 1963 stated most directly in his "Message to the Grass Roots," "When you want a nation, that's called nationalism."[35] According to Malcolm X's estimation, without the establishment of a black nation, there would be no black liberation. "Revolution is based on land. Land is the basis of all independence. Land is the basis of freedom, justice, and equality."[36] Similarly, Wilson Jeremiah Moses, one of the premier historians of U.S. black nationalism, argues in *Classical Black Nationalism* that black nationalism is a very specific political ideology "whose goal was the creation of an autonomous black nation-state, with definite geographical boundaries—usually in Africa."[37] For those scholars who fall within this school of thought, any definition that neglects to recognize the desire for the formation of a nation-state as a fundamental principle of black nationalism risks an interpretation so broad as to lose its denotative meaning as a political ideology. "The alternative has been to conceive of a more amorphous, generalized black nationalism that would take in all black peoples everywhere," explains Theodore Draper in his 1969 book, *The Rediscovery of Black Nationalism*. "The trouble with stretching the term too far is that it takes in too much to be an effective nationalism."[38]

Indeed, there is much evidence in the oral and literary texts of black nationalists to support this point of view. The idea of nation formation—both within and outside the United States—is featured prominently in the work of many black nationalist theorists, particularly those that advocated emigration or "internal statism."[39] In fact, nineteenth-century black nationalist Martin R. Delany's emigrationist efforts and his declaration that African Americans are a "nation within a nation" are the primary reasons why many scholars refer to him as the "father of black nationalism" and consider his 1852 publication, *The Condition, Elevation, Emigration, and Destiny of the Colored People of the United States Politically Considered*, to be the inaugural black nationalist document. It is also why Delany figures so prominently in most books written on black nationalism in the United States. Other well-known black nationalists whose position on the necessity of a strong black nation-state were just as spirited and/or militant include charismatic leaders like Bishop Henry McNeal Turner, Marcus Garvey, and Elijah Muhammad, and organizations and groups like the 1854 Emigration Convention, the Exodusters movement, the African Blood Brotherhood, and the Republic of New Africa.

There is no question that emigrationism and the nation-state concept are recurrent and prominent ideas within black nationalist thought; however, limiting the scope of nationalists to those who advocate these tenets excludes or minimizes the importance of theorists and activists who were anti- or nonemigrationist yet clearly nationalist. While the impulse to put forth a definition of black nationalism that is (over)determinant is understandable, particularly when this is done in an attempt to describe and explain it as a political tradition, it is unnecessary to draw strict lines of demarcation, for they are not reflective of lived experiences. Political thought and practice are processes that are more fluid and complex than narrow readings would suggest. More and more, scholars have begun to recognize this dynamic (most likely because of recent studies revisiting the evolution and effects of the Black Power movement) and, as a result, are modernizing interpretations of black nationalism. "The complicated phenomena we struggle to name as black nationalism, cultural nationalism, and neonationalism have now been so reconfigured that our essentially nineteenth-century, or maybe even eighteenth-century, understanding of them has to be abandoned," cultural critic Paul Gilroy clarifies. "Everywhere, as a result of both internal and external pressures, the integrity of the nation-state, as the primary focus of economic, political and cultural action, has been compromised."[40] Therefore, as cultural studies scholar Wahneema Lubiano suggests, it is most efficacious to think of U.S. black nationalism as being "plural, flexible, and contested."[41]

This project falls in line with scholarship produced by Paul Gilroy (1993), Wahneema Lubiano, Sterling Stuckey (1972, 1987), William L. Van Deburg (1992, 1997), and Komozi Woodard (1999), all of which recommend that definitions of black nationalism go beyond the nation-state configuration and be comprehensive enough to include its cultural manifestations. This approach enables scholars to envision black nationalism in ways that are inclusive of various forms of expression, from those of territorial nationalists to those of cultural nationalists and from oral performances to literary stylings. It also allows researchers of black nationalism to circumvent the privileging of the elite and to recognize popular forms of political dissemination, which are equally important to our understanding of the way black nationalist ideology moves within and between black communities. Therefore, without further ado, it is necessary to provide a working definition of black nationalism. This definition—an amalgam that builds on the efforts of previous practitioners and scholars—informs my interpretation of the shape and content of black nationalist ideas, as well as the strengths and shortcomings of these ideas, and guides my assessments of scholarly works on black nationalism and its leaders.

At its most fundamental level, black nationalism is a political philosophy that promotes group self-consciousness and advocates group self-determination. "A nationalist must be obsessed with the principle of self-determination," announced Maulana (Ron) Karenga, founder and leader of the Black Power movement's cultural nationalist US Organization.[42] While the struggle for the formation of a separate nation-state is extremely important, it is the envisaging of a black "nation" that is central to black nationalist ideology. At times, it is evoked literally, while at others, it is figurative. It is most efficacious, then, to think of black nationalism as operating out of what Benedict Anderson styled an "imagined community." In his appropriately titled book, Anderson proposes a most imaginative explication of the "nation" concept as it relates to the nationalist standpoint. He describes the nation as "an imagined political community—and imagined as both inherently limited and sovereign."[43] This explanation is one of the most beneficial ways of conceptualizing black nationalism in the United States, because it avoids many of the problems associated with a definition dependent upon the nation-state configuration. For example, as previously stated, American blacks who consider themselves "nationalists" are a nation within a nation, or as sociologist Rod Bush aptly observes, a "nation against a nation."[44] Therefore the "nation" in U.S. black nationalism is "imagined" because its boundaries are demarcated by racial lines, which are socially constructed and historically determined (its membership constituted by the "one drop" rule), and because its demands for sovereignty are usually based not on the desire for national independence from a foreign nation but on an appeal for the actualization of American democratic principles.

Because the "nation" is an ideological construct, some scholars and political analysts attempt to discredit black nationalism as a mode of politicking, as if it were merely suggestive of a collective artificial consciousness. The "nation" in black nationalism may be perceived and understood as an "imagined community," but its existence and its consequences are very real. In fact, Anderson issues a warning to those who may misread the nationalist phenomenon and put forth the argument that nationalism "is not the awakening of nations to self-consciousness: it invents nations where they do not exist."[45] Nationalists may imagine communities, Anderson writes, but invention must not be confused with "'fabrication' and 'falsity,'" for "[c]ommunities are to be distinguished, not by their falsity/genuineness, but by the style in which they are imagined."[46]

This approach is useful for the study of black nationalism in the United States, because black nationalist theory is founded upon the conviction that black people in the Diaspora—by virtue of African ancestry, a common historical experience of slavery, as well as a legacy of racial oppression in the forms of political disfranchisement, economic exploitation, social discrimination, and cultural degradation—share a cultural identity and therefore constitute a nationality, or nation, separate and distinct from other (read: white) Americans. "Nationalism is the belief that Black people in this country make up a cultural Nation," Maulana Karenga articulated in 1967. "The cultural nation is a people with a common past, a common present and, hopefully, a common future."[47] For many of Karenga's counterparts, both past and present, the issue of black liberation extends beyond the boundaries of the United States. Pan-Africanism, black nationalism's ideological kindred, interlocks the freedom of Africans and African descendants throughout the Diaspora and has been intimately connected to black nationalist thought in the United States since its inception. "A-F-R-I-C-A, Puerto Rico, Haiti, and J.A. / New York and Cali, F-L-A / No it ain't 'bout where you stay, it's 'bout the motherland," illustrate black neonationalists dead prez in their 2000 song, "I'm a African."[48] Prominent nineteenth century Pan-Africanists include black Americans like David Walker, Henry Highland Garnet, Alexander Crummell, Martin Delany (who made the legendary proclamation, "Africa for the African race, and black men to rule them"), and James T. Holly, Afro-Caribbeans like Edward W. Blyden, and the West African Africanus Horton. During the twentieth century, Pan-Africanism in the States welcomed its most influential propagandists with the appearances of Marcus Garvey and W. E. B. Du Bois on the global political stage.

Tales from the Darkside: The Rationale and Rationality of Black Nationalist Thought

In the late 1980's/early 1990's, raptivists reintroduced black nationalism and Pan-Africanism to a new generation of African Americans. But the politics of the period weren't the only throwback: hip-hop observers and scholars revived the debate over definition as critics questioned the legitimacy of raptivism as a form of black neonationalism. Another question of concern in the historiography of U.S. black nationalism that is of special interest for this project is the issue of motivation. Many researchers have paid particular attention to the social psychology of black nationalism, especially those whose treatment of the subject is unsympathetic. Yet much of the dialogue on the rationality—or, most often, the nonrationality—of black nationalism is tinged with racism and/or classism, especially those accounts that insinuate that black nationalism is a nonintellectual political discourse and/or that classify it as "pathology." (During the late 1980's/early 1990's, this characterization of black neonationalism was amplified by portrayals of hip-hop artists and audiences as low-class, pathological, and anti-intellectual.) Depictions of nonelite, working- or "lower"-class black nationalists as emotional/nonrational—or, even more bluntly, as "simple"—reveal a supposition that black people's (re)actions are instinctual rather than intellectual. Thus it is imperative that scholars critically engage black nationalist discourse.

It is just as important that they not underestimate its emotional import. Striking a balanced regard for the rationale and the rationality of black nationalism has proven a difficult task for scholars, as many tend to oversimplify the former. Consequently, a significant number of writers and researchers of U.S. black nationalism conclude that its source of inspiration is rooted in hostility, or some other dark mood that lurks deep in the subjective mind of black communities. Disillusionment may be a significant instigator of black nationalist sentiment, for as Black Arts pioneer Amiri Baraka once theorized (in overtly gendered language), "*promise* is a dying bitch with rotting eyes."[49] Yet a deconstructive interpretation leaves no room for an appreciation of the affirmative potential of black nationalist thought or an accurate assessment of a style of politicking that can be both productive and destructive. Embracing this dualism is vital to understanding black nationalist thought as a social and political phenomenon. Black nationalist orators and writers have been able to invoke a passionate response from their audiences, but their skill should also be measured by their adeptness at articulating a commonality of experience. "People believed and followed Malcolm [X] not out of an emotional attachment to his charisma," explains scholar William W. Sales, Jr. "The basis of his leadership was that he gave back to his followers, in a more highly refined and clarified form, ideas and insights which in fact were rooted in their experiences."[50] As Sales suggests, the power of black nationalist ideology lies in its ability as an identity politics to seduce its audiences both cognitively and intuitively; and that power was exponentially increased when politics met popular culture during the golden age of rap nationalism.

Despite this facility and flexibility, many scholars write the history of black nationalism in the United States as though it is a political trend reflective of a collective black mood, as if the ascendancy of black nationalist thought at any given historical moment is a measure of the level of despair and hopelessness in African America. It is an issue so preeminent in the historiography of black nationalism that it inspired historian John H. Bracey, Jr. to dissent and write a minority opinion apart from his coeditors in the landmark 1970 compilation *Black Nationalism in America*. The historical narrative generated by writers and researchers like August Meier and Elliot Rudwick (and Theodore Draper, Wilson Jeremiah Moses, Victor Ullman, Gayraud Wilmore, and William Julius Wilson, to name a few) concludes that an escalation of racial terrorism by white America, more often than not, provokes an expansion of nationalist sentiment in black America. One drawback of this approach, so common among historians, is that it produces a gendered reading of the political expression of black nationalism. It is a masculinist methodology that highlights a few good men and simultaneously undermines black agency.

Here is a brief and simplified account of the history of American black nationalism as written by many who subscribe to this point of view: The "protonationalistic" phase of black nationalism—inspired by the contradiction between the "War of Independence" for America and state of dependence of African America—is represented by (1) the eighteenth-century movement for independent black institutions, from the "black church" to mutual aid societies and fraternal organizations, (2) post–Revolutionary War legislative petitions for manumission and emigration by slaves and free blacks in Boston in 1773 and 1787, respectively, (3) the emigrationist efforts of Paul Cuffe in Sierra Leone in 1815, and (4) the antebellum cultural expressions of southern slaves in sacred and secular (con)texts.

These protonationalist expressions matured, culminating in the appearance of classical black nationalism in the 1850's, a political phenomenon best represented by the 1852 publication of Martin R. Delany's *The Condition, Elevation, Emigration, and Destiny of the Colored People of the United States Politically Considered*. The birth of classical black nationalism is then attributed to the intense racial paranoia that characterized the 1850's, an emotional state symbolized by both the enactment of and the reaction to the Compromise of 1850 and the 1857 Dred Scott decision. However, the Civil War and Reconstruction resolved the collective black anxiety and resulted in the first significant decline in black nationalist sentiment as political advancements led to an increased faith among African Americans in the potential of the American democratic system. Martin Delany is, once again, used as an example of the political moment; his stint as a major in the Union army during the Civil War and as a Republican politician during Reconstruction is believed to personify the state of black optimism during these revolutions.

Nevertheless, this hopefulness was short lived. The dismantling of Reconstruction inaugurated the "nadir" of African American history when severe forms of antiblack social, political, and economic violence compelled the accommodationist black politics characterized by Booker T. Washington and the Tuskegee machine. The racial terrorism of the post-Reconstruction era may have inspired a small resurgence of black nationalist sentiment, particularly in the form of migration and emigration movements, but the social-political environment was so oppressive that it would take another generation and Marcus Garvey's Universal Negro Improvement Association (UNIA) for black nationalist ideology to once again capture the imagination of an impressive segment of the black population. The popularity of the UNIA in the United States is considered a consequence of the disenchantment of southern migrants and West Indian immigrants, whose expectations for a better life in the northern Promised Land were thwarted by economic exploitation, political corruption, and social alienation.

However, civil rights/integrationism would, once again, eclipse the black nationalist moment, as American involvement in both world wars generated economic prosperity and inspired social positivism. Black nationalism would not reappear on the political scene with any import until the mid- to late 1960's, when the modern Civil Rights movement failed to produce substantial change in the economic and social lives of black Americans, particularly in the urban areas outside the South. The disappointment and disillusionment experienced by many African Americans in the post–World War II period reached a pinnacle with the assassination of Martin Luther King, Jr.—a violent end to a nonviolent life. Black youth across the country responded to that hypocrisy with a call for "Black Power," a slogan exemplified by their postmortem spiritual leader El-Hajj Malik El-Shabazz, better known as Malcolm X. (As a postscript, it is easy to incorporate the development of rap nationalism in this historical account as young black men and women in the hip-hop generation—suffering the contradictions of postapartheid America and under attack from their Civil Rights predecessors—responded to the social, political, and economic warfare unleashed by the Reagan and Bush administrations.)

This may be an effective way to historicize the development of black nationalism in the United States, but it is problematic for a number of reasons. One problem with the standard narration of the history of U.S. black nationalism is its overemphasis on external forces as a determining factor in the rise and fall of nationalist thought. Racial terrorism—be it social, political, economic, or physical—is a defining feature of the African American experience and is not limited to those historical moments described as nationalist. Thus, the presence or absence of racism is not a precise gauge of when and/or where black nationalist sentiment will appear. In fact, antiblack violence was so common during the Civil Rights movement that leaders and activists integrated it as a movement strategy, utilizing white hostility to dramatize the moral corruption that racism engenders. So, as Black Power movement theorist Maulana Karenga articulated, "Nationalism is not merely a response to white oppression, but a need for Black people to come together."[51] As such, it should be recognized as a constant and appreciable force in African America.

A second problem with the historical periodization common among scholars of U.S. black nationalism is that its exaggerated focus on influential men, particularly those who were leaders and theorists, distorts the reality of the way African Americans engage in black nationalism as a political and cultural phenomenon. In fact, this approach leads many scholars, like Wilson Moses, to assess black nationalism as a top-down, aristocratic movement that combines "messianic self-conception" with an "authoritarian collectivism," or as the "belief that all black people could and should act unanimously under the leadership of one powerful man or group of men, who would guide the race by virtue of superior knowledge or divine authority."[52] Moses's conclusion, however, is skewed by his emphasis on a black leadership class that was almost exclusively male and whose members were ("more than incidentally")[53] ministers, a profession that is not only historically phallocentric but was also purposefully restricted to men. It is true that in both the nineteenth and twentieth centuries clergymen dominated black nationalist leadership. However, by focusing on ministers, Moses and others advance a male-centered perspective that renders invisible other significant supporters of the black nationalist tradition—including women, slaves, and nonliterate blacks.

For example, where does this historical method leave the contributions and critiques of a nineteenth-century black nationalist-feminist like Mary Ann Shadd Cary? As the first black woman to publish a newspaper in North America, she is at least as significant as her male peers for her pioneering role in the abolitionist and nationalist black press. Shadd Cary, the cofounder of Canada's second black newspaper, the *Provincial Freeman*, is also noteworthy as an emigrationist who challenged the masculinist discourse of classical black nationalists like Martin Delany, reasoning that "coloured men are as merciless as other men, when possessed of the same amount of pride, conceit, and wickedness, and as much, if not more ignorance."[54] Despite her innovative spirit, the modest recognition of Shadd Cary in the literature on black nationalism demonstrates how women have gone largely unnoticed by many scholars, not only because of the elite and masculine character of black political leadership but also because of social scientists' focus on black male leadership. Yet as nineteenth-century black feminist pioneer Anna Julia Cooper's warning echoes forth from the past, "[O]ur present record of eminent men, when placed beside the actual status of the race in America to-day, proves that no man can represent the race."[55]

Scholars' preoccupation with black (male) leaders has also had the effect of depreciating the collaboration and/or participation of common, everyday black people, for the political consciousness of the layperson usually materializes in the cultural realm. Cultural critic Wahneema Lubiano even suggests that black nationalism in contemporary African America functions as "common sense" or, as she describes it, as "a cultural narrative that explains many black Americans' understanding of themselves."[56] While this is probable, without traditional forms of documentation, the collectivist ethics of African America become more difficult to track. Nevertheless, historians like Sterling Stuckey (1972, 1987), Lawrence Levine (1977), and Robin D. G. Kelley (1994) have made significant inroads into the study of quotidian resistance and nationalist sentiment among the black nonelite—focusing particularly on nineteenth-century slaves and the twentieth-century working class.

For these reasons and more, the cultural production of the hip-hop generation is, thus, another site through which to examine the infrapolitics of African America; and rap music, particularly black neonationalist rap, is an invaluable lens through which to observe postmodern, postindustrial (dis)continuities in black cultural politics and political cultures.

Conclusion: In Search of Our Nation's Manhood

With working definition and historical background in place, it is possible to begin discussing some of the consistencies and inconsistencies in the tradition of American black nationalism—in particular, its latent and manifest gender and sexual politics. For many black nationalists, racial identity has been shaped by conventional gender norms, roles, and expectations, and the African American experience has been interpreted through gendered language, a point illustrated by Poor Righteous Teachers' front man Wise Intelligent during a 2002 interview: "Just being a black man in America I put my race first that's just the bottom line. That's the way man should be, in my opinion. We have to do for self. That's the way that I think, that's the way I operate."[57] Wise Intelligent's rationalization of his political philosophy typifies rap music's black neonationalism and is a standpoint dissected in the next chapter, "'We Men Ain't We?' Mas(k)ulinity and the Gendered Politics of Black Nationalism." To contextualize the race/gender politicking of rap nationalists, chapter 2 explicates how, historically, American black nationalism has been configured by the theories and praxis of race and gender. It focuses on classical and modern black nationalists and defines the "crisis of masculinity" that influenced their preoccupation with the reclamation of black manhood. Chapter 3, "Brothers Gonna Work It Out: The Popular/Political Culture of Rap Music," chronicles the emergence of black neonationalism in post–Civil Rights, post–Black Power African America by highlighting the golden age of rap nationalism. It surveys the development of rap nationalism and analyzes the politicization of rap music that occurred during the late 1980's/early 1990's. While chapter 3 investigates the ideological and political influences of rap nationalists, chapter 4 provides a more in-depth explanation of how these cultural workers figured as the legitimate heirs to the tradition of U.S. black nationalism. "Ladies First? Defining Manhood in the Golden Age of Rap Nationalism" documents the masculinist discourse of rap nationalism. In particular, it focuses on how raptivists' gendered pronouncements resemble those of the classical and modern periods and spotlights the multiple ways rap nationalists privilege heteronormativity. Chapter 5, "Representin' God: Masculinity and the Use of the Bible in Rap Nationalism," reveals how raptivists claimed the black nationalist–masculinist tradition by using the Bible as a (re)source of power and a blueprint for empowerment. The conclusion, "Be True to the Game: Final Reflections on the Politics and

Practices of the Hip-Hop Nation," speculates upon the potential for and influences of the popular/political culture of raptivism as it illuminates the dialogic relationship between musical artists and grassroots organizers. The book closes with my observations and assessment of the race/gender politics of black nationalism.

2

"We Men Ain't We?"
Mas(k)ulinity and the
Gendered Politics of Black Nationalism

The 1989 film *Glory* dramatized the story of the Massachusetts 54th, one of the first all-black Union regiments of the American Civil War. It was a tale of the human spirit, of triumph and heroism—of glory—against enormous odds. Yet despite its billing as a war epic, *Glory* unwittingly revealed a lot about American political culture and black cultural politics. In particular, terrific moments of clarity enable the student of gendered realities to explore not only how war is figured as a rite of manhood but also how manhood is figured by the act of war. The most fascinating revelation of this compelling story (and the most relevant for this book) was its conspicuous display of the race and gender politics of the Civil War era. In a war that is emblazoned in the American memory as pitting (white) brother against (white) brother, it was black men who stood to lose the most. For in this contest of masculine will theirs was a battle for freedom, and—as *Glory*'s histrionics illustrated—this freedom was defined in terms of both the right to self-determination *and* the right to exercise masculine privilege. These ex-slaves, freedmen, and free men risked their lives to claim their humanity and demonstrate their manhood.

The cinematic moment that brings this point to light most dramatically is the scene that leads into the film's culminating event: the Massachusetts 54th's courageous but fatal assault on the Confederacy's Fort Wagner in South Carolina in 1863. The evening before the men of the 54th commence their "heroic" death march, they gather around a campfire for a moment of inspiration and reflection before battle. In a style assumed to be familiar to the slave quarters of the antebellum South, these soldiers break out into an improvised melody (as black folks in movies are so prone to do) and begin to conjure God through song and sermon. While harmonizing "Oh my Lord, Lord, Lord, Lord" to the syncopated rhythm of hand clapping, tambourine shaking, and washboard scraping, they ask Him for the strength and courage to face the battle ahead—a battle they sense they are destined to lose.

There are three testimonials in this scene, the first by Jupiter Sharts, the Sambo/coon who is a good-hearted but dim-witted runaway from South Carolina. His Christianity, the kind of simple and unadorned religiosity the public expects from a field hand, is demonstrated by his one and only request of God: "Tomorrow we go into battle," he states, his illiteracy punctuated by a speech impediment, "So Lord-y, let me fight with the rifle in one hand, and the good book in the other."

The second testimonial is delivered by John Rawlins, a character molded in the tradition of Harriet Beecher Stowe's Uncle Tom, his masculine exterior balanced by a feminine interior. Rawlins, played by actor Morgan Freeman, has a "gentle, domestic heart,"[1] and it is as a mother/father figure that he gains his position as an honorable and respected elder among the men in his company. Yet in this scene Rawlins is also the organic minister of the group. Equipped with the growls and rhythmic delivery distinctive of African American preaching styles, Rawlins asks the Lord for His blessings, which he invokes in terms of manly courage. If the next day should be their last, Rawlins prays,

> Oh Heavenly Father, we want you to let our folks know, uh, that we died facing the enemy! We want 'em to know that we went down standing up . . . amongst those that are against our oppression! We want 'em to know, Heavenly Father, that we died for freedom!

The final, most emotionally raw testimonial in this spontaneous secular/sacred prebattle worship is delivered by Trip, the bad-ass nigger/runaway slave. Portrayed by Denzel Washington, Trip is *Glory*'s counterpart to trailblazing African American historian John Blassingame's "Nat"—a "not-Sambo" recognizable by his defiant will and righteous anger. He exists outside of what social scientists consider the traditional institutions of the black community: he has no religion ("I ain't much about no prayin' now") and no family ("kill'd off my momma"), and it is because of this independence from familial and community attachments that Trip is able to openly challenge authority—both white and black. Yet despite his history of loss, Trip maintains the one thing that white folks could not take away from him: his manhood. Prompted to testify by Rawlins ("You better get your butt on in there boy!") Trip stands before the campfire in this riveting scene as a man before men; his gendered script is short, but to the point. And he concludes with a pointed statement that provides the audience with valuable insight into the minds of the men, both black and white, who risked their lives in America's wars.

"It ain't much a matter what happens tomorrow, 'cause we men ain't we?" he declares with pause: "We men ain't we?"[2]

What Trip's speech lacks in eloquence, it makes up for in poignancy. On that fateful evening, when he comes face to face with his mortality, Trip's only comfort is the belief that the heroic sacrifice of the 54th will confer upon them manly recognition. It is a sentiment indicative of a desire that seduced 180,000 African American men to enlist in the ranks of the Union army during the Civil War. By participating in the ultimate display of masculine contestation and aggression, the black soldiers of the Massachusetts 54th, and of other black Union regiments, hoped to acquire the privileges of male power and patriarchal authority enjoyed by (many) white men during the antebellum era. For them, the spoils of war ranged from citizenship (or male representation in the public sphere) to manly respect (and male repositioning in the private sphere). As gender historian Gail Bederman notes, these black men enlisted in the Union army despite "unequal and offensive treatment" because they understood what was at stake, "that enlisting was their most potent tool to claim that they were men and should have the same rights and privileges as all American men." But most importantly, she stresses, they did so because they recognized the gendered realities of nineteenth-century America. "These African Americans understood that the only way to obtain civic power was through gender—by proving that they, too, were men."[3]

By breathing life into the stereotyped supporting roles around Matthew Broderick's Colonel Shaw, the black actors of *Glory* bore witness to the burdens and privileges of black manhood during the antebellum and Civil War period. In fact, this narrative is so meaningful because the Civil War provided the first major backdrop for the public staging of strong black masculinity; it marked the beginning of an enduring claim by African American men to hegemonic masculinity that was summed up in one compelling line: "We men ain't we?" In the form of a query, these four words unmask the uncertainty and instability in the status of black manhood in the United States and give the historian of the African American experience some insight into an issue that is not only omnipresent but accorded primacy in black culture and politics. Often expressed in the singular and in the affirmative, "We men ain't we?" becomes the declarative statement, "I'm a man," recognizable in multiple expressions of African American popular and political culture. For instance, in Spike Lee's 1992 film interpretation of the life of Malcolm X, Malcolm's father, a Garveyite and Baptist preacher, bellows, "I'm a man!" while unloading his gun in the air and forcing night riders to retreat from their attack on his home. On the music scene, James Brown, also known as "The Godfather of Soul," wailed "I'm a man! I'm a man!" as he threatened to exact revenge on the brother trying to steal his money and his "honey" in the 1973 hit "The Big Payback"; and '80s R & B crooner Alexander O'Neal softly assured his lady that he is a sensitive and attentive lover while countering, "I'm a man! I'm a man!" in the background of the 1991 hit "All True Man." Meanwhile, in the political arena, this pronouncement can be found, among other places, in the nineteenth-century publications of black nationalism's premier theorists David Walker ("we are MEN") and Martin Delany ("I am a man") and could be understood as the overarching theme of the 1995 Million Man March. This masculinist politicking is not the sole province of black nationalists. The photographic record of the 1968 Memphis Sanitation Strike is so powerful because the workers' struggle for manly dignity was signified by their protest placards that read simply "I Am A Man."

Nevertheless, as political discourse black nationalism is an ideology that has historically proven itself to be inspired by a crisis of masculinity and translated in a manner akin to what psychologist Alfred Adler deemed "masculine protest."[4] Claims to the social, political, and economic power of patriarchy highlight a rhetorical dependence on the subordination of the feminine in the oral and literary works of black nationalists. Many feminist scholars concentrate on sexism in black nationalism, specifically the subordination of women, and attempt to amend androcentric historical accounts by spotlighting the political activism of women and women's organizations; here, however, I focus on the masculine ideals that both influence and emanate from black nationalist theory and praxis. Rather than demonstrate how black nationalist discourse works to exclude women and/or relegate them to the margins of black nationalist movements, organizations, and (consequently) histories, I scrutinize the masculinist ways in which black nationalist ideologues consistently and systematically shape the black political agenda. My particular interests are in how black power in the United States is defined in terms of what women's studies scholar Anne McClintock deems a "politics of substitution"[5] (or the tendency among African male nationalists to covet, or displace, the social, political, and economic position of European male colonials), as well as in how the process of black empowerment is defined in terms of violent resistance.

Black nationalism has, historically, proven itself to be a politics obsessed with (and therefore limited by) the reclamation of black manhood; as we will see, like the black men in the soldier's story *Glory*, black male nationalists are in an undying struggle over the question, "We men ain't we?"

Rediscovering the Phallic Nation: Black Nationalism as a Politics of Masculine Protest

Until recently, scholars of U.S. black nationalism have mistakenly assumed that its significance as a political theory is based simply on its positioning as a racial politics. Yet if, as sociologist R. W. Connell suggests, the definition of gender politics can be deduced to be an "embodied-social politics,"[6] black nationalism must be recognized as a race *and* gender politics, for "gender is the modality in which race is lived."[7] It has become quite clear among feminist scholars, male and female, that people do not experience life in the disjunctive and/or hierarchical categorizations that have become the great analytical triumvirate of race, class, and gender, but instead move through their lives as black *and* female *and* middle class, for example. In the United States, life chances are shaped, in part, by class and corporealities, for among Americans, power and privilege are largely determined by the ways in which race and gender are inscribed on the body. And because power relations have a tremendous effect on material and cultural realities, it is only logical to assume they will also affect political activism, particularly the way people organize and why they do so.

Not surprisingly, feminist theorists and social scientists, particularly women of color, forged new ground during the 1980's and '90s in exploring the interlocking forces of race and gender on the body politic. Despite these important inroads, studies of the impression of race and gender on the American political terrain continue to focus on the efforts and activism of women while its imaging and existence as a masculinist domain is comparatively underexplored.[8] Investigating women's influence on the development and transformation of the American public sphere is extremely important work. It is equally important to understand the seduction of race and gender appeals, because race and gender circumscribe the space in which people move politically and have inspired alternative means of political expression. Although explicating the historical significance and ever shifting meanings of these power relations is difficult at best (we still struggle with the language to explain them as social phenomena), black nationalism provides an opportunity to study the dynamics and dialectics of an embodied-social politics.

With virtually exclusive access to the public sphere, black men have, historically, enabled themselves with the power and authority to determine the black political agenda. Many among the ranks of black nationalists have consistently abused that power and defined the boundaries of the imagined black nation in terms of a sexual politics that institutionalized male domination and the subordination of the "feminine." For instance, black women's sexuality was the subject of scrutiny by classical black nationalists like Alexander Crummell, who intimated that one of black women's primary (political) duties was to protect their virtue and maintain sexual purity, while modern black nationalist Stokely Carmichael conversely asserted that the only position for women in his movement was prone.[9] In the masculinist discourse of black nationalism, the construction of gender is dependent upon the construction of (hetero)sexuality; therefore its phallocentric politics necessitated the subordination of not only women but "effeminate" men as well. In an attempt to prove their manhood ("We men ain't we?"), black heterosexual male nationalists strictly patrolled the borders of their masculine domain. This fact is manifest in the heteronormativity displayed by nineteenth-century theorists like Henry Highland Garnet, who demanded both freedom and franchise in terms of patriarchal privilege, and is confirmed by the explicit homophobia exhibited in the mid-twentieth century by Black Power advocates who deemed homosexuality "counterrevolutionary." This sexual politics continued throughout the late twentieth century, as evinced by rap nationalist Ice Cube's pronouncement, "true niggas ain't gay."[10]

Whether the hypermasculine positioning of black nationalists is mildly disagreeable or violently offensive, it is meaningful because it stands as evidence of a self-perceived crisis among black men present in black political culture. Cultural studies scholar Paul Gilroy characterizes this phenomenon as a movement to counteract manly dispossession: "An amplified and exaggerated masculinity has become the boastful centerpiece of a culture of compensation that self-consciously salves the misery of the disempowered and subordinated."[11] The preoccupation with masculine status described by Gilroy betrays a semiotic approach to a race and gender politics dominated by men who have been historically denied access to the signs and symbols of "manhood"—particularly the ability to provide for and to protect their families and communities. Because this symbolic castration transcends time and space in African America, black nationalists from the early nineteenth to the late twentieth century projected "manhood" as a signifier for their liberation politics. Among those black nationalists, the definition of what constitutes "manhood" has remained, in effect, static: masculinity was/is defined as not-femininity. Thus black nationalism evolved as a politics that, more often than not, sanctioned the subordination of the feminine, symbolized by women, gay men, and all that is emotional/nonrational.[12] It is an embodied-social politics—and an identity politics—that many times reveals a thinly veiled crisis of manhood among black men. And that crisis is resolved through "masculine protest."

Take, for example, the sexual politics of two black nationalist periods, the classical and the modern, which on the surface appear to be contradictory. With few exceptions, black nationalists have been, and continue to be, conscientiously conservative—almost puritanical—about issues of gender and sexuality, in part as a response to white supremacist stereotypes that rationalized sexual terrorism against black men and women. This was especially the case among black leaders, nationalist and integrationist, male and female, during the post-Reconstruction era. After slavery, many men and women in the black elite enthusiastically embraced conventional gender standards in an effort to re-present African America to white America and as a form of resistance to antiblack propaganda popularized, for example, by minstrelsy. As Gail Bederman explains in *Manliness and Civilization*, for men during this period "manliness," characterized by rational self-restraint, was the ideal representation of manhood. It is therefore easier to understand why classical black nationalists like Alexander Crummell, who were trying to defy racial characterizations of black Americans as savage, intellectually backward, and sexually depraved, comported themselves with cosmopolitan refinement.[13] "If black men were seen as beasts, as rapists, as bodies out of control," feminist scholar bell hooks writes, "reformist movements for racial uplift countered these stereotypes by revering the refined, restrained, desexualized black male body."[14] Likewise, for women the gender standard was modeled after a bourgeois Victorian ideal that was discussed in terms of sexuality and defined by words like "morality," "social purity," and "chastity."

During the late nineteenth century some members of the black elite set out on a political project to regenerate black womanhood, in part by redeeming black women's sexuality. And many, like Crummell, who was an Episcopalian minister, sought to impose Victorian sexual ethics on what he considered the nation's most neglected population: "The Black Woman of the South." Victims of "rude, coarse labor of men" and "ruthlessly violated" by white men, southern black women were subject to a "gross barbarism which tended to blunt the tender sensibilities, to obliterate feminine delicacy and womanly shame," Crummell argued.[15] Thus, he declared the need for a "domestic revolution." Crummell urged upstanding Christian women of the North to travel south, for only women with "intelligence and piety," with "delicate sensibility and refinement," could restore the "instinct of chastity" in their degraded sisters. Without this rehabilitation Crummell believed there could be no racial uplift, presaging the Nation of Islam's adage that a nation can rise no higher than its women: "If you want the civilization of a people to reach the very best elements of their being . . . you must imbue the *womanhood* of that people with all its elements and qualities."[16]

For Alexander Crummell, like the bourgeois feminists in the black women's club movement, racial uplift was defined by the fulfillment of conventional gender roles because, in his words, according to some white men, "black men have no *rights* which white men should regard, and black *women* no virtue which white men should respect!"[17] It is interesting, but fitting, that Crummell chose to appropriate the language of the 1857 Dred Scott Supreme Court decision in this context, during his discussion of the sexual exploitation of black women, for it aptly frames the defining struggle of the race: black men aspire to "manhood rights," a form of empowerment that necessitates black women's subordination in the public and private spheres. A critical part of this coveted patriarchal role, as described by Crummell, is the right to protect the "virtue" of black women, that is, the right to sovereignty over the sexual (re)production of black women.[18]

While classical black nationalists like Alexander Crummell responded to stereotypes by systematically contradicting them, modern black nationalists like rhetoricians in the Black Panther Party defied these representations, ironically, by engaging them. The Victorian manliness Crummell exhibited during the late nineteenth century was no longer the masculine ideal during the mid-twentieth century. As economic conditions shifted during the mid- to late nineteenth century, so did attitudes toward manliness.[19] Some middle-class white men, deeming the Victorian ideal "effeminate," felt a need to "revirilize" society. So at the turn of the century, "masculinity" became an alternative to "manliness," the former signifying a male identity that idealized aggression and virility—ideals that are more congruent with contemporary conceptions of manhood. In the mid-1960's many young black nationalists responded to what they perceived to be an emasculated sensibility among Civil Rights advocates by embracing this masculine model of manhood, choosing militancy over nonviolent resistance, a political method they judged effeminate. Two poems written by Black Arts leader Amiri Baraka provide an extreme example of this assessment. Baraka castigates Civil Rights pioneer Bayard Rustin not only for his politics, but for "switchin like a fag" in his poem "The Dance of the Toms," and labeled Roy Wilkins, then leader of the NAACP, an "eternal faggot" in his "CIVIL RIGHTS POEM": "His spirit is a faggot," Baraka wrote, "his projection / and image."[20] In fact, as literary and cultural studies scholar Phillip Brian Harper notes, "so well understood was the identification between inadequacies of manhood and black consciousness in the Black Arts context that this poem needed never render explicit the grounds for its judgment of NAACP leader Roy Wilkins, for the perceived racial-political moderation of both him and his organization clearly bespoke his unforgivable 'faggotry.'"[21] At this time, shedding a feminized male gender identity was critical, for it was not the characters popularized by minstrelsy that haunted many black activists and intellectuals. Instead, modern black nationalists were compelled to address another, no less damaging representation of African America: the matriarchal black family. As a result of an "open weapon of ideological warfare"[22] unleashed in 1965 by sociologist and future U.S. senator Daniel Patrick Moynihan, the rehabilitation of black manhood became a primary issue on the political agenda.

Inspired by the Civil Rights movement, the federal government commissioned a research project to investigate the race problem in the United States. That study, *The Negro Family: The Case for National Action* (dubbed the "Moynihan Report" after its lead researcher), concluded that racial inequalities were the result of a "tangle of pathology" precipitated by slavery and perpetuated by the structure of black families. Moynihan branded black women matriarchs whose autonomy psychologically emasculated black men, because "[o]urs is a society which presumes male leadership in private and public affairs."[23] The impact of his judgment was both immediate and far reaching. Case in point: the Black Panther Party. During the early stages of the organization's development, its leaders, from cofounders Huey Newton and Bobby Seale to Minister of Information Eldridge Cleaver, were profoundly influenced by the controversial "Moynihan Report." From the group's beginnings in 1966, the men of the Central Committee set forth to reclaim their manhood through macho rhetoric and virile display—a gender phenomenon bell hooks calls the "'it's-a-dick-thing'" version of masculinity."[24] The creation of phallic/ies was central to Panther ideology: witness Seale's statement that "power comes out of the barrel of a dick,"[25] or the praxis of the community-patrol program. In fact, Panther leaders were so successful at this ideation, the Party was never able to overcome its early imaging as a macho gang of pistol-packing, "pig"-hunting, hypersexual black men. Yet as impressive as their masculine performance in the public arena was, it was matched by their demonstrative gender politics.

Eldridge Cleaver's work is a good example of the tone that characterized race/gender theorizing during the Black Power movement. And like the writings of Alexander Crummell, Cleaver's work implicates black womanhood and black women's sexuality. While he embodied the black male rapist in *Soul on Ice*, Cleaver propagandized the black female Jezebel in an essay entitled "Pronuciamento." In this address delivered at the Berkeley Community Center in 1968, he describes the rationale behind "Pussy Power," a recruitment strategy with which Panther women were to (re)produce members. To illustrate his point, Cleaver analogizes the biblical narrative of Adam and Eve, concluding that Eve could have altered the course of humanity if she had only utilized her powers of seduction.

> So Eve was a jive bitch. Because if she had been hip to Pussy Power, all she had to do was just sit down and say well you just go on and jack off because I'm gonna stay right here and fuck the devil. If Eve had done these things I'm sure that Adam wouldn't have held his ground.[26]

The profane nature of the above excerpt shows how far Black Power theorists strayed from the gender politicking of their predecessors as Cleaver encouraged black women to flaunt their sexuality—not repress it. Nevertheless, his speech reflects a radical departure in rhetorical style, not substance; for while it may evidence a shifting sexual ethic, it also reveals

the conservation of patriarchal authority, confirming the dynamic reproduction of cultural traditions Paul Gilroy names the "changing same."
The conceptualization of "Pussy Power" was deceptively disempowering—it was not, as bell hooks imagined thirty years later, "power to the
pussy."[27] Instead it represented a continuing, contemporary manifestation of an effort to control black women's sexuality: female bodies were
subject to male desire and the object of male consumption.

The sexual politics of classical and modern black nationalists Alexander Crummell and Eldridge Cleaver exemplify a phenomenon R. W. Connell names "protest masculinities." Protest masculinities, according to
Connell, can be a response to a perceived sense of powerlessness—particularly among men in marginalized communities (communities of color,
impoverished communities) whose limited access to resources jeopardizes
their claim to a gendered position of power.[28] For many black men, this
"crisis" of masculinity is inspired by a material reality—specifically, a history of political disfranchisement, economic exploitation, and social discrimination—that has denied them the patriarchal "right" to provide for
and to protect their families and communities. The proscriptions of
racism contributed to a sense of gendered deprivation that is consistently
reflected in the oral and literary work of nineteenth- and twentieth-century black nationalists. A 1967 article written by Huey Newton, cofounder and Minister of Defense of the Black Panther Party, illustrates
this point. In this article, descriptively called "Fear and Doubt," Newton
laments the self-perceived state of emasculation among men in modern
African America: "As a man he finds himself void of those things that
bring respect and a feeling of worthiness," he explains. This lack of manly
respect, according to Newton, was due to the depressed economic conditions of black communities.

> In a society where a man is valued according to occupation and material
> possessions, he is without possessions. He is unskilled and more often
> than not, marginally or unemployed. . . . He is, therefore viewed as quite
> worthless by his wife and children. His is ineffectual both in and out of
> the home. He cannot provide for or protect his family. He is invisible, a
> nonentity. Society will not acknowledge him as a man.[29]

As this quotation demonstrates, for many black nationalists, hegemonic masculinity—a political economy of male domination that ranges
from influence to exploitation—becomes an ideal that is embraced and/or

exaggerated. Eldridge Cleaver's rationalization of rape as an "insurrectionary act"[30] and his diagnosis of male homosexuality as a "sickness" not unlike "baby-rape"[31] in *Soul on Ice* are examples of the lengths to which black nationalists have gone in an effort to prove their manhood. Yet as extreme as Cleaver's work is (and it is clear that *Soul on Ice* is evidence of a crisis), it illustrates an integral element of masculine protest: performance. For what is masculinity if not camp? Witness Alexander Crummell, who was recognized for his display of genteel and civilized manliness during the mid-nineteenth century, or Huey Newton and Bobby Seale, who were infamous for their spectacle of virile and dangerous masculinity during the mid-twentieth century.

The difference in male representation portrayed by Alexander Crummell and the cofounders of the Black Panther Party highlights the historical dynamics of gender identity. If, as historian Gail Bederman suggests, gender is the process that links identity to anatomy,[32] black nationalists like Crummell, Newton, and Seale show that in a politics based in race and gender rationales this process is often projected into the public domain as a performative, or demonstrative, politics. Gender provides the guise—the mask—through which the male theorist/activist translates his social role into a political one. This explanation is not intended to minimize the stimuli for and consequences of gender performance, for the script, the actors, and the audiences are very real. As Black Arts movement theorist Larry Neal wrote about the Black Panther's theatrical media tactics, "it's some rather serious shit. Even though it may have started as a dimly perceived game," he assured, "when you get right down next to it, up under its skin, it ain't no game. No kind of way."[33]

While black nationalism is a politics that creates a sense of collective identity, it is deceptively hierarchical; for as a form of masculine protest, black nationalist ideology has been shaped, in part, by a hegemonic masculinity that undermines a communal ideal. "We say male supremacy is based on three things," cultural nationalist Maulana (Ron) Karenga evidences, "tradition, acceptance, and reason."[34] Karenga's proselyte Amiri Baraka echoed this sentiment, adding biological determinism. "[W]e do not believe in 'equality' of men and women," he wrote of his organization, the Congress of African People, which was founded in 1970. "We could never be equals . . . nature has not provided thus."[35] These paradigmatic statements reveal an embodied-social politics that demarcates not only race but also gender and sexuality. As a result, black nationalism recreates a system of domination and exploitation. This is illustrated by the symbolic and symptomatic sexual politics of Maulana Karenga's US Organization. Along with Kawaida and Kwaanza, Karenga created an "Africanized" ritual in which women were to "salimu" or "submit" to their male comrades as they passed, that is, they were expected to bow while crossing their arms across their breasts. In addition, women in the US Organization were instructed to dress seductively and embrace polygamy. Amiri Baraka also recalls that Karenga consistently degraded women, "calling them 'freaks' and commenting loudly on their physical attributes."[36] Although notorious, the sexual division of labor that characterized the US Organization is not inconsistent with the black nationalist tradition. The work of women and gay men has proven essential to the progression of the black nationalist agenda; however, they have been silenced, marginalized, harassed, and/or persecuted, and the struggle for their rights independent of what is called the "black liberation movement" has largely been subverted, trivialized, or simply ignored. "All the black women in those militant black organizations deserve the highest praise," repents Baraka in his autobiography. "Not only did they stand with us shoulder to shoulder against black people's enemies, they also had to go toe to toe with us, battling day after day against our insufferable male chauvinism."[37]

This is not to suggest that black nationalists were the sole perpetrators of sexist and homophobic beliefs and behaviors in the black political sphere. The handling of Ella Baker by the Southern Christian Leadership Conference and Bayard Rustin by the organizers of the March on Washington provide primary examples: both played a critical role in mobilizing and organizing these movements, yet both were mistreated by the male leadership of the modern Civil Rights movement. Furthermore, according to historian V. P. Franklin, Martin Luther King avoided sharing a public platform with James Baldwin—on a television program and at the March on Washington—because of his homosexuality.[38]

Aside from sexism and homophobia, the politics of representation played a key role in shaping problematic public policies on gender and sexuality in both the Civil Rights and black nationalist movements. These failings among black nationalists stem from the fact that, as a politics of masculine protest, black nationalist theory has been consumed with demands for the reclamation of black manhood. From the issues of abolitionism and enfranchisement to the platforms of black Communists and the Million Man March, manhood rights—defined as a (natural) right to male superiority in the public and private spheres—have figured prominently in the black nationalist agenda.[39] For instance, in 1830 a group of thirty-eight free blacks met in Philadelphia to determine a course of action for their antislavery activism. Their conclusion: elevate black manhood. "[O]ur forlorn and deplorable situation earnestly and loudly demands of us to devise and pursue all legal means for the speedy elevation of ourselves and our brethren to the scale and standing of men."[40] This sentiment would be echoed by black male nationalists throughout the nineteenth and twentieth centuries. In fact, David Walker's fixation on the need for black men to establish themselves as "men" among (white) men was prevalent throughout his 1829 *Appeal to the Colored Citizens of the World*, proving that his work was indeed a seminal piece of black nationalist thought in more ways than one: "[T]he Americans," he insisted, "are waiting for us to prove to them ourselves, that we are MEN, before they will be willing to admit the fact."[41] In certain passages of the *Appeal* Walker's commitment to this subject seems frantic, even desperate, as in this passage in which he strongly asserts that servitude is antithetical to manhood: "Are we MEN!!—I ask you, O my brethren! are we MEN? . . . What right then, have we to obey and call any other Master, but Himself?"[42]

Even W. E. B. Du Bois, who is known as an early champion of women's rights, was prone to masculinist imaging. In fact, in an insightful critique of *The Souls of Black Folk*, American Studies scholar Hazel Carby assesses its gendered language and composition and concludes, "There is, unfortunately, no simple correspondence between anyone's support for female equality and the ideological effect of the gendered structures of thought and feeling at work in any text one might write and publish."[43] Du Bois's association of race, nation, and manhood did not end with *Souls*. After the death of Bishop Henry McNeal Turner in 1915, Du Bois lamented the loss of a hero. In his tribute to Turner's memory, he engages in the type of hero worship R. W. Connell, a scholar of gender and sexuality, has called the "production of exemplary masculinity."[44] Connell believes this creative process is central to the maintenance of hegemonic masculinity; and judging by the nature of Du Bois's eulogy, a politics of hegemonic masculinity is central to the political ideal of black nationalism. Du Bois immortalizes Turner in a manner reminiscent of John Henry, one of the original black American folk heroes.[45] "In a sense Turner was the last of his clan," Du Bois testified, "mighty men, physically and mentally, men who started at the bottom and hammered their way to the top by sheer brute strength."[46]

The preoccupation with the status of black manhood was not the sole domain of nationalist men. Black women have also stressed the need for black men to reclaim their manhood. In her 1833 "Address at the African Masonic Hall," Maria Stewart told her male audience in no uncertain terms that they must prove themselves worthy of manhood rights in order to receive them: "Talk, without effort, is nothing; you are abundantly capable, gentlemen, of making yourselves men of distinction; and this gross neglect, on your part causes my blood to boil within me." For Stewart, action spoke louder than words, and without (male) action there could be no results: "Here is the grand cause which hinders the rise and progress of people of color. It is their want of laudable ambition and requisite courage."[47] As a woman who defied gender conventions and appeared on the political scene during a time when the "cult of domesticity" bound genteel women to the home, Stewart was one of the first black women to publicly advocate women's rights. Yet despite her burgeoning feminist views, she continued to reinforce patriarchal norms by daring black men to fulfill their "manly" duties: "Had our men the requisite force and energy, they would soon convince [white Americans] by their efforts both in public and in private, that they are men, or things in the shape of men."[48]

More than a hundred years after Stewart appropriated the masculinist discourse of her male peers, black women continued to uphold the idealized "traditional" roles that characterized nineteenth-century race/gender theory—particularly that which endorsed an aggressive expression of masculinity. "The Black Man in America has been quiet for so long that it seems almost unbelievable that he will ever make a decisive move toward his manhood and in that very process challenge the white man to be a human being," Louise Moore, the Vice President of the Domestic Personal Service Workers, taunted in the black militant newspaper *The Liberator*. Like Maria Stewart's 1833 speech at the African Masonic Lodge, Moore's 1966 article "When Will the Real Black Man Stand Up?" uses provocation to bolster her point, showing that even among women, the reclamation of black manhood has proven to be one of the most potent forces behind the conceptualization of black nationalist thought. In the midst of a controversy surrounding the myth of the matriarchal black family, Louise Moore embraced mainstream American gender ideals and challenged black men to stand up and be accountable as men. "A mature leader will be he, that has thrown off the yoke of his family's oppression, the yoke of the white man's oppressive culture and who has risen above his own fear of death and feels within himself that he is a man who wants to join with all real men to make possible all things," she explains. At a time when the rehabilitation of "emasculated" black manhood figured prominently on the black political agenda, Moore did not hesitate to exploit the source of this perceived psychic dismemberment—the castrating black bitch—to inspire black male activism: "Will the real Black man stand up or will the Black woman have to make this revolution?"[49]

Despite historical shifts in social, economic, and political contexts, proponents of black nationalism throughout the nineteenth and twentieth centuries have overwhelmingly placed a premium on maintaining standard gender conventions, or as Paul Gilroy notes, "The integrity of the race is thus made interchangeable with the integrity of black masculinity, which must be regenerated at all costs."[50] The toll, more often than not, was exacted at the expense of those who were not black, heterosexual, and/or male. Black feminist pioneer Toni Cade Bambara's assessment of improper male and female behavior in 1970 reveals the parameters of gender expectations among Black Power advocates: "if a woman is tough, she's a rough mamma, a strident bitch, a ballbreaker, a castrator. And if a man is at all sensitive, tender, spiritual, he's a faggot."[51] For many black nationalist theorists and activists the re-masculinization of black men would be achieved, as Malcolm X declared, by any means necessary. And it was in Malcolm's memory that Eldridge Cleaver warned, "We shall have our manhood. We shall have it or the earth will be leveled by our attempts to gain it."[52]

Violent resistance, or the threat of violent resistance, has been a pivotal theme in masculinist black nationalist discourse. Just as the hunger for male power and authority determined the direction of black nationalism, the masculine values of competition and aggression would determine its method. For example, Student Nonviolent Coordinating Committee Field Secretary Julius Lester wrote (in his appropriately titled *Look Out, Whitey! Black Power's Gon' Get Your Mamma!*) that as "the ideology for the confrontation," black nationalism "says, like the song the old folks used to sing about Samson (undoubtedly thinking of others than Samson), 'If I had my way, I'd tear this building down.'"[53] The struggle to redeem black manhood and a strong belief in the redemptive power of militancy in that struggle have shaped black nationalist strategy and framed black nationalist politics as a politics of violent resistance.

"The War Must Go On": Black Nationalism as a Politics of (Violent) Resistance

In the aftermath of World War I and a season of antiblack violence that earned the historical title the "Red Summer" of 1919, Marcus Garvey thrilled his audience in Newport News, Virginia, by exposing the hypocrisy of white Americans who declared the wartime effort as a victory for democracy abroad, when black Americans could not enjoy their constitutional right to life and liberty at home. Being no stranger to pomp and circumstance, Garvey was a master of oratory. He was known, and is remembered by many, as a "demagogue," a leader who could exploit the emotional needs of the "masses." While this may be true, Garvey was also able to tap into the political awareness of many black (im)migrants, exposing the contradictions between American democratic principles and America's undemocratic practices. Therefore, when he demanded the extension of constitutional rights to all black Americans in October 1919, his battle cry was met with cheers. "We new Negroes of America declare that we desire liberty or we will take death," he pronounced, appropriating the most celebrated slogan of the American Revolution. Yet despite the diehard lust for equality exhibited in this quotation, Garvey's true passion was, apparently, equality among men. For his declaration of war was conceived not as a war to liberate all black peoples but as a diasporic war to determine—unequivocally—the status of black manhood. "The war must go on," he insisted, "the war will go on . . . to decide once and for all in the very near future whether black men are to be serfs and slaves or black men are to be free men."[54]

For black nationalist leaders, their mission was well worth mortal sacrifice, because as Garvey attests, dying with dignity is preferable to living in emasculated shame. Garvey's words illustrate the militant imagery that has been a popular tool in androcentric black nationalist discourse. Among those who advocate gender domination in the name of racial equality, "The war must go on." The masculinist discourse of war provides black nationalist rhetoricians with the vocabulary and symbolism with which to translate a politics of liberation into a politics of violent resistance; and with the invocation of violence, the quest to reclaim black manhood is immediately transformed from an idle threat into a mortal proposition. "[I]t'll be ballots, or it'll be bullets," Malcolm X announced in 1964. "It'll be liberty, or it will be death."[55] Or as Eldridge Cleaver advanced four years later at a Peace and Freedom rally in Los Angeles, "I don't say 'Give me liberty or give me death'; I say 'Give me liberty or I'm gonna pick up a gun.'"[56] Under these do-or-die circumstances, black nationalist politics becomes not only an example of performative masculinity but the ultimate form of masculine protest. Thus, as Larry Neal explained in the Black Power classic *Black Fire: An Anthology of Afro-American Writing* (1968), among black nationalists there is a "sense of being at 'war.'" For the "tension, or double consciousness, is most often resolved in violence, simply because the nature of our existence in America has been one of violence."[57]

Many black nationalist theorists used violence, or the threat of violence, to purge an emasculated sense of (male) self. While Black Power advocates may be the usual suspects, their contemporaries in the Black Arts movement were subject to literary renderings of violent resistance. For example, Amiri Baraka utilized a language of violence in his endorsement of poetry as a revolutionary weapon. "We want 'poems that kill.' / Assassin poems, Poems that shoot / guns," he wrote. "Airplane poems . . . Setting fire and death to / whities ass."[58] This poetic styling was not exclusive to men. Black Arts pioneer Nikki Giovanni also framed black nationalism as a politics of masculine protest and advocated violence as a welcomed approach to revolutionary struggle. "Nigger / Can you kill," she challenges, "Can a nigger kill / Can a nigger kill a honkie / Can a nigger kill the Man." In this poem Giovanni not only intimates that assassination is an essential step in the Negro-to-Black conversion-of-consciousness experience but identifies it as a rite of passage for black men: "Learn to kill niggers / Learn to be Black men."[59]

The rationale of using violence as a counterstrategy to violence has its roots in a historical and perduring shame about slavery, a shame that puts the burden of enslavement on the male slave. Even in those cases where black nationalists discuss the enslavement of women, the topic is addressed in terms of its castrating effects on black manhood. W. E. B. Du Bois's discussion of white men's sexual exploitation of black women in *The Souls of Black Folk* provides a good example of this phallocentric discourse. Du Bois conceived the "Negro problem" in the post–Civil War era to be threefold. "His" was a burden of poverty, ignorance, and the "red stain of bastardy." Like his mentor Alexander Crummell, who described the degraded condition of black women subject to the "lustration" of white men in "The Black Woman of the South," Du Bois believed this private shame had grave effects on public advancement. For Du Bois, the "systematic legal defilement of Negro women" was a problem because it stood as evidence that, as a consequence of enslavement, black men had been stripped of their right to dominate black women. "This 'hereditary weight,'" Hazel Carby writes, "is the burden imposed on black men by history because they could not control the sexual reproduction of black women. Under this weight of betrayal by black women, most black men stumbled, fell, and failed to come into the full flowering of black manhood."[60]

A slave metaphor figures prominently in the masculinist discourse of violent resistance. At this point the race/class/gender positionality of the nationalist subject is most apparent. From David Walker to LeRoi Jones, the distance between the reality of the free and that of the enslaved contributed to the dictate of death before submission, suggesting, as bell hooks writes, that "the worst that can happen to a man is that he be made to assume the social status of a woman."[61] Huey Newton's recollection of a statement made by Eldridge Cleaver illustrates many black nationalists' severe and unreasonable judgment of male slaves' masculinity: "[A] slave who dies of natural causes will not balance two dead flies on the scales of eternity."[62] Contrary to black nationalists' assumptions, however, the cultural production of slaves indicates that—for better or worse—slave men were subject to "traditional" gender conventions. A "Hymn of Freedom" sung during an 1813 slave revolt off the South Carolina coast illuminates male slaves' sense of manliness and masculine duty to their wives and children:

> Look to Heaven with manly trust
> And swear by Him that's always just
> That no white foe with impious hand
> Shall slave your wives and daughters more
> or rob them of their virtue dear
> Be armed with valor firm and true
> Their hopes are fixed on Heaven and you
> That truth and justice will prevail
> And every scheme of bondage fail.[63]

This hymn reveals standard gender expectations among male slaves and shows that they internalized threats to their manhood. Yet due to extreme circumstances, slave men were compelled to express their masculine identity in alternative ways. More often than not, the human instinct of self-preservation took precedence over an ill-advised attempt to affirm their masculinity through violence—at least violence against whites. Despite this exercise of sound judgment, many black nationalist theorists insist that one of the most destructive legacies of slavery is the inheritance of an emasculated "slave mentality."

As defined in 1963 by LeRoi Jones (who later changed his name to Amiri Baraka to signify a shift in "radical" consciousness), a "slave mentality" was "the most socially unfortunate psychic adjustments that the slave had made during the two hundred years of slavery." Jones believed that "two hundred years of bending to the will of the white man had to leave its mark. And that mark was indelibly on the very foundations of the new separate Black society."[64] Many historians, black and white, legitimated the mythology of the "slave mentality" and bought into the idea that slavery left a lasting impression upon the manhood of the black race. By perpetuating a masculinist definition of "resistance" (i.e., equating violence with "manhood"), traditional slave studies incriminated slave men for their enslavement.[65] Distorted portrayals of slave behavior (most specifically the overcharacterization of slaves as childlike and submissive to account for the comparatively lower number of slave insurrections in British North America) and the relative scarcity of alternative representations had a significant impact on black nationalists' reconstructions of the history and legacy of slavery in the United States. This misrepresentation has led them, as historian of black nationalism Sterling Stuckey notes, to "exaggerate the degree of acquiescence to oppression by the Black masses."[66]

A striking example of a masculinist reading of the slave experience in an academic study is Eugene D. Genovese's essay "The Legacy of Slavery and the Roots of Black Nationalism." Originally delivered at the September 1966 Second Annual Socialist Scholars Conference, this paper was an attempt to explain what Genovese perceived to be the lack of a radical political tradition among African Americans (as opposed to Afro-Caribbeans or Afro-Brazilians, for example). In this presentation, Genovese insisted that the American slave system, which he believed was characterized by a paternalistic relationship between master and slave, pacified African America and made its leaders accommodating to the will of white men: "Slavery and its aftermath emasculated the Black masses; they are today profoundly sick and shaking with convulsions," he argued. After the height of Civil Rights protests and at the beginning of the Black Power era, Genovese suggested that the reclamation of black manhood was at the center of African American politics. "Those who believe emasculation is the figment of the liberal imagination ought to read the words of any militant leader from David Walker to W. E. B. Du Bois, from Frederick Douglass to Martin Luther King, from Robert F. Williams to Malcolm X. The cry has been to assert manhood and renounce servility."[67]

As Genovese observed, this historical reductionism is readily apparent in the writings and speeches of black male political leaders during the nineteenth and twentieth centuries, a point highlighted by Nation of Islam minister Malcolm X's critique of his male contemporaries in the Civil Rights movement. "When I listen to Mrs. [Fannie Lou] Hamer, a black woman—could be my mother, my sister, my daughter—describe what they had done to her in Mississippi, I ask myself how in the world can we ever expect to be respected as *men* when we will allow something like that to be done to our women, and we do nothing about it?" he inquired. "No, we don't deserve to be recognized and respected as men as long as our women can be brutalized in the manner that this woman described, and nothing be done about it, but we sit around singing 'We Shall Overcome.'"[68] Malcolm X's statement shows, however, that for black nationalists the need to reclaim black manhood involves more than a desire to renounce servility. They conclude that the only way black men can overcome the "slave mentality" and claim their gendered right to political power and patriarchal authority is through violent resistance. Eldridge Cleaver's review of Algerian anticolonialist and revolutionary theorist Frantz Fanon's canonical text *The Wretched of the Earth* (1963) demonstrates this homeopathic strategy. "What this book does is legitimize the revolutionary impulse to violence," Cleaver wrote in 1967. "It teaches colonial subjects that it is perfectly normal for them to want to rise up and cut off the heads of the slave masters, that it is a way to achieve their manhood, and that they must oppose the oppressor to experience themselves as men."[69] Six years later, theologian Gayraud Wilmore echoed this viewpoint in his esteemed work *Black Religion and Black Radicalism*, presenting the 1831 Nat Turner insurrection as a divinely inspired blow against the emasculation of black manhood during slavery. In his celebration of violent resistance as the antidote for endangered black masculinity (and in protest of William Styron's compromising representation of a nationalist hero), Wilmore wrote, "Nat Turner discovered his manhood by unveiling the God who liberates. His fanatical attempt to authenticate that manhood in blood was the inevitable consequence of the fanatical attempt of white men to deny it."[70]

The endorsement of violence as a weapon in the war against the personal/political castration of black men constantly (re)appears throughout the oral and literary tradition of black nationalist thought in the United States. In fact, it was the motivation behind one of the most provocative publications in the history of American black nationalism, Henry Highland Garnet's *Address to the Slaves of the United States of America* (1848). Like most black nationalists, Garnet strongly believed in divine retribution for the sins of white America. Yet he did not suspend this belief in hopes of judgment in the hereafter. Garnet—a Presbyterian minister—insisted that the slavocracy pay for its crimes against "God and man" in the here and now. Like David Walker, he concluded that the enslaved should avenge the murder, brutality, and exploitation perpetuated by their enslavers. Yet Garnet did so by casting doubt upon the "manliness" of male slaves. Like most nineteenth- and twentieth-century black nationalists, he did not recognize quotidian resistance and misinterpreted slave dissemblance as submission. In a polemic that reads as if it were penned by Nation of Islam minister Louis Farrakhan (at least Farrakhan circa the late 1980's/early 1990's), Garnet challenges the manhood of slave men.

> You act as though, you were made for the special use of these devils. You act as though your daughters were born to pamper the lusts of your masters and overseers. And worse than all, you tamely submit while your lords tear your wives from your embraces and defile them before your eyes. In the name of God, we ask, are you men?[71]

According to Garnet's account, by failing to perform their most important male role—protecting their wives and daughters—slave men were rendered impotent to the will of their masters. Yet in his *Address* Garnet provided a means for his bonded brethren to erect their male status: the act of rebellion. Insisting that it was God's testament, he proclaimed, "Heaven would frown upon the men who would not resist such aggression, even to death."[72] This riotous revelation shocked Garnet's abolitionist peers, for moral suasion was the principal strategy of the antislavery movement in the 1840's. Nevertheless, he took his cultural cues from the ancestors and his political lessons from the American Revolution and concluded that only through violence could black men redeem their manhood. "However much you and all of us may desire it, there is not much hope of redemption without the shedding of blood. If you must bleed, let it all come at once—rather *die freemen, than live to be slaves.*"[73]

While Garnet believed that the remasculation of slave men was a matter of do or die, for some black nationalists, it was kill or be killed. In 1829 David Walker's message to slave insurgents was clear.

[I]f you commence, make sure to work—do not trifle, for they will not trifle with you—they want us for their slaves, and think nothing of murdering us in order to subject us to that wretched condition—therefore, if there is an attempt made by us, kill or be killed.[74]

Walker's command was fearless, but not unfounded. The boundary between slavery and freedom was secured by a constant threat of violence, and any attempt to cross that line could result in death. Walker recognized the gravity of his proposal; however, he rationalized that it was a calculated risk. He deemed counterviolence a necessary evil in the crusade to fulfill both manly and Christian duty.

Look upon your mother, wife and children, and answer God Almighty; and believe this, that it is no more harm for you to kill a man, who is trying to kill you, than it is for you to take a drink of water when thirsty; in fact, the man who will stand still and let another murder him, is worse than an infidel, and, if he has common sense, ought not to be pitied.[75]

As this passage shows, among black nationalists violent resistance was considered not a sin but a divinely ordained crusade—even at the turn of the century. When lynching became a social/economic prescription for destabilized race relations, for many black leaders the desire to aggressively pursue manhood rights was suppressed by the will to live. Yet in an era dominated by the "accommodation politics" of Booker T. Washington, the threat of mob action did not intimidate everyone. Bishop Henry McNeal Turner was proving himself a "fearless confrontationist in an age of compromise,"[76] and in 1889 another black preacher assured his colleagues that "the surest guarantee of respectability for Negroes was for every black man to purchase a gun and use it at the slightest provocation."[77]

What is intriguing about the aggressive stance assumed by these turn-of-the-century black clergymen, particularly that taken by the latter, is its apparent contradiction of the gospel of the New Testament, the foundation of modern black Christian teachings and preaching. However, what these black nationalist ministers and others bring to light is an alternate reading of the New Testament that adapted the story of Jesus to address the needs of their black congregations. It is the religious manifestation of black cultural politics that James H. Cone termed "Black theology" in 1969, and it reflects a knowledge system—a standpoint—that is both pragmatic and radical. Modern problems call for modern solutions, or as Cone points out in *Black Theology and Black Power*, "we cannot solve ethical questions of the twentieth century by looking at what Jesus did in the first."[78] While this realization does not necessitate abandoning or avoiding the work and words of Christ, it does require a reorientation of the Christian en-visionary. For example, in his 1968 book *The Black Messiah*, Albert B. Cleage, Jr., founder of the black nationalist church Shrine of the Black Madonna, demonstrates the revolutionary potential of New Testament doctrines by quoting chapter 11, verse 34 from the Gospel of Matthew: "Do not think that I have come to bring peace on earth; I have not come to bring peace, but a sword." Like his nationalist predecessors Cleage is resourceful, using the Bible as a conjure book in the struggle for black liberation.[79] He unveils Jesus as a "troublemaker" and represents conflict as being as much a part of New Testament doctrine as compassion.[80] Christian righteousness, most often translated in terms of love and forgiveness, can also be expressed through resistance against injustice, Cleage argues. "The question is a very simple one. If we are afraid of conflict then anyone who is not afraid of conflict is our master." Therefore, Cleage concludes, like Walker, Garnet, and Garvey before him, that violent times demand violent measures, for "[a]nyone who is willing to use violence can make anyone who is afraid of violence his slave."[81]

An extensive knowledge of the Bible has proven extremely adaptive to the masculinist discourse of black nationalism. Yet it also reflects the (de)constructive/revisionist, object-to-subject positioning characteristic of the black nationalist tradition. While the Bible is used as an interpretive tool to explain black historical experiences, the slave metaphor is used as an analytical tool to describe the symbolic emasculation of black men in America. The fact that the master/slave analogy continues to have currency in contemporary black politics speaks to the sense of manly dispossession black men have experienced, even as it condemns the slave for the condition of enslavement. One of the most powerful examples of the impact of these sensitivities on black nationalist-masculinist protest is the Black Power movement. No period of black nationalism is more notorious for its proliferation of militant activists than the late 1960's, and no black nationalist organization is more infamous for its advocacy of militant resistance than the Black Panther Party for Self-Defense.

From Pussy Power to Penis Envy: Black Nationalism as a Politics of (Ex)slave Resistance—A Case Study

> [T]he black panthers are the holy men of our time.
> —Sarah Webster Fabio, *The Black Panther*, 1968

During the mid-1960's sexual politics took center stage in the public sphere as America's youth, both black and white, pushed the boundaries of America's consciousness around gender and sexuality. Sex itself became a political act: as white college students raised eyebrows with a sexual revolution that introduced "love-ins" to the North and West, black (male) student activists raised ire with their own form of sexual revolution that involved interracial "love-ins" in the South and West. And if the practice was hot, the theory was even hotter. For at no time in the history of U.S. black nationalism had gendered language been as provocative— or as outrageous—as during the Black Power movement. And at the forefront of this movement was the brazen sexual politics of the Black Panther Party.

"We say that political power, revolutionary power grows out of the lips of a pussy," the party's Minister of Information Eldridge Cleaver announced to an audience at Stanford University in October 1968.[82] Interestingly enough, this statement could be interpreted as a progressive, although audacious, reading of the centrality of women's participation in political struggle. However, a couple of months earlier, in Los Angeles, Cleaver clarified his position on "pussy power" as a tool in the liberation of African America. Because women had "the power to bring a squeaking halt to a lot of things that are going on,"[83] Cleaver instructed them to avoid sexual contact with their apolitical (presumably) male partners: "Until he['s] ready to pick up a gun and be a man, don't give him no sugar." Cleaver concluded by adding even more of a retrogressive twist to his rampant (hetero)sexism: homophobia. "I don't know how you can stand to have them faggots layin' and suckin' on you," he wondered aloud of his female listeners. But in the black revolution, Cleaver assured these women, "You can always get a real man."[84]

At the same time that Eldridge Cleaver was performing masculine prowess and promoting the sexualization of his female comrades with the theory and practice of "Pussy Power," many of his peers in the Black Power movement discouraged extramarital female sexual activity (at least in theory). In fact, within the black nationalist tradition, the political role of black women has been historically defined in terms of their reproductive capabilities. Like their nineteenth- and early-twentieth-century forefathers, most Black Power organizations made official policy out of exalting black motherhood. They argued that it was women's duty to reproduce and raise warriors for the revolution or, as poet Kay Lindsay critiqued in 1970, "[n]ow that the revolution needs numbers / Motherhood got a new position / Five steps behind manhood."[85] In fact, the celebration of motherhood in the Black Power movement was bolstered by the belief that birth control and abortion were genocidal plots of "The Man." "Educate your woman to stop taking those pills," Panther member Evette Pearson enjoined her male peers in January 1969. "You and your woman—replenish the earth with healthy black warriors."[86] Meanwhile, during the early years of the Congress of African People, gender roles in the organization corresponded with the "separate spheres" doctrine of the nineteenth century. The women of the Committee for a Unified NewArk, the parent organization of the Congress of African People, asserted in a pamphlet titled *Mwanamke Mwananchi (The Nationalist Woman)* that "[n]ature has made women submissive" and that a woman's duties—inspiring her husband, educating her children, participating in the "social development of the nation"—were confined to the private sphere. Highly influenced by Maulana Karenga, these women, who referred to themselves as the "Malaikas" (a Swahili word that means "angels"), validated their position with a passage from *The Quotable Karenga*: "What makes a woman appealing is femininity and she can't be feminine without being submissive."[87]

While the US Organization, the Congress of African People, and other Black Power activists conformed to the Victorian sexual ethic popular among their nineteenth-century predecessors, the leadership of the Black Panther Party defied tradition and modernized the sexual politics of U.S. black nationalism. Yet, as previously stated, the two standpoints—the pious and the profane—are more congruous than they may appear, for they both endow black men with the right to determine the parameters of black women's sexuality. The propagation of "pussy power" during the early period of the Black Panther Party's development shifted the symbolic role of male nationalist from protector to pimp. In fact, the San Francisco chapter of the Black Panther Party had to defend itself from allegations that it prostituted its female members during a 1969 conflict with the San Francisco Black Guard. "We do not pimp our women," one party member countered. "They are our other half which makes up the whole."[88] Pimping may not be a revolutionary act, but it is a role that both contradicted and conformed to the imagining of patriarchal power integral to the black nationalist tradition.

As previously discussed, one of the catalysts behind the "changing same" of the Black Panther Party's sexual politics was the publication of the "Moynihan Report," an influential yet erroneous study that misinterpreted black women's pragmatism as domination. Borrowing from sociologist E. Franklin Frazier's influential study *The Negro Family in the United States* (1939), Moynihan claimed that black men's inability to earn a family wage throughout the nineteenth and twentieth centuries impelled black women into the workforce and propelled them into a more equal role in the household. Yet instead of recognizing this family dynamic as a consequence of sheer necessity (or as evidence that black women "do what they have to"),[89] Moynihan overestimated black women's prerogative and argued that they had not learned to submit to black men. Subsequently, the myth of the black matriarch, and its concomitant characterization of black women as castrators of black men, was widely circulated in the politics and practices of the early Black Power movement. For example, Eldridge Cleaver used it in combination with the masculinist discourse of war to explain his take on the political economy of racial domination. "There is a war going on between the black man and black woman which makes her the silent ally, indirectly but effectively, of the white man," he theorized. "That's why, all down through history, he has propped her up economically above you and me, to strengthen her hand against us."[90] Moynihan's conclusions, although not cited, are also a perceptible influence on cultural nationalist Larry Neal. Like Cleaver, Neal identified an economic conspiracy against black men and diagnosed its affliction on gender relations within black communities. "Since he cannot provide for his family the way white men do, she despises his weakness, tearing into him at every opportunity until, very often, there is nothing left but a shell." He then concluded, "The only way out of this dilemma is through revolution."[91]

Because of the widespread dissemination of this supposed gender "dilemma," those women who attempted to challenge sexism in the movement found it necessary to navigate the political minefield of the matriarch thesis and engage the language of the Moynihan Report lest they be scapegoated and accused of emasculating black men. "I think, historically, even at this time, even for women in the [Black Panther] Party, to say we want full share and full responsibility is *kind of* difficult and *kind of* touchy because of our society," one Panther women confessed with apparent hesitation.

> Our men have been *sort of* castrated you know. The responsibilities that they rightfully should have had before, were taken away from them—to take away their manhood. We've had to fight all this before. Our men are constantly thinking or saying that maybe if we assume a heavier role, a more responsible role, that this, in turn, will sort of take away their responsibility and it's such a touchy thing, that we have to be sure that the roles are evenly divided.[92]

It is evident that this unidentified Panther is cautious; she struggles to advocate gender equality but is careful to avoid a charge of racial treason. Her conscientiousness demonstrates the extent to which black women were besieged by the allegations of the Moynihan Report and its adherents. Not all black women were as indulgent. In a 1965 article published in *The Liberator*, writer Betty Frank Lomax candidly discussed the precarious position of women caught between economics and the experts. Although black women were being accused of being matriarchs and emasculators, she wrote, "we all know . . . no man is dominated by his woman unless it appeals to his *neurotic* need for some kind of sexual phantasy, or some expiation of his guilt and hence, brutality passed off as masculine dominance."[93] Despite Lomax's protestations, many black men and women endorsed the race and gender theories initiated by the Moynihan Report. Angela Davis, a feminist survivor of the Black Power movement, commented upon the detrimental effects the matriarch/female castrator concept had on African American movements for social change: "Black men and women alike remain its potential victims—men unconsciously lunging at the woman, equating her with the myth; women sinking back into the shadows, lest an aggressive posture resurrect the myth in themselves."[94]

In the oral and literary texts produced during the early years of the Black Power movement, black women were presumed guilty before proven innocent, a dire consequence of the matriarch thesis. As Davis intimates and the unnamed Panther woman confirms, black women were not immune to the hype. Many were compelled to be complicit, at least rhetorically, in their own gender subordination. For example, at a 1965 conference held in Harlem called "The Role of the Black Woman in a White Society," a panel of black women expressed their desire to restore "traditional" family roles and the virtue of black women. "Black women must reject the insidious castrating, feminist concept that now prevails in America," they insisted. One panelist, Myra Bain, a writer for the conservative magazine the *National Review*, claimed, "the Black woman's role in society is supplementary to and defined by the role of the Black man."[95] Black Panther Gloria Bartholomew agreed in a 1968 article published in the party's newspaper. "What is a Black woman's chief function, if it is not to live for her man?" she asked. "The Black woman must drop the white ways of trying to be equal to the Black man. The woman's place is to stand behind the Black man, so in the event that he should start to fall she is there to hold him with her strength."[96] And in the early 1970's, the female members of the Congress of African People defended black men's right to patriarchal power and privileges and supported the implementation of conventional gender roles within their organization. In 1971 the Malaikas, informed by "African" cultural values, reasoned that black men were the leaders of the "house/nation" because their mental and physical capacities were greater than women's. "After all," they maintained, "it is only reasonable that the man be the head of the house because he is able to defend and protect the development of his home."[97]

While these women responded to the "crisis of masculinity" articulated by Moynihan and the thesis of black matriarchy by "returning to tradition," their male counterparts excavated the praxis of black nationalism as a masculinist discourse and, once again, envisioned it as a politics of (ex)slave resistance. Over one hundred years after the publication of David Walker's *Appeal*, Black Power advocates continued to revive the slave metaphor, particularly the concept of the "slave mentality" and its effect on national identity. The perduring shame over slavery drove cultural nationalists like the US Organization to historical revisionism about their "glorious African past"[98] and prompted revolutionary nationalists like the Black Panther Party to theorize about the peculiar institution's repercussions on black-white race relations. From "Pussy Power" to "penis envy," the official version of the Black Panther Party's sexual politics was directly and indirectly shaped by an attempt to purge the burden of emasculation triggered by a historical memory of slavery. Eldridge Cleaver's *Soul on Ice* provides a prime example.

Even though it was written before his affiliation with the organization, Cleaver's seminal composition made a significant imprint on the literary and oral stylings of the Black Panther Party. In *Soul on Ice* the slave metaphor reemerges as the ideological linchpin of the masculinist discourse of black nationalism, as Cleaver testifies that the slave experience dehumanized black men and undermined black manhood. Take, for example, his construction of race/gender theses—particularly his characterization of black men as the "Supermasculine Menial" and white men as the "Omnipotent Administrator"—to explain the dialectic of power in the United States, an approach that was disseminated throughout early Panther literature. Cleaver proclaims that by determining the value of male slaves in terms of their corporeal—or "masculine"—capabilities, slaveholders deprived them of cognition, which white men then conferred upon themselves. This process emasculated black men, he argues, because by alienating them from their minds, white men robbed male slaves of their right to self-determination in the private sphere. Of the impact of this transformation on the relationship between black men and black women, Cleaver writes, "Having no sovereignty over himself, he hasn't that sovereignty over her which our traditional patriarchal myths lead her to believe he should have."[99] In contrast to the debased status of slave men, Cleaver alleges that black women were empowered by enslavement; according to his historical narrative, the female slave metamorphosed into an "Amazon" who, alongside her "psychic bridegroom" the Omnipotent Administrator, consummated the deed of black male oppression.

Yet Panther rhetoricians deciphered a miscalculation in the plan to deconstruct black manhood that would be the key to its reconstruction: penis envy. Party leaders contended that in their scheme to disengage the mind from the body, white men participated in their own castration. "This caused the slave-master to become very envious of the slave," Newton told Party members, "because he pictured the slave as being more of a man, being superior sexually, because the penis is part of the body."[100] The historical legacy of penis envy informed the contemporary racist imagination and, therefore, racial discrimination, added Chairman Bobby Seale in a 1969 interview. "A good part of racism is the absurd psychological fears on the part of people who think that the black man has a bigger penis than the white," he asserted. "Thus male supremacy on the basis of sex organs can be connected to racial supremacy arrived at through the notion of sexual differences by race."[101] The Panthers' theorization of "penis envy" betrays an underlying motivation behind the embodied-social politics of black nationalism, a politics that reduces race relations to a cockfight between black and white men. At this point, the movement becomes less about a politics of liberation than about a "politics of substitution," the objective being defined in terms of masculine appropriation. Penis envy (officially labeled "manhood rights") is latent in the call for patriarchal power and manifest in the appeal for sexual access to white women; but while the former is discussed explicitly, the latter is an explicit discussion that evidences just how personal the political is, particularly for men in the Black Power movement.

In "The Allegory of the Black Eunuchs," a concluding chapter in *Soul on Ice*, Eldridge Cleaver portrays what he perceived to be an illicit sexual desire among black men, a desire he had earlier labeled "a revolutionary sickness." Cleaver attempted to explicate the psychology of interracial heterosexual relationships through a character named "the Infidel," an inmate alternately identified as "Lazarus" to signify his political (un)consciousness. He is the antagonist of the story and the arch enemy of a group of young black radicals Cleaver christened "the Eunuchs." In contrast to the Black Eunuchs, the Infidel embodies the a/politics of an older, presumably Civil Rights, generation. Yet at issue in "The Allegory of the Black Eunuchs" is not the political strategy of the Infidel but his sexual depravity. The Infidel is shameless in his lust for white women. According to his estimation, black liberation is measured by his freedom to engage in sexual relations with The Man's woman, a freedom he defends by invoking the slave metaphor: "I know that the white man made the black woman the symbol of slavery and the white woman the symbol of freedom," he professed. "I will not be free until the day I can have a white woman in my bed and a white man minds his own business. Until that day comes, my entire existence is tainted, poisoned, and I will still be a slave—and so will the white woman."[102]

Cleaver's exposition of this "triangle of desire"[103]—comprised of the black man as Subject, the white man as Other, and the white woman as the object of the Other—epitomizes the positioning of black nationalism as a politics of masculine protest. It is an example of the covetous manner in which power has been defined by black male nationalists and helps to explain why black empowerment has been framed as a struggle for re-masculation, or a politics of substitution. Freedom for black male na-tionalists has been equated with free access to the symbols of white male power, and as the Infidel declares in "The Allegory of the Black Eu-nuchs," "Until that day comes . . . I will still be a slave." This perceived power struggle between black and white men over the symbols of man-hood—this penis envy—reveals a method to the madness of black na-tionalism as a politics of (ex)slave resistance. It demonstrates the role of "unconscious phantasy as a structuring principle of our social, emo-tional, and political life."[104] For a preoccupation with the "triangle of de-sire" is also recognizable in the pronouncements of other premodern, modern, and postmodern black nationalists. Among those who have gone out of their way to express disfavor for the "forbidden fruit" are David Walker, who insisted in 1829, "I would not give a pinch of snuff to be married to any white person I ever saw in all the days of my life"; a follower of Maulana Karenga, who proudly reported in 1967 that, be-cause of his mentor, "I no longer have to want those stringy haired, col-orless, white women"; and Ice Cube, who in his 1993 song "Cave Bitch" announced, "Stringy hair, no derrière / frontin' and fakin' with your sili-cone pair / Do I wanna fuck? Not hardly."[105] Therefore, while cultural studies scholar Kobena Mercer insists that it is important to recognize white "Fear of a Black Penis," it is equally as important to recognize black men's internalization of and response to cultural anxieties over the (sur)reality of black masculinity. In the case of U.S. black nationalism, particularly as explicitly articulated by leaders in the Black Panther Party, penis envy is phallus/y that has determined the means by which black male artists, intellectuals, and activists have pursued their political ambi-tions. Or as Huey Newton rationalized in a 1968 interview published by *The Movement*, "If he can only recapture his mind, recapture his balls, then he will lose all fear and will be free to determine his destiny."[106]

Like their nineteenth-century predecessors, Black Panther leaders maintained that the only process by which the (ex)slave could reclaim his manhood—that is, recapture his mind/balls—is through violent resis-tance. While the future Minister of Information highlighted the theme of interpersonal relations in *Soul on Ice*, the Minister of Defense focused on the political arena. Influenced by the words and work of Malcolm X and Mao Tse-tung, Huey Newton advised party members that liberation would be realized by any means necessary. "We say the only way we're going to be free is by seizing political power which comes through the barrel of the gun."[107] The men of the Central Committee, inspired by anticolonial freedom fighters in Africa and Asia, declared violence a necessary tool of liberation politics. And like their black nationalist forefathers in the United States, Black Panther leaders preferred death to submission—at least in theory. "As far as we are concerned we would rather be dead than go on with the slavery that we're in. Once we compromise we will be compromising not only our freedom, but also our manhood," Newton explained in a manner reminiscent of antislavery nationalists like David Walker and Henry Highland Garnet. "And this is the basic point," he concluded. "Either we will win or we will die trying to win."[108]

Conclusion: Y La Lucha Continua . . .

From the community patrol campaign to the free breakfast program for school children, the popularity of the Black Panther Party was built on the projection of its members into the patriarchal role of provider/protector. Although its liberatory praxes represented the party's most impressive work in various local communities, it was the outrageous masculinist "it's-a-dick-thing" sexual politics of the Panther leadership that left a lasting impression on the community at large. Yet despite its phallocentric approach to the discourse of black nationalism, the Black Panther Party proved appealing to black women, as well as men, in the early years of its organizational development. "Check it out sister, what is it we've all wanted from our Black males and Black brothers for so long?" member Ida Walston inquired of her fellow female comrades. "Going back as far as the days of slavery we've wanted our men to stand up and be heard, to be the one to determine his own destiny and the destiny of the people, haven't we worked for this, stolen, lied and whored for this?"[109] Former Panther leader Elaine Brown also bore witness to a desire to observe strong black men in defense of their communities. In fact, she acknowledged that it was the spectacle of Black (male) Power—the antithesis of the emasculated man—that attracted her to the movement. "Here were men who were saying listen, we are willing to take charge of our lives, we are willing to stand up," she recalls in the compelling documentary *Eyes on the Prize*. "That had a certain subjective appeal to my psyche and to my emotional need to say, yes, there were men in this world, black men, who cared about the community and wanted to do something and were willing to take it to the last degree."[110]

While patriarchal protection was attractive to some black women who, like a number of black men, felt they had been denied the benefits associated with their traditional gender roles, many women in the Black Power movement paid the price for their collusion with a political theory and practice based upon male domination. For example, a sexual division of labor relegated black women to menial positions during the developmental years of the Black Panther Party, the Revolutionary Action Movement, and the Congress of African People. The responsibility of women in these organizations and others was restricted to office-related work like typing, filing, and producing and distributing pamphlets and flyers—not to mention cooking and cleaning. For example, during the early years of the Committee for a Unified NewArk, organizational divisions developed according to traditional gender roles. Women led the Social Organization Council, the African Free School (and its 24-hour nursery), the Chakula Ujamaa (a collective kitchen), and the Ushoni Ujamaa (a sewing collective that tailored African attire). Alternately, the men led the departments of economics, politics, and security. In retrospect, women's adoption of these subordinate roles may appear disempowering, but such simplified or superficial readings underestimate the appeal of the race/gender politics of black nationalism. It is important to bear in mind that many female black nationalists, like their male counterparts, "are attracted to the affirmation of blackness and the open confrontation with white supremacy offered by black nationalist ideologies."[111] Literary scholar Farah Jasmine Griffin cautions feminists who critique black nationalist women for embracing a political ideology that focuses on patriarchal rights and privileges: support should not always be interpreted as sanction of the masculinist discourse of black nationalism. For although most black feminists fail to differentiate among conservative, liberal, and radical black nationalists, she writes, "[m]any black women see room to negotiate gender roles within this continuity."[112]

This is, in fact, what happened in the Black Panther Party. In the early years "Pantherettes" were rarely seen working in the field, giving speeches at universities, or representing the organization at conferences, with the exception of Kathleen Cleaver, the Party's Communication Secretary, who ran with Newton and Seale on the Peace and Freedom Democratic Party ticket for California state office in 1968. The patriarchal tone of the national agenda began to shift, however, in 1969 as women in the organization began to challenge its counterrevolutionary gender theories and practices. That year Party leaders Huey Newton, Bobby Seale, and Fred Hampton publicly denounced male chauvinism, and a year later, Newton advised Panther members to set aside their homophobia and build coalitions with gays and lesbians.[113] Therefore, while the Black Panther Party is probably best remembered for its hypermasculine public image, it was one of the first black nationalist organizations to reject sexism in theory and practice. Although imperfect, its leadership and its rank and file struggled with issues of gender and sexuality in ways that defy simple, linear explanation.[114] For example, the most symbolic moment of the Black Panther Party's attempts at gender equality occurred in 1974 with the promotion of Elaine Brown to the position of national chairman. Second only to founder and Minister of Defense Huey Newton, Brown became the acting leader of the Black Panther Party while Newton was in political exile. And yet this promotion did not go uncontested. Many male members of the Black Panther Party begrudged Elaine Brown's leadership, and by her account, this resentment was one of the catalysts for the party's demise. In her controversial autobiography, Elaine Brown describes the hostility she experienced after she advanced to the position of party chairman, recalling that she heard "echoes of the men's accusations that Huey had let some bitch run their shit, intrude upon their world, where aggression and violence defined manhood."[115]

The Black Panther Party represents the best and the worst of black nationalist politics. Its sexual politics and struggle with gender issues reveal, as Kobena Mercer and Isaac Julien articulate, that "[a]lthough black men have been able to exploit the contradictions of the dominant ideological regimes of truth, the political limitations of remaining within its given structure of representation became acutely apparent in the context of black liberation movements of the 1960s."[116] The story of the Black Panther Party demonstrates the dynamic nature and radical potential of black political culture, from the leadership's rhetorical dependence on sexism and homophobia to reconstruct a weakened sense of masculine identity to their willingness to transform the party's patriarchal and heterosexist platforms.

Unfortunately, this legacy was short lived. When black nationalism returned to the forefront of the black political arena during the late 1980's/early 1990's, this was not the reincarnation of the Black Panther Party embraced by young black men and women. In fact, the legend of the Black Panther Party that prevailed in the imagination of a post–Black Power generation of neonationalists ignored these shifts in Panther ideology. Just as male activists during the Black Power era cultivated a masculinist memory of Malcolm X, raptivists during the golden age of rap nationalism romanticized the historical memory of the Black Panther Party as an organization of militant thugs. This "production of exemplary masculinity"—this hero worship—again became a necessary tool in the attempt to rehabilitate black manhood during the late 1980's/early 1990's, when the focus of black nationalist politics shifted from the emasculated black man to the black man as an "endangered species." "Our vision of heroism is not for the timid, the insecure, or the introverted," writes rap documentarian Nelson George of *Hip Hop America*. "We like them bold, we like them to embody our blasculinity, and, be they revolutionaries or rap stars, we like to know they are ready to die—even though we truly don't want them to."[117]

3

Brothers Gonna Work It Out

The Popular/Political Culture of Rap Music

In the 1988 Public Enemy release "Party for Your Right to Fight," rap nationalist and lead lyricist Chuck D ushered in a new moment in hip-hop history when he defiantly stated,

> Power equality and we're out to get it
> I know some of you ain't with it
> This party started right in '66
> With a pro-black radical mix.[1]

As a trailblazer of the consciousness movement within rap music, Chuck D claimed his legacy as the political progeny of the Black Panther Party. The Black Panthers, remembered by the hip-hop generation as righteous revolutionaries, are deified and located among an elite class of politicized "prophets of rage." They are black nationalists whose standard for black manhood is preserved and emulated. In fact, Chuck D told a *Toronto Sun* reporter in May of 1998 that when he and his friends from Adelphi University entered the rap game they did so in a deliberate manner. "We wanted to be known as the Black Panthers of Rap, we wanted our music to be dissonant."[2] With songs like "Party for Your Right to Fight," "Fight the Power," and "Power to the People," these pioneers of rap nationalism purposefully invoked the rhetorical and political styling of the Black Panther Party and the Black Power movement of the late 1960's, complete with its envisioning of black nationalism as a politics of masculine protest. Like their idols, Chuck D and his crew believed that they were the representatives of a "revolutionary generation," a group of in-dangered young black males considered by the state to be "Public Enemy

#1."[3] And as public enemies, Chuck D argued that it was black men's responsibility to "get mad, revolt, revise, realize" for black liberation;[4] for, as he stated on their 1990 album *Fear of a Black Planet*, "it takes a man to take a stand."[5]

Although the use of rap music as a form of cultural expression was not a revolutionary idea (that musical movement began over ten years prior to the introduction of rap nationalism), the use of rap music as a site for political expression was radical. And in politicized rap music demonstrative race and gender politics reemerged with a vengeance, thrusting "it's-a-dick-thing" masculinity into the public sphere and propelling black political/popular culture into the national spotlight. "It is the forcefulness of rap's insurrection that allows it to *penetrate* white defenses," insists Jon Michael Spencer, using the same kind of sexualized masculinist language found in the lyrics of the artists he spotlights.[6] From East Coast groups such as Public Enemy, Boogie Down Productions, and X-Clan to West Coast artists like Ice Cube, Paris, and Kam, rap nationalists intentionally conjured a tradition of model, and militant, black manhood. Utilizing black nationalist politics and hip-hop culture, these artists and others offered young black males the opportunity to reassert a masculine presence in the public domain. This effort was, in part, a response to the popular music of the mid-1980's when black male artists like Michael Jackson and Prince dominated the charts. "When rap came out I thought it was the perfect thing for me," exclaimed Brand Nubian's lyricist Lord Jamar. With rap music "a lot of masculine men said, 'Yeah, this is the way I can sing without singing, and this is a way for me to write poetry without being a poet, like a soft poet.' And that's why rap is so popular because you can still keep your masculinity."[7] Public Enemy's "Sister of Instruction" Sister Souljah agreed. "Rappers are bringing back the notion of strong, masculine voices," she declared, singing the praises of hip-hop music in a manner that intimated how she envisioned her (secondary) role as a woman within the rap nationalist movement. "You will not find a black male rapper who sounds like DeBarge or some other soprano singer."[8] Souljah's view of the masculinist impulse shaping rap nationalism as a counterpoint to the effeminate representation of black men in popular culture was affirmed by her bandmate Chuck D. In the 1991 hip-hop documentary *Tour of a Black Planet*, Chuck proclaimed that the "black man is already emasculated and this standard is projected to black males" through R & B music. Therefore, according to Chuck D, black men needed counterimages, an "intellectual, pro-black point of view" symbolized by men like Malcolm X, Louis Farrakhan—even Martin Luther King, Jr.[9]

As rap artists rebelled against the black male image in popular culture, there was a noticeable void in the black political arena. Black men and women held more electoral positions on the local, state, and federal level; however, political representation did not translate into a marked difference in the material conditions of life for many African Americans, in part because the move from protest politics to electoral politics after the Second Reconstruction rendered black political leaders and organizations—rigidified in Civil Rights strategy—ineffective and ill prepared to address the multifaceted needs of African America, particularly those of the poor.[10] "Most people I grew up with in Newark grew up under black rule," attested hip-hop activist and spoken word artist Ras Baraka. "They didn't grow up under [white mayor, Hugh] Addonizio. They grew up under [black mayors, Kenneth] Gibson and Sharpe James, with predominantly black city councils, black police directors, black county prosecutors, and went to Malcolm X Shabazz or George Washington Carver elementary school." Meanwhile, the deputy mayor of Newark explained, "[black] folks are still disenfranchised. People thought if blacks gained power in the city then somehow that translated into power for all black people. And it did not."[11] In fact, while the gap between the white haves and the black have-nots widened during this period, there was a deafening silence in the black political arena that led one political scientist to conclude *We Have No Leaders*.[12] This crisis in black leadership, which intensified during the Reagan and Bush administrations, did not go unnoticed by the hip-hop generation. "Back in the '60s, there was a big push for black senators and politicians, and now we have more than we ever had before, but our communities are so much worse," reported raptivist Talib Kweli. "A lot of people died for us to vote, I'm aware of that history, but these politicians are not in touch with people at all. Politics is not the truth to me, it's an illusion."[13]

As disillusionment and alienation began to permeate the political imagination of the post–Civil Rights generation, rap artists idolized the words and works of political personalities like Marcus Garvey, Malcolm X, and Louis Farrakhan, men whose uncompromising public personae and urban, poor/working-class roots stood as an example to those whose masculine status was being undermined by a postindustrial capitalist economy.[14] "God knows, when I heard Farrakhan, I had never heard a black man talk like that. It blew my mind, absolutely blew my mind," hip-hop journalist/activist Kevin Powell recalled of his introduction to Farrakhan during the mid-1980's. "It was intoxicating, as intoxicating as crack was for a lot of people in our community in the '80s." For Powell that event at New York City's Madison Square Garden was affirming; it bolstered his sense of manhood and gave him an opportunity to—at least symbolically—defy white male domination. "I really believe that a lot of black nationalism that is embraced by black men has to do with fear," he confessed, speaking directly to the sense of emasculation experienced by many young black men during the mid-1980's. "You feel powerless your entire life. And all of a sudden you have this space. You can be Marcus Garvey, and talk stuff to white folks. You can be Malcolm X and talk stuff to white folks."[15]

Powell's experience reveals how, for some males (and females) in postindustrial, post–Civil Rights African America, the masculinist discourse of black nationalism begat a feeling of empowerment. Within the context of the perceived crisis of masculinity that arose, in part, due to the popular and political culture of the mid-1980's, it is not surprising that within hip-hop communities during the late 1980's and early 1990's rap music became a vehicle for the dissemination of black neonationalist politics. It was a tool used to both inspire and translate what French philosopher Michel Foucault called an "insurrection of subjugated knowledge," the sometimes radical, always subversive thinking and/or activism that characterizes the politics of dominated and exploited peoples. "With the forced exile, incarceration, and execution of black leaders, rappers have become the spokesmen for the black community," reported Disposable Heroes of Hiphoprisy frontman Michael Franti.[16] Much like their nineteenth- and twentieth-century predecessors, these artists and activists in the Hip-Hop Nation used an embodied-social politics to impart meaning and significance to the increasingly depressed state of urban black America. They interpreted the effects of postmodern, postindustrial, post–Civil Rights social, political, and economic transformations with a language of masculine dispossession and, thus, endorsed a masculinist agenda for empowerment.

Bring(in') the Noise: The Politicization of Rap Music

> The power and consciousness of the Hip Hop movement flow
> through the circle of leadership they offer to the current generation.

> It is imperative that we recognize that it is no coincidence that this
> cultural movement explodes after a full decade of cultural implo-
> sion.   —Joseph Eure and James G. Spady, *Nation Conscious Rap*

The resurgence of nationalism in black communities during the mid- to-
late 1980's may strike some historical observers as odd, since it appeared
on the heels of the legal gains made during the Civil Rights movement.
However, in the period immediately following the Second Reconstruction, much like that which immediately followed Reconstruction, the
conservative antiblack backlash was quick and severe, both legally and
extralegally. Those who were never exposed to the kind of institutionalized racism outlawed by the Civil Rights Act of 1964 and the Voting
Rights Act of 1965 nevertheless experienced segregated spaces and disfranchisement. This postapartheid generation of black youth grew up
with the rhetoric of integration politics yet nonetheless felt the sting of
marginalization, alienation, and the contradiction of inner-city segregation. These stark realities were compounded by the economic devastation
inspired, in part, by federal policies that made the exploitation of foreign
labor more appealing than that of local labor—a trend that, as we have
seen, was not alleviated by the growing number of local and national
black elected officials, which in turn contributed to widespread disillusionment with the political process. Meanwhile the Reagan-Bush administrations unleashed class warfare as affirmative action and community
programs were dismantled and the criminalization of poverty underwrote
the prison industrial complex.

Ironically, even the social experiments that resulted from the Civil
Rights movement did not necessarily read as progress for those working-
and middle-class black youth who—through busing and suburban relocation—found themselves isolated in predominantly white neighborhoods and secondary schools. Furthermore, public confusion over racial
loyalty in the 1991 Anita Hill–Clarence Thomas sexual harassment hearings revealed that in a desegregated African America, race could no
longer ensure political allegiance. The overall social, political, economic,
and cultural transformations of the post–Civil Rights, postindustrial,
postmodern period from which rap nationalism emerged demonstrate
that "we bear witness to a more insidious and complex structure of domination."[17]

Nationalism became a logical response for those in the hip-hop generation seeking to make sense of the chaos that characterized the 1970's and

'80s. "I think you have to be separate first," reckoned Lord Jamar of Brand Nubian. "Integration is not working, and to pretend that it is, is just a lie."[18] However, as nationalist sentiment evolved into a hip-hop movement, some critics—in comparing it to other freedom struggles—measured its significance in terms of its ability to motivate and mobilize social activism, and in finding no mass movement, judged it a failure and/or a fraud.[19] This is both a legitimate and a limited assessment. While it is true that this genre of rap music did not immediately galvanize a youth movement and that its political promise is circumscribed by its commercialization—or as Nelson George argues, rap artists are "entertainers whose viability and effectiveness as messengers are subject to the whims of the marketplace"[20]—it is also true that its political potential was expanded by its mass dissemination and ability to reach global markets. Years after rap nationalism ceased to be a recognized force within hip-hop culture, disfranchised and dispossessed youth regardless of race, ethnicity, class, gender, and nationality embraced rap music as a forum for politicking, and that phenomenon began with raptivists like Public Enemy and Boogie Down Productions.[21] This success is due to the fact that, as feminist scholar Wahneema Lubiano recognizes, for cultural workers in the business of black nationalism "[p]erformance equals the wished-for destiny but it also equals the strategy by which that destiny literally comes into being at the moment of consumption of cultural production."[22] So while there is no denying that rap nationalists were not social activists or political leaders, they were perceived as worthy spokespersons for a generation disillusioned with "liberal integrationism"[23] who were intent on defining their own history and determining their own political moment distinct from that of their parents.

This was no small feat. Rap music has proven to be a theater of intergenerational warfare over the future of African America as middle-aged, middle-class black men and women grieve for the political culture of their past and over the perceived transgressions of the cultural politics of the present. During the 1990's the Civil Rights generation returned to the public arena to protest the cultural production created by the beneficiaries of their political labor. Unfortunately, they had tunnel vision, equating "rap music" with "gangsta rap," the most controversial and sensationalized of rap genres. "To such young people," bemoans literary historian Sandra Hollin Flowers, "the regimen of a rigorous, disciplined political agenda would seem an unattractive alternative to the freedom of day-to-day existence driven by drugs, 'scoring,' 'gang banging,' spontaneous aggression, and the rhythms of rap music."[24] In their movement against what they perceived to be the profane and pornographic nature of rap music, community elders used the most powerful moral ammunition in their arsenal: they invoked the names of their s/heroes in an attempt to censor the music that would come to represent the post–Civil Rights generation. "I believe that African American women such as Harriet Tubman, Rosa Parks, Ella Baker, Sojourner Truth and Fannie Lou Hamer, among others, did not struggle and jeopardize their lives to give young black music artists the temerity to refer to black women as bitches and whores and, with abandon, characterize African American people as niggers," wrote Reverend Calvin Butts of Abyssinian Baptist Church in Harlem.[25]

Butts, pastor of the oldest black Baptist church in New York, led a highly publicized campaign against hip-hop music in 1993. That summer Butts received media attention for threatening to steamroll thousands of rap music compact discs, although he insisted that he did not advocate censorship, "just common decency and favoring high culture over low."[26] The following year, fellow baby boomer C. Delores Tucker also created media frenzy with her antirap crusade. As the president of the National Council for Black Women, Tucker successfully lobbied Congress for two hearings before the Subcommittee on Commerce, Consumer Protection, and Competitiveness in an attempt to ban—not censor—gangsta rap. The transcript of these hearings stands as evidence of the intergenerational conflict raging within black communities during the late twentieth century. Tucker, like Butts, believed there are limits to the civil liberties gained by African Americans during the 1950's and '60s. "This freedom," she testified, "freedom from responsibility and accountability, is not the kind of freedom that Dr. King, Medgar Evers, John Lewis, James Farmer, Rosa Parks and so many others risked their lives for."[27] Apparently even Rosa Parks agrees, for in 1999 she sued Atlanta-based rap artists OutKast for defamation of character. Parks objected to the group's use of her name as the title of one of their songs, because as her lawyer argued "hip-hop is disrespectful to establishment figures."[28]

According to black baby boomers, rap music's list of violations is long, but as sociologist Rod Bush observes, this "[d]ismissive sniping by the elders, lamenting youth's failure to follow the trail that *we* blazed, has always generated more heat than light."[29] Recognizing that the criticism launched by the Civil Rights generation was tinged with sanctimoniousness, the hip-hop generation did not submit to the moral conviction of their elders. "You blinded by cultural ignorance and steady judging," charged KRS-One in his 1995 song "Free Mumia." "But judge not, lest ye may be judged."[30] Using C. Delores Tucker as an example, hip-hop journalist Kierna Mayo Dawsey exposed just how anachronistic and self-satisfied the Civil Rights generation had become: "Although some of us will, it's a little scary that Dr. Tucker would assume that Snoop Doggy Dogg, or me for that matter, cares that she marched with King," she wrote. "At this very moment, the gap between the generations in black America is as wide as the Sahara. 'Kids have it better today,' she tells me. Really?"[31]

While Civil Rights veterans perceived decades of work unraveling before their eyes, young scholars and artists of the hip-hop generation responded by challenging their elders' sense of political "progress." Bill Stephney, cofounder of Public Enemy and president of StepSun Music, contends that during the late 1980's the hip-hop generation was responding not only to the retrogressive race politics of the Reagan-Bush era but also to what they perceived to be "some terrible choices [made] by the Civil Rights generation." Stephney evaluated the political strategy of the Civil Rights movement and deemed it short-sighted: "our success is just access to white institutions that [they] told us were wrong in the first place."[32] Other rap nationalists also expressed frustration with the generational conflict over hip-hop music in terms of what they perceived to be the political limitations of the Civil Rights movement. Coming of age after the Second Reconstruction, they called into question the self-righteous attitude of their detractors. "A lot of people feel that people from the 60's took their eyes off of the prize in the 70's," explained Ice Cube. "And we picked it up ourselves, now they want to show us how to do it. They want us to do it the same way they did it, and it didn't work. So you have kids who don't want to listen."[33] In an interview that predated the "gangsta" rap controversy, Chuck D described what he identified as the unfinished business of the Civil Rights and Black Power movements. Like Ice Cube and Stephney, he betrayed a hint of historical regret: "There was a sense of complacency in the early '70s: 'Okay, we've fought, we've reached our goal.' These people thought they were on an equal plane, or equal status. So you had a lot of people brainwashed during that period of time. So they didn't teach their young. But the young learn the hard way."[34]

For better or worse, rap music became a forum for black nationalist thought. The music reflected a political consciousness that developed in response to the social, political, economic, and cultural conditions confronting young black Americans during the late 1980's/early 1990's, conditions that were partly the result of gains made by the Civil Rights movement. The dissemination of politicized rap music was aided by an increasingly advanced communications technology (which ironically also signaled its declining significance in the political arena),[35] making hip-hop culture a legitimate tool for transmitting political thought to a generation whose attention span was increasingly being challenged by multimedia stimuli. "The basic assumptions and tactics that guided the African-American middle class for several generations no longer reflect the actual economic, social, and political conditions challenging the Black community," articulates historian Manning Marable.[36] Ras Baraka, who lost a bid for Newark city council in 2002, agrees: new times call for new measures. "There's a difference between the thinking of young black people and older black people, because they dealt with complete segregation and disenfranchisement by white people," he stated. "There is a serious and complete lack of understanding about where this generation should go, what we should be doing."[37] For the first time in the history of African America, civil rights were no longer an integral part of the black nationalist agenda as young, working- and middle-class black men and women attempted to redefine and revise liberatory politics at the end of the twentieth century. "There was a time for boycotts," pronounced rap artist Talib Kweli. "But once the people who did that handled their business, it became time for their children to find new ways of dealing with shit."[38] While the absence of civil rights as a political platform is probably the most significant shift in the postmodern manifestation of black nationalism, the emergence and evolution of neonationalist sentiment in rap music demonstrate that there are also political ideologies and methodologies that survived the premodern and modern periods.

Although the social activism of old-school DJ Afrika Bambaataa during the mid-1970's stands as evidence of his early recognition of the possibilities of merging hip-hop culture and political consciousness, the politicization of rap music evolved slowly and unevenly during the 1980's.[39] It first appeared via social criticisms of ghetto life in rap classics like Kurtis Blow's "The Breaks" (1980) and Grandmaster Flash and the Furious Five's "The Message" (1982). In 1983 the politics of rap music became more explicit, as manifested in the "nation-conscious" release "How We Gonna Make the Black Nation Rise" by Brother D and in Keith LeBlanc's "No Sell Out," which, although produced by a white man, utilized samples from the speeches of Malcolm X.[40] Four years later, hip-hop pioneers Run-DMC wrote the spirited cultural nationalist song "Proud to Be Black," emphatically stating for their audiences, "Ya know I'm proud to be black ya'll / And that's a fact ya'll."[41]

But it wasn't until 1988 that two groups—Public Enemy and Boogie Down Productions—fully realized rap music's potential as a vehicle to express black rage and represent a legacy of militant, masculinist black politics. As Jon Pareles observed in the *New York Times*, the power of these two groups lies in their ability to read the social, political, and economic concerns of young African America. "Public Enemy and Boogie Down Productions registered the sense of urgency as urban ghettos grow increasingly desperate and audiences want to know why and what to do."[42] Highly regarded by music critics, the lyrical innovation of these two groups is also acknowledged by their fellow rap artists, some of whom they inspired. In an interview published in *Nation Conscious Rap* (1991), rap nationalist Paris paid respect to these hip-hop pioneers. "It was only a matter of time before our people started to come around," he maintained, "and I think as far as hip hop was concerned I think it was sparked by brothers such as KRS-One [of Boogie Down Productions], and brothers such as Public Enemy." Paris contextualized the groundbreaking contributions of these artists, describing the tremendous influence they had on the consciousness of black youth communities during a time when, for most male rap artists, success was measured by conspicuous consumption and sexual conquests. "It made it okay to be conscious where before everybody was talking about women and the gold chains they had, and the Benz they rolled around in," he attested.[43]

Paris's enthusiasm revealed the promise of a new political moment in hip-hop history. While Public Enemy's *It Takes a Nation of Millions to Hold Us Back* and Boogie Down Productions' *By All Means Necessary* exchanged one form of gendered politicking for another, they nevertheless established hip-hop culture as an uncompromising voice for black (primarily male) youth.

Although Public Enemy's first album, *Yo! Bum Rush the Show*, was released in 1987, it was not until 1988 that songs like "Bring the Noise," "Prophets of Rage," and "Party for Your Right to Fight" appeared on the rap scene, introducing Public Enemy to their peers as "one of the most politically and socially conscious artists of any generation."[44] The group's impact on the hip-hop movement was monumental: rap scholars lavish praise on the group (William Eric Perkins enthusiastically maintains that

Public Enemy should be recognized as "social revolutionaries"),[45] rap journalists wax eloquent about their cultural and political impact (Greg Tate proclaimed, "Chuck is the music's answer to the sheets-of-sound oratory Baraka bequeathed to the black poetry movement for love of Coltrane"),[46] hip-hop activists claim the group as inspiration for their commitment to community organizing (Kevin Powell bore witness that "'Rebel without a Pause' had a huge impact on changing my life and making me a deeper black nationalist"),[47] and other rap nationalists credit the group for raising their political consciousness (Paris declared, "1990 / fresh outta college / Public Enemy is hittin' niggas up with knowledge / and I love it / 'cause without them there would be no me"; and Speech of Arrested Development testified, they "came into my house with a boomin' bass and broke down my door and grabbed me by the neck and said, 'Wake up!'").[48]

The 1988 release of *It Takes a Nation of Millions to Hold Us Back* is cited as one of the most influential LPs responsible for the transformation of hip-hop culture into a medium for transmitting black nationalist thought. Popular culture scholar Jeffrey Louis Decker even proclaims that it gave "black nationalism in the United States its first widely publicized expression in nearly two decades."[49] The release of *Fear of a Black Planet* (1990) and *Apocalypse 91 . . . The Enemy Strikes Back* (1991) further solidified Public Enemy's position at the vanguard of rap nationalism and, ironically, secured their commercial success as these three LPs went multiplatinum.[50] Nevertheless, according to Public Enemy's manager Bill Adler, the group's mission far outweighed their celebrity status: "They're not out to be stars, they're out to save Black America."[51]

Adler's proclamation aside, the formation of Public Enemy as a rap group is an interesting story that highlights rap music as both a cultural politics and a commercial culture; its creation was a conscious exercise in using cultural production as both politics and commodity. What became "Public Enemy" actually began with a crew of Long Island DJs called Spectrum City, founded by Hank Shocklee in the mid-1970's. In 1979 Shocklee recruited Charles Ridenhour, a young Adelphi University student with "microphonitus," to be the first emcee in Spectrum City. A few years later, Spectrum City was invited to spin at a popular hip-hop radio show at Adelphi University's WBAU. The show, hosted by Bill Stephney, began experiencing unprecedented success, so when Stephney was promoted to the position of WBAU's program director he launched the "Super Spectrum Mix Hour." It was during this late-night Saturday show that Ridenhour—or "MC Chuckie D"—met future bandmate William Drayton, the man who would become known as trickster extraordinaire Flavor Flav. Meanwhile, in 1985, a year after Stephney left Adelphi University to become beat box editor for *CMJ New Music Report*, he became head of promotions for a new record company named Def Jam. The fledgling Def Jam label, which at the time was interested in signing diverse acts, had already had great success with Run-DMC and was working with upcoming artists LL Cool J and the Beastie Boys. Def Jam cofounder Rick Rubin was intrigued by Chuck D's "sound"[52] so he assigned Stephney, who was responsible for introducing Ridenhour to the WBAU audience, the task of recruiting him to the Def Jam label. Chuck D was initially reluctant to sign a contract, preferring to remain behind the scenes. Rubin persisted, and after a successful negotiation in 1986, it became time to create a niche for the band.

When asked in 1990 if Public Enemy's politics prompted him to offer the group a contract, Rick Rubin was amused. "Politics? There wasn't any politics in the music at the time."

> [Chuck D] was just doing some real good, real funny raps, about driving around in his (Olds) 98. And I think that's the real spirit of that whole first album. I think the politics became very much of an angle. They were looking for something to make them different from the other rap groups. They were a little bit brighter, had gone to school and they thought the political side of things would be a good way to go.[53]

As Rubin suggests, the concept of "Public Enemy" grew out of the political and educational experiences of those who were instrumental in forming the group. The Public Enemy posse was mostly made up of college-educated young men who grew up in burgeoning black suburbia and who, being older than most rap music enthusiasts (all were born in the early 1960's), had direct contact with grassroots Civil Rights and Black Power experiments during their developmental years. For example as preteens, Ridenhour, Shocklee, and Richard Griffin (aka Professor Griff) attended the Afro-American Experience, a summer educational program sponsored by the city of Roosevelt and held at Adelphi and Hofstra Universities during the early 1970's. According to Chuck D's memoir, this program, coordinated by college students and activists from organizations like the Nation of Islam and the Black Panther Party, was based on an Afrocentric curriculum conceived to supplement the education black children received in the public school system. Reminiscing about their college years, Bill Stephney described his crew as "pseudo-intellectuals" who "would sit in a room that had all these drum machines and turntables and ten thousand records and talk shit about everything, about relationships, about politics." They felt strongly about the pervasive black bourgeois mindset they felt invalidated the freedom struggles of the 1950's and '60s and the social-climbing, "post-Civil-Rights-*Jeffersons*-we're-moving-on-up attitude" of many of the black students at Adelphi University in the early 1980's. "They weren't talking about the immense problems of the world, or the effect of Reaganism on the black community like we were at nineteen years old. So we had all these designs and delusions attached with our love for this developing genre that we came up with."[54] This was the breeding ground of what was to become Public Enemy: a race- and class-conscious examination of post–Civil Rights African America.

Therefore, when assigned the task of crafting an identity for the new act signed to Def Jam, Bill Stephney was interested in fashioning a rap group that was a combination of his two favorite groups at the time: Run-DMC and The Clash.

> The Clash was very political. They had done *Sandinista!* [released in 1980], which was a very successful sociopolitical record that sold a gazillion copies, and Run-DMC, they were the cool rap-rock group, that had the coolness of a white rock group, but they were rappers. So if you could somehow combine the two, we thought we'd do something interesting. So [I] presented that concept to Chuck and Hank, and out of that Public Enemy was born.[55]

Thus in a manner that further complicates the issues of origins and authenticity in postmodern culture, Public Enemy, the most successful political rap group of this generation, was conceived as a combination of a countercultural movement of black working-class youth in New York and a countercultural movement of white working-class youth in London.

According to all accounts, the name came before the concept. "The sociopolitical meaning of Public Enemy came *after* we decided the group would be called that, because the meanings and connections of what we were about fit right in," Chuck D clarifies in *Fight the Power*.[56] Hank Shocklee suggested the group adopt the name "Public Enemy" from the single "Public Enemy #1," a battle record Chuck D recorded with Flavor Flav in late 1984. It worked precisely because it also represented black men; as Chuck D recalls, "rap music back then was looked upon just like Black men were looked upon: scum of the earth."[57] By tapping into the political consciousness of their audiences, the group found a way to take advantage of the commodification of black popular culture that was underway during the late 1980's. "Our initial direction was to market nationalism," writes Chuck D. "I knew that people in music like trends. Our concept was to wear African leather medallions or something other than gold because people were getting their heads taken off for wearing gold back then."[58] Therefore, at Public Enemy's inception, Ridenhour, Shocklee, and Stephney recognized the powerful potential of cultural commodities in a globalizing marketplace; and Public Enemy seized the opportunity to invert popular culture in meaningful and deliberate ways just as it began increasingly to encroach upon the daily lives of people throughout the world.

Chuck D and company entered the rap industry at a time when touring was just as important as music videos in establishing an artist's image. While the promotion of contemporary rap artists narrows the field to a proven formula—that is, new artists are recruited and promoted on the basis of their similarity to commercially successful artists—in the mid-1980's groups that entered the hip-hop arena were marketed on the basis of their stylistic differentiation from their peers. "That's how groups were judged," explained Chuck D. "You had to carve your own niche, and that's what we were doing, carving our own niche. That was the key back then."[59] The group wanted to be distinct, so they envisioned a "theatrical" approach.[60] That commercial sensibility combined with their political intention and Ridenhour's graphic arts and cartoonist background produced rap nationalism's founding fathers: Public Enemy. This is not to suggest that the group's formation was a completely smooth process. For example, when deliberating over the concept and constitution of "Public Enemy," Bill Stephney objected to the inclusion of William Drayton as "Flavor Flav," contending that Drayton's comedic personality jeopardized the potent dynamic of the group. (Stephney's instincts were partially correct. College-educated black fans criticized Flavor Flav's role in the group because, as Chuck D explained, "they didn't understand the psychology behind it.")[61] However, Shocklee and Ridenhour, who refused a solo contract with Def Jam, believed Flavor Flav was just what Public Enemy needed. They felt, as Stephney recalls quoting the classic

Disney musical *Mary Poppins*, that "a spoonful of sugar helps the medicine go down." Shocklee and Ridenhour insisted that if Public Enemy was going to be a hard-hitting, militant political group, Flavor Flav could help "balance them out, because we're still in the music business." In retrospect, Stephney recognizes that it was the right decision: "Flavor turned out to be the right sort of foil to balance the seriousness of Chuck."[62]

With Chuck D and Flavor Flav in place, the Public Enemy package was made complete by the illustrated statement of their logo, a black male silhouette in the crosshairs of a rifle, and with the visual impact of their security team the S1Ws (Security of the First World), a militant cross between the revolutionary nationalists of the Black Power movement and the religious nationalists of the Nation of Islam. "I was always making up names and titles, so I gave everybody a title to create more of mystical aura and approach," clarifies Chuck D. The DJ, Norman Rodgers, was christened Terminator X, and for the head of the S1Ws, Richard Griffin, Chuck D selected a title that paid homage to his political idols: "I was into Black Nationalism thoroughly so I called [Professor] Griff the 'Minister of Information,' which is a takeoff of Eldridge Cleaver and the Black Panther Party."[63] (Griffin was also dubbed "The X Minista" in honor of the Nation of Islam.) When Public Enemy recruited community activist Sister Souljah (Lisa Williamson) in 1991, they introduced her as the group's "Sister of Instruction."[64] It is no wonder, then, that when Public Enemy entered the hip-hop arena armed with militant politics and the sonic arsenal of producer Hank Shocklee, their publicist and "Media Assassin" Harry Allen announced, "This ain't the future of hip-hop—this is just a nagging reminder of a past imperfect."[65]

Chuck D was extremely media savvy. What could potentially be alienating to a mainstream audience was instead a public sensation. Ironically, critics and consumers—especially white males—adored Public Enemy. "We knew how to keep an audience on our side but at the same time say enough to make them feel guilty, then at the end make them feel like they're with us even though they fucked up," Chuck D discloses.[66] Richard Harrington of the *Washington Post*, nevertheless, cited critics wary of "the thin line between the Prophets of Rage and the profits of rage." "After all," he wrote, "what's a rebel without applause, and what better way to court controversy than to revive an explosive issue like black nationalism?"[67] Cynicism aside, the fact that marketing played a role in the creation of Public Enemy did not undermine their desire to situate black nationalist politics within the hip-hop scene. Those scholars and journalists who condemned Public Enemy as being disingenuous, or "manufactured," worked under the assumption that commercialism negates or neutralizes all political possibilities. This underlying expectation—that to be sincere *and* subversive means working outside the mainstream—is unrealistic and unlikely for those who have never really had the luxury of being *in*, especially for those who have come of age with the illusion of inclusion. "We're capitalists," reasoned Stephney. "I don't think there was any time when we said we are Marxist revolutionaries who want to change the means of production and make sure that the people control shit, but also we want to rock the crowd and sell twenty thousand tickets at the Nassau Coliseum [in New York]. We always thought those people were crazy."[68] What Public Enemy was able to envision and enact was a post–Civil Rights, postmodern, postindustrial strategy. Like other artists who emerged from what George Lipsitz refers to as "aggrieved communities," they were able to "subvert or invert the very instruments of domination necessary for the creation of a new global economy—its consumer goods, technologies and images."[69]

And yet, it is important not to underestimate power relations in a capitalist economy. For as extraordinary as it was to stage a cultural insurrection, it has proven easier to co-opt the politics of that cultural production precisely because it was staged in the capitalist marketplace. "We knew that this music was a blessing and a curse," recalled Chuck D. And that curse "has been the hardest thing to reverse."[70] As Dick Hebdige observes in relation to white consumption of reggae music, the commercialization of political music produced within the African Diaspora—by virtue of its decontextualization—can reduce what was conceived of as cultural resistance into an issue of style over substance.[71] As with reggae, the evolution of rap music invites discussion over the meaning of style in popular culture. For example, as previously mentioned, the commodification of gangsta rap destabilized and eventually inverted its social impact. Once hijacked by major corporations, gangsta rap, which began as a critique of the criminalization of black male youth, became increasingly devoid of its subversive edge and, unfortunately, started to contribute to the very dehumanizing representations of black men that some of its originators intended to deconstruct. As a result of its metaminstrelsy, gangsta rap became the most popular genre of rap music and contributed to the decline of rap nationalism as a marketable force in the rap music business. Bill Stephney believes that Public Enemy may have actually contributed to the industry's transition from rap nationalism to gangsta rap. He contends that by projecting theatrical representations of militant political activism and promoting violence in the form of self-defense, Public Enemy paved the way for the literal and figural representations of intracommunity violence that would be articulated by gangsta rap. Stephney claims that by doing so, Public Enemy laid the foundation for the commercial success of gangsta rap.

> We provided a bridge from a symbolic standpoint, from a sociopolitical and ideological standpoint, to [gangsta rap]. There is no N.W.A. without Public Enemy. It's not an accident. That angry, violent culture that comes up in the early 1990's—as typified on one end by N.W.A. and moving into Death Row [Records] and some aspects of Bad Boy [Records], namely Biggie—became very interesting to white kids, even more interesting than Public Enemy was. Because it's even more exotic and more dangerous than Chuck's position. It's completely voyeuristic.[72]

For Stephney, that radical transformation—the beginning of the end of the golden age of rap nationalism—is simply the nature of the (capitalist) beast: "We are subject to the vagaries of our successes," he submitted. "We always wanted to sell millions of records, we always wanted to sell to everybody. It didn't matter: black, white, Latino, Asian. But unfortunately there are ramifications."[73] Chuck D's theory on the music industry's promotional shift from consciousness rap to gangsta rap has more insidious implications: he believes that corporations—not consumers—demanded a change in product. Regardless of the rationale, both Bill Stephney and Chuck D speak to the hazards of using commercial culture as an insurrectionary tool.

Despite the risks inherent in engaging the mainstream popular culture arena, rap nationalism represents one of those breakthrough moments—a "saturnalia of power"—when the hidden transcript becomes public.[74] As Chuck D states, "We knew that if our people were going to be trendy we could at least make it trendy to have them learn about themselves and their history . . . that's what we tried to sell: intelligence."[75] Public Enemy stands as an example of the conscious manipulation of culture as commodity. Like other politicized artists in the postindustrial, postcolonial, globalized arena of popular culture—e.g., Nigeria's Fela Kuti or Panama's Ruben Blades—Public Enemy was part of a movement among contemporary musicians who "[take] commodity culture for granted" and represent "the emergence of a kind of cultural practice that aspires to political significance."[76] Their influence transcended geopolitical boundaries for "a lot of different reasons," concluded Chuck D, but primarily because "oppression is a world issue."[77]

Sites of oppression may be global, but sites of resistance are extremely localized. Chuck D's poetic compositions fall squarely within the tradition of U.S. black nationalism. Public Enemy's political rhetoric is a fusion of the religious nationalism of the Nation of Islam, the revolutionary nationalism of the Black Panther Party, and the cultural nationalism of the Black Arts movement, which is no surprise considering that its primary lyricist's "crucial developmental years," by his own admission, "took place right smack-dab in the middle of the Black Power Movement." Chuck D remembers attending the Panthers' free breakfast program when visiting family members in Harlem as a child. "My parents were young in the 1960's, and had radical ideas," he recalled. "My mother wore an Afro, and I remember wearing an Afro myself, as well as singing the 'Free Huey Newton' song."[78] The founders of Public Enemy believe that their age facilitated their political standpoint, and therefore contributed to their success. "I was actually considered 'too old' when I cut my first recording in 1987 at the age of twenty-six," Chuck remembers, "but while my age may have appeared a disadvantage to some, it was actually an advantage based on what I knew."[79] Stephney agreed. "The reason we were confident about Public Enemy is [that] we knew we weren't part of an elite, that we represented a whole, rather numerous, generation of black folks, particularly young black men, who had gone to college or had been educated by the last vestiges of the '60s and '70s," he said. "For me, as part of that generation of kids who sung 'Lift Every Voice and Sing' every morning in a school with nothing but black teachers, to do Public Enemy is a no-brainer. The question is, how come someone didn't do it before us?"[80] As young witnesses of the civil disobedience of the late 1960's and '70s and recipients of the social experiments of the Civil Rights and Black Power movements, the members of Public Enemy were in a unique position to introduce political ideology into an evolving youth culture. "For many young people who are a part of the Hip-Hop Nation today, the Vietnam War and the turbulent 1960s is a period that they read about in history books—not for me," Chuck D writes in his autobiography. "I actually lived through that and was personally affected and shaped by the pervasive antiwar, civil rights, and Black Power sentiments as a child."[81]

Chuck D's influences are evident in his work. For instance, in "Party for Your Right to Fight" he translates the political persecution of black radicals (the Black Panthers, Malcolm X, and Martin Luther King, Jr.) through the teachings of the Honorable Elijah Muhammad. Chuck D uses the Nation of Islam's Yakub creation story and attributes the demise of African American freedom fighters to the wicked ways of "grafted devils" and their conspiracy against the "Black Asiatic Man."[82] This ideological patchwork exemplifies the political beliefs of Chuck D, whose neonationalism is, for the most part, a bricolage of the theories of his political heroes, in particular Malcolm X, the Black Panther Party, and Louis Farrakhan.[83] His militant standpoint is an adept crafting of historical memory that, as scholar Jeffrey Louis Decker observes, is "at best, an uneasy cultural-political alliance—one which is as contradictory as it is creative, as prone to historical amnesia as it is to constructive historical revision."[84]

The ideological tension between Chuck D's mentors (and, by extension, the mentors of other rap nationalists) is not as great as it first appears: the tie that binds them is Malcolm X. The Malcolm who was deified by the Black Power movement in the 1960's and '70s is the Malcolm who is idolized by the Hip-Hop Nation in the 1980's and '90s—the Nation of Islam Malcolm who also instructed and groomed a young Minister Louis Farrakhan in the mid- to late 1950's. He is the highly mythologized standard for strong and defiant black masculinity whom Ossie Davis eulogized mournfully as "our manhood, our living, black manhood!"[85] Like their nineteenth- and twentieth-century predecessors, rap nationalists are extremely involved in the "production of exemplary masculinity,"[86] and Malcolm X is more often than not at the center of their hero worship. His name is a veritable fixture in the lyrics and liner notes—the "shout outs"—of rap nationalists like Public Enemy, KRS-One and Boogie Down Productions, X-Clan, Brand Nubian, Ice Cube, and Paris, young black men who conjure, as Michael Eric Dyson asserts, "his masculinity, his blackness, and his ghetto grounding."[87] Yet the myth-making machine of "Malcolmania"[88] defined which moments of Malcolm X's life were deemed significant; and it was his advocacy of violent resistance (not to mention his violent death) that rap nationalists invested with the most meaning. This representation of Malcolm X—frozen in time—signifies rap artists' investment in a politics that equated power with violence and violence with manhood, for they did not acknowledge

Malcolm X's political maturation after his break with the Nation of Islam. Many scholars have speculated upon Malcolm X's ideological growth during this short period of his life, particularly his gender politics. But the post–N.O.I. Malcolm X does not fit as neatly into the masculinist discourse of post–Civil Rights U.S. black nationalism, and therefore that history is prone to erasure. So for those in pursuit of a symbol for militant black manhood in postindustrial America, the legacy of Malcolm X became most associated with the veiled threat underlying his celebrated declaration that black liberation should be realized "by any means necessary."

An example of this kind of masculinist invocation of Malcolm X is Boogie Down Productions' *By All Means Necessary*. When KRS-One of Boogie Down Productions entered the ranks of political raptivism in 1988 he did so quite deliberately: "When rap music needed to have a teacher, I became it." Never one to shy away from self-aggrandizement, KRS claimed his role in rap music history during a 1992 interview with rock critic Roger Catlin. "Before I came out, there was no such thing as a black consciousness movement. . . . Kids on the street didn't know who Malcolm X or Martin Luther King was until rap let them know."[89] Tapping into the collective memory of Malcolm X as a vision and as a visionary, with *By All Means Necessary* KRS appropriates not only Malcolm's words but his image as well. The cover of Boogie Down Productions' second effort features KRS-One in a defensive stance, cautiously looking out of a window with an Uzi submachine gun in hand. It is a calculated visual transfiguration of the now infamous photo taken of Malcolm X after his home was mysteriously firebombed in 1965. This representation is the kind of symbolic action described by literary critic Kenneth Burke as "incantatory," or that which "invite[s] us to make ourselves over in the image of the imagery."[90] Through his imag(in)ing, KRS situates both himself and Malcolm within the masculinist discourse of black nationalism as patriarchal protector, not only of his family but of the extended communal black family as well. This recontextualization (of what was probably, and ironically, one of the most terrifying moments in Malcolm's life) signifies upon the militant "it's-a-dick-thing" masculinist politics popularized by Black Power advocates in the 1960's and '70s using the overexploited metaphor of the gun as an extension of black male power. "People wanna know how come / I've got a gat and I'm lookin' out the window like Malcolm," rejoins KRS-One's fellow raptivist Ice Cube. Because like Malcolm, rap's neonationalists were "ready to bring that noise."[91]

While KRS-One drew upon the image of Malcolm X as warrior, like the real (as opposed to the imagined) Malcolm, his position on violence was pragmatic—and sometimes contradictory. Boogie Down Productions' first album, *Criminal Minded* (1987), is widely accepted by hip-hop scholars as a pioneering album of the "gangsta," or hardcore-reality, rap genre. Cultural critic Russell Potter praises *Criminal Minded* for producing "knowledge raps with a gangsta edge," while hip-hop journalist Nelson George places it within its social and historical context, describing *Criminal Minded* as the "first album-length exploration of the crack-fueled criminality of Reagan's America."[92] Hip-hop activist Kevin Powell also paid tribute to Boogie Down Productions' first album; he considers it a milestone in the annals of black music. "That's [KRS-One's] most brilliant work to me," he insisted. "I think *Criminal Minded* did for hip-hop what be-bop did for jazz."[93] Yet despite KRS-One's reception as one of the first "gangsta"-styled rap artists, his second release, *By All Means Necessary* (1988), reintroduced Boogie Down Productions' lyricist as a philosopher of antiviolence and advocate for self-defense. KRS-One's perspective on violence shifted after the tragic 1987 shooting death of his DJ, Scott La Rock. "I'd have to be a fool to have had my DJ killed by the 'Criminal Minded' lifestyle and then continue the criminal lifestyle," he told *Pittsburgh Post-Gazette* reporter Scott Mervis. "I had to clean my act up."[94] In fact, KRS-One was instrumental in the now-defunct Stop the Violence Movement organized in response to the 1988 stabbing death of a teen at a Long Island, New York, rap concert. Yet—and here is where the discrepancy lies—despite his notorious antiviolence stance, in 1992 KRS-One and the Boogie Down Productions' crew assaulted Prince Be, a member of the R & B group PM Dawn, after he criticized KRS-One during an interview for *Details* magazine. ("Public Enemy and people like that, they just make mountains out of molehills," Prince Be commented. "KRS-One wants to be a teacher, but a teacher of what?") When questioned about the incident, KRS-One responded, "They got disrespected. There are some who disagree with my actions, but we're not trying to win a peace prize, we're trying to revolutionize people."[95] Nevertheless KRS-One, a staunch advocate against black-on-black crime, remained flexible on the issue of violence. He concluded that in the attempt to attain "a positive destiny" circumstance may dictate strategy. "Whether peace by war or peace by peace," freedom must be had "one way or another. By all means necessary."[96]

By All Means Necessary established KRS-One as one of rap music's leading intellectuals and, according to reporter Chris Heim, transformed him into "the prime exponent and chief theoretician of educational rap and its militant message of pride, empowerment, knowledge and up-lift."[97] To be clear, KRS-One considered himself to be not a nationalist but a humanist: "I manifest as a black man but I'm universal."[98] Despite his resistance to being labeled "pro-black," black nationalist ideology was infused throughout his lyrics. The 1989 Boogie Down Productions' classic "You Must Learn" is a nationalist manifesto for incorporating black history in America's public schools. Three years later KRS-One professed to "create organizations, [because] without organizations there'll be no black nation."[99] Throughout most of his career, KRS-One's lyrics have consistently exhibited black nationalist politics, even though—unlike some of his peers—his racial politics are anti-essentialist. For example, in his 1990 song "The Racist" KRS-One challenged those blacks who label all whites as antiblack ("You can't blame the whole white race / for slavery, 'cause this ain't the case"), and in his 1992 song "Build and De-stroy" he argued that the actions of Clarence Thomas and Colin Powell prove that evil is not limited to white people ("You talk about being African and being black / Colin Powell's black, but Libya he'll attack").[100] This type of critical thinking was not new to black nationalist thought: nineteenth-century black nationalists like David Walker demonstrated that racial essentialism is not fundamental to black nationalist ideology. So while KRS-One may not have considered himself a black nationalist, his body of lyrical work places him squarely within the black nationalist tradition.

After Public Enemy and Boogie Down Productions radicalized rap music with their "self-conscious racial pedagogy"[101] and launched the "revolutionary wave"[102] of the hip-hop movement in 1988, there was a proliferation of rap artists who entered the music scene armed with a black nationalist perspective. For example, 1990 witnessed the introduction of neocivilizationists such as Brand Nubian, Poor Righteous Teachers, and X-Clan, who, in the spirit of nineteenth-century black nationalists Martin Delany and Edward Wilmot Blyden, celebrated the legacy of ancient African empires. A year later, controversial "gangstAfronationalist[s]"[103] like Ice Cube and Paris exploded on the scene, exploiting white fears and using hardcore lyrics to express their pro-black political stance.

Like the literary tradition of black nationalism, the development of raptivism was a notably regional phenomenon, highly concentrated in the urban North, and in particular among artists in the New York metropolitan area. Rap nationalists like Public Enemy, KRS-One, Brand Nubian, and X-Clan were all from New York, and each devoted entire songs to their neonationalist politics. On the other hand, the lyrics of West Coast rappers focused more on local concerns. Los Angeles– and Bay Area–based raptivists like Ice Cube and Kam or Paris and Tupac tended to weave their political consciousness into lyrical narrations on gang violence or police brutality. This is not to overstate the case. The correlation between coast and style was not absolute: not all rap nationalists were from the east, and not all gangsta rappers were from the west.

Jeffrey Louis Decker has distinguished between two types of nation-conscious rap: "sixties-inspired hip hop nationalism" and "Afrocentric hip hop nationalism."[104] This distinction may be helpful, but it is also a little misleading—all rap nationalism was "sixties-inspired." Despite their different approaches, raptivists identified most with the militant nationalism of the Nation of Islam Malcolm X and its reincarnation in revolutionary nationalist "sons of Malcolm," like the Black Panther Party.[105] However, in form and function, their work was more reminiscent of cultural nationalists, particularly the musicians, poets, and scholars of the black aesthetic who came of age during the diffuse Black Arts movement.[106] In fact, Kwame Ture (Stokely Carmichael) once advised Chuck D to value the dialogic relationship between culture and politics. "Hip-Hop borrows from Black people's culture," he counseled. "So since you're doing Hip-Hop, you should only do Hip-Hop for one reason: to excel in it and put it back in your culture to progress your people. If you don't do that, it's self-defeating, it's non-progressive."[107] Both the Black Arts and hip-hop movements considered their mission to be that of re-educating African America. They believed cultural production to be the critical means to an end that involved the transformation of black political consciousness. During the Black Arts movement, artists-activists used literary, visual, spoken word, and theatrical arts to introduce the black nationalist political standpoint to their audiences. A generation later, liberation remained the message and music was the method: "We want to continue the paths of the revolutionists and activists before us," Brother J of X-Clan attested in a 1989 interview. "And this time we have a tool, it's called music, the universal language."[108] As Ice Cube articulated in 1991, many raptivists believed that culture was the key to reversing the legacy of the so-called slave mentality—a state of mind characterized by ignorance and submission—as it was manifest in the hip-hop generation. "The reason I say nigga is because we are mentally dead. . . . We have limited knowledge of self so it leads to a nigga mentality." In order to overcome this racial unawareness Ice Cube issued the *Death Certificate*, an inspired concept album during which, with the help of the Nation of Islam, he undergoes a psychological transformation—a nigga-to-black conversion of consciousness: "Soon as we as a people use our knowledge of self to our advantage we will then be able to become and be called Blacks."[109]

The "Nigga-to-Black" Conversion: Black Power Meets the Hip-Hop Movement

> What is teaching but sparking curiosity?   —Chuck D, 1988

More than Malcolm or Huey, the prototypes for raptivism are the freedom songs of the Civil Rights movement, the politicized R & B of James Brown, Marvin Gaye, and Curtis Mayfield, and, most importantly, the poetry-in-motion of Gil Scott-Heron and the Last Poets, artists who "developed a spoken style that turned words into bullets."[110] Chuck D recalls singing one of his favorite songs, James Brown's "Say It Loud—I'm Black and I'm Proud," as a child with his classmates "like there was no tomorrow."[111] Yet the work/ethic of politicized rap artists in the hip-hop movement also parallels that of the artists-activists in the Black Arts movement, the spiritual sister of the Black Power movement. In fact, it is interesting to note the similarities between movements, for the intragenerational conflict over rap music discussed earlier was initiated by the very generation of activists whose legacy rap nationalists claim—the men and women who came of age during the Civil Rights and Black Power movements.

The politicized youth culture that would come to be identified with the Black Power movement developed in urban America, particularly in the states of New York and California, among blacks who dealt with a more subtle, yet no less tangible, institutional racism than their southern counterparts that was manifest in mass unemployment, substandard housing, and ever present police brutality. And like rap music's ghettocentrists, the black insurgents of the late 1960's/early 1970's were a group of young "citi-fied" black folk who renounced black bourgeois ideals in favor of what they imagined to be the more aggressive and expressive style of the working and nonworking poor. The politics of these young men and women, many of whom came from middle-class backgrounds, were cultivated largely in response to the protest strategies of the Civil Rights movement. Perceiving nonviolent civil disobedience as a sign of submission, Black Power advocates rejected its most recognized practitioner, Martin Luther King, Jr., and idealized the more militant approach to activism and oration identified with the memory of Malcolm X. Therefore, what developed in the cities of the American North and West was a style of organization and leadership unique to the geographical and generational context of a neophyte corps of freedom fighters.

The artist-activists of the Black Power and hip-hop movements have more in common than their geographic and generational origins. Both rejected an "art for art's sake" philosophy of cultural production and were committed to the belief that art should be functional, a mechanism to inspire and sustain black empowerment. During the late 1960's/early 1970's, cultural nationalists believed that a Negro-to-Black conversion of consciousness—that is, a psychological and spiritual revolution—among the masses was of paramount importance to the black struggle; without this step they believed the liberation of black folks from their enslavement to white supremacy would never be realized. To cultural nationalists like Maulana Karenga of the US Organization and Amiri Baraka of the Congress of African People, this destruction of African America's "slave mentality" was fundamental to revolutionary struggle, and the new black aesthetic would be the catalyst for black empowerment. "[T]he first violence will be internal," Larry Neal vows in the Black Power classic *Black Fire*. "But it will be a necessary violence. It is the only thing that will destroy the double consciousness—the tension that is in the souls of Black folk." Through his allusion to violence as a spiritual healer, Neal emphasized the cultural nationalist belief that the initial revolution would be targeted toward the black mind. By doing so, he simultaneously defined the connection between art and activism promoted by the Black Arts movement and positioned black artists at the vanguard of the revolutionary struggle. "The artist and the political activist are one," he asserts. "They are both shapers of the future reality. Both understand and manipulate the collective myths of the race. Both are warriors, priests, lovers and destroyers."[112]

Over twenty years later, some rap artists (perhaps unwittingly) embraced the spirit of the Black Arts movement and its "politics of transvaluation,"[113] defending the connection between cultural production and psychological liberation and utilizing music as a mechanism for inspiring revolutionary action. Just as Larry Neal conjured *The Souls of Black Folk* and deconstructed double consciousness for African America in the late 1960's, Ice Cube invoked Du Bois to explain the spiritual and mental state of African America in the early 1990's: "You say Ice Cube is a problem—well you're right, he's two people in the same body, one African, one American," he wrote for the liner notes of his 1992 release, *The Predator*. By virtue of a political awakening, Ice Cube was no longer afflicted by the "unreconciled strivings" that once plagued the souls of black folk ("I see myself through the eyes of Africa and I will continue to speak as an African," he proclaimed), and this newly discovered consciousness allowed him to confront the contradictions between racial rhetoric and racial realities in post–Civil Rights movement America: "I will become African American when America gives up oppression of my people."[114] Chuck D, perhaps appropriating Black Arts movement rhetoric, also expressed a need for "a bloodless coup, a mind revolution." In typical Public Enemy fashion, Chuck D stressed the importance of psychological liberation in a style that combined the cultural nationalism of the Black Arts movement with the religious nationalism of the Nation of Islam. "[I]t's gotta be a mind revolution, and that's what Armageddon is all about, the war to end all wars. Everybody first of all has to win the war with themselves."[115]

While rap nationalists of the late 1980's/early 1990's claimed the rhetorical legacy of Black Power activists, without a movement to support their political standpoint, they appeared to be all talk and no action. "Rappers represent the community, but I would not say they're the new Black Panthers," observed James Bernard, former senior editor of *The Source* magazine. "That's not fair to them. They're not there trying to lead organizations or stage organized rallies."[116] The precarious position of the raptivist, as Last Poet Abiodun Oyewole intimated in his 1994 conversation with Ice Cube, is that the politicized artist should be situated within a politicized environment. In the absence of community activism—without the support of leadership and organizational structure—the role of the rap artist as a political observer is skewed. "The difference between you and me and then and now is that my whole thing was specifically from a political arena," Oyewole told Ice Cube. "The Last Poets came on to rebel against a system that had us all in check, whereas the kids like you all have been seen as coming on as a cartoon."[117] Yet as a spoken word artist whose work was inspired by movement politics, Oyewole recognized the value of hip-hop culture's stylized race politics and claimed its performers as "our warriors." "This is our army," he affirmed. "These brothers are looking for rites of passage."[118]

While Oyewole was cautiously optimistic about the hip-hop movement, cultural studies scholar Paul Gilroy's criticism of its poets laureate is more cautious and less optimistic. In an evaluation of what he hesitates to call "neonationalism," Gilroy assesses the shift in U.S. black nationalist discourse from the modern to the postmodern period in terms of its substance (or lack thereof): "The 'ism' in that nationalism is often lacking," he argues. "[I]t is no longer constructed as a coherent political ideology. It appears more usually as a set of therapies—tactics in the never-ending struggle for psychological and cultural survival." Gilroy's criticism is valid. However, it is important to note that by emphasizing the importance of decolonizing the black mind from white domination, the artist-activists of the Black Arts movement, like their hip-hop descendants, were also focused on psychological and cultural survival. The difference is that they did so within the context of a movement. And many, like Amiri Baraka and Haki Madhubuti, were experienced community organizers. By contrast, as Gilroy argues, for the raptivist politics "is now more a matter of style, perspective, or survivalist technique than a question of citizenship, rights, or fixed contractual obligations (the things that defined nationality in earlier periods)."[119]

Gilroy is right; times have changed. Nevertheless, poverty, segregation, slumlike living conditions, and underfunded and overcrowded public schools continued to define the material conditions of life for many in African America. Meanwhile, liberal discourse masked comparable social relations, and black political participation was circumscribed to symbolic representation just as lobbying and interest-group politicking reinscribed "the possessive investment in whiteness."[120] So, as Nelson George documents, the hip-hop generation is "a generation coming of age at a moment of extreme racial confusion—in these years since official apartheid was legislated out of existence and de facto segregation grew—who have been grappling with what equality means during the worst economic conditions for the underclass since the Depression."[121] During the late 1980's/early 1990's, popular culture became a very public forum for negotiating some form of clarity for "schizophrenic, post-civil rights movement America."[122] Without the experience and/or support of community activism, rap nationalists were more dependent upon the word than their action. These artists' music represents a form of symbolic protest not unlike labor union songs, antiwar songs, or Civil Rights movement songs, for as KRS-One stated, music is "a revolutionary tool for changing the structure of racist America."[123]

While that is indeed significant, the presence of black nationalist thought in rap music substantiates the supposition made by scholars like William Van Deburg and Mark Anthony Neal that the lasting impression of the Black Power movement was not its politics, but its style.[124] Take, for example, hip-hop organizer Rosa Clemente's memory of her days as a student activist at Albany State University in the early 1990's: "I always loved Public Enemy, because of the politics. That was the time when everybody was wearing the African medallions and it was about knowledge of self and everybody was reading Malcolm and people were talking about nationalism and struggle."[125] In the absence of a movement (and in the attempt to define one), it is not surprising that rap nationalists appropriated and adapted Black Arts movement concepts and strategies— particularly rhetoric concerning the need for psychological liberation from white domination. Cultural nationalism had become increasingly vital for young African America during the mid-1980's, a period defined by a politics of conservatism that pushed racial assimilation while promoting anti–affirmative action and shaped by a politics of liberalism that obscured racial dynamics in the name of "multiculturalism."

Consequently the Negro-to-Black conversion of consciousness, as Ice Cube suggests in *Death Certificate*, was (post)modernized as the nigga-to-black conversion of consciousness, framing black nationalism as a politics of (ex)slave resistance. The need to create a countercultural movement to decolonize the minds of black youth was evident in the lyrics of a number of raptivists during the golden age of rap nationalism. For example, in their frenetic song entitled "tolerate," the rap collective Freestyle Fellowship announced that it was their intention to "liberate state / of mind . . . we're reachin' out so we can free the blind,"[126] and in "Come Clean" Jeru the Damaja maintains that rap music is his "verbal weapon": "my attack is purely mental / and it's nature's not hate / it's meant to wake you up / out of your brainwashed state."[127] Harmony, a former member of Boogie Down Productions, outlined the mission of rap nationalists and described black liberation as the ultimate objective of raptivists. "Revolution. Revolution. To change. We're talking, and doing, and moving. That's revolution. Not being stagnant, not being still. Motion, changing, not rearranging but changing."[128]

And while revolution was on the minds of many, some rap nationalists went so far as to condemn any rap music that was not political as counterrevolutionary. Defiant Giants invoked the revolutionary tactics of Mao Tse-tung in China and the Mau Mau of Kenya to illustrate their conviction that rap music must be dedicated to facilitating the liberation of black America.

> In the Chinese Revolution when Mao Tse Tseung [sic] led the Chinese Revolution all cultural art forms, all poetry, all plays that were not totally intertwined and geared towards the revolution of the Chinese people were wiped out. In the Mau Mau Revolution in Kenya, if your drum wasn't playing to the revolution, if your dance wasn't dancing to the revolution, they busted up your drum, they busted up your dance, and they busted you up too. This is the direction that hip hop music is going. Making the artists accountable.[129]

While the impulse to make all artists—particularly those who are participating in a commercial art form—accountable is certainly idealistic, most rap nationalists were not this extreme. Nevertheless, as hip-hop culture became more and more politicized in the late 1980's/early 1990's, many artists became conscious of their role and of the music's potential as a vehicle for transmitting liberatory thought within black communities.

In a 1991 *Essence* magazine article Sister Souljah explained what she believed to be the calling of rap music in African America. Its purpose, as KRS-One noted a year earlier, was "Edutainment." Rap music provided young black people with a system of knowledge that counterbalanced the misinformation they received in the public school system, Souljah contended—a school system, she added, that was funded by a government that did not have black folks' best interests at heart. "I think the purpose of any educational system in any country is to uphold and maintain the power of the state. Because we are in America and the state is racist, white, and capitalist, the educational system is a racist, white, capitalist educational system."[130] Her bandmate Chuck D agreed and referred to public schools as the "killing fields": their "cultural one-sidedness," he writes, is "killing the minds of our youth."[131] As the vice-principal of an elementary school in Newark, New Jersey, hip-hop activist Ras Baraka was intimately aware of the preparatory training received by black youth living in major metropolitan areas. He spoke of the paradox of public schools and schooling in the post–Civil Rights/Black Power era: "It's possible to grow up in a predominantly black city like Newark and go to Harriet Tubman Elementary, George Washington Carver Middle School, Malcolm X Shabazz High School and have no political consciousness at all. These people are not even studied in those schools, and we have to ask why." His answer: "Because the people in power are not interested in that at all. It's neocolonialism in these inner-cities."[132]

Distrust of the public educational system was widespread in the Hip-Hop Nation and was perhaps fostered by the fact that many—if not most—raptivists, unlike their nineteenth- and twentieth-century black nationalist predecessors, were not formally educated. Learned black nationalists of the past represented an exception in African America. They were, as W. E. B. Du Bois articulated, the "Talented Tenth." By contrast, in their time, rap nationalists represented the rule. For example, although Chuck D, Sister Souljah, and Paris have baccalaureate degrees from Adelphi University, Rutgers University, and the University of California, Los Angeles, respectively, most rap nationalists either never attended a college or university (e.g., KRS-One, Wise Intelligent, Lord Jamar, Talib Kweli) or did not finish their degrees (e.g., Ice Cube, Sadat X, M-1 of dead prez). This deprivation reflected the institutional neglect—the "savage inequalities"[133]—of the public school system, which, in the post–Civil Rights era, remained separate and unequal, the result of widespread underfunding and overpopulation in America's inner-city schools. And yet raptivists worked this situation to their advantage. Although they were imperfect, much as political scientist William W. Sales, Jr., writes of Malcolm X, as organic intellectuals these rap artists demonstrated to their "street constituency . . . the essence of the intellectual endeavor without the mediation of formal academic institutions and processes."[134]

Nevertheless, it's the content, not the context, of public education that is of major concern to rap nationalists, whether it be Public Enemy's "Brothers Gonna Work It Out" ("History shouldn't be a mystery / Our story's real history, not his story") or the Jungle Brothers' "Acknowledge Your Own History" ("Lookin' for the true black days of glory / That's history—that's his story.")[135] Boogie Down Productions' "You Must Learn" was another prime example. In his 1989 classic KRS-One, otherwise known as the "T'cha" (Teacher), exposed the irony of the prevalence of lily-white curricula in predominantly black classrooms.

> It seems to me that in a school that's ebony
> African history should be pumped up steadily
> but it's not and this has got to stop
> see Spot run, run get Spot.

For KRS-One, this universal (read: white) approach is "insulting to a black mentality / a black way of life or a jet-black family." So like most raptivists, he proposed a complete restructuring of America's public schools. This radical reformation would involve the institution of a pro-black course of study or, as KRS-One advised, "one that teaches to a black return / 'cause you must learn."[136]

From KRS-One's "You Must Learn" to Grand Puba's "Proper Education," most rap artists in the hip-hop movement suggested that the American educational system is in fact a government conspiracy designed to keep black people subordinate and dependent. Raptivists dead prez, who reintroduced raptivism to the hip-hop scene almost a decade after the decline of the golden age of rap nationalism, compared the public school system to both the institution of slavery and the prison industrial complex. "The schools ain't teachin' us nothin' but how to be slaves and hard workers for white people," they lectured, "to build up they shit, make they businesses successful while it's exploitin' us."[137] The self-proclaimed "Black Panther of hip-hop" also maintained that public institutions of primary and secondary education in the United States are involved in the conspiratorial indoctrination of black youth. In the liner notes of *Guerrilla Funk* Paris accused "Amerikkka's school system" of "mentacide," a term he defined as the "deliberate and systematic destruction of a group's mind with the ultimate purpose being the destruction of that group." Paris strongly urged his audience to "[f]orget what you learned—learn what you forgot!"[138] According to rap nationalists, this mentacidal plan is exacted on the innocents: school-aged children whose self-consciousness is not yet strong enough for them to defend themselves against the exploitative mechanisms of white supremacy. Politicized rap artists believed that the diabolical plot to impose white cultural hegemony on black youth is executed through a curriculum that combines both the ignorance and ignoring of Africa with misinformation about black America. For instance, in "Proper Education," Grand Puba put forth the common argument that in schools across America the history of "The Black Man" is stripped of its dignity and reduced to the period of enslavement.

Now let me tell you folks just exactly what I mean
the way they try to lower the Black man's self-esteem
put us in their schools and I call 'em mental graves
when they teach us about ourselves, all we learn that we were
slaves.[139]

This sentiment was repeated time and time again. It even appeared in an editorial published in the self-proclaimed source of "Hip-Hop Music, Culture & Politics." In 1989 journalist Barry Deonarine wrote an opinion piece for *The Source* magazine in which he expressed his position on the institutionalization of racism in America's schools. He denounced the ways in which U.S. history is taught and insisted that black Americans be informed that "[w]e are not the descendants of slaves, but the descendants of kings and queens who were kidnapped by white Europeans hungry for money."[140] Eight years later in *Fight the Power*, Chuck D reiterated the importance of the relationship between historical memory and representation. "Most people are familiar with the African slave trade, and believe that the history of Black people begins with the colonial period and the slave trade," he testifies. "Without a knowledge of the past, not just the slave past, people around the world will continue to hold a warped and negative view of Black people."[141] However, for Chuck D, the black image in the black mind is just as consequential as the black image in the white mind, because "[a]n honest review of history reveals the potential greatness of Africa and African people for self-determination and self-rule."[142]

As these examples demonstrate, for rap nationalists the antidote to "trick knowledge"—a concept borrowed from the Nation of Islam that refers to the devious ways and means white supremacy is maintained— was "proper education."[143] "Proper education" was a multifaceted issue in the hip-hop movement. For most raptivists it took the form of instruction in black American cultural and intellectual achievements, especially in the worlds of science and mathematics and, in particular, in the great civilizations of Africa. (Like their nineteenth-century predecessors, rap nationalists placed a premium on an African ideal that is largely a product of the African American imagination.) This reinterpretation of the history and ancestry of African America is important in the tradition of black nationalism, because black nationalists' "revisionist" history, or what literary scholar Henry Louis Gates, Jr., calls an "imaginative reconstruction" of the past,[144] is a purposeful search for historical narratives that can be used to structure a more positive consciousness of self and community.

For example, KRS-One argued that it is important for black children "to know that they come from a long race and line of kings, queens and warriors," for this knowledge will make them "have a better feeling about themselves."[145] Chuck D concurs and reasons that the youth of African America are in dire need of self-love—of black pride—"so they won't submit to the bullshit of the American shit-stem."[146] Like Chuck D, hip-hop artist-activists dead prez took a no-nonsense approach to the issue of transforming "They Schools" and addressed the high drop-out rate of young black men in America's urban areas: "Until we have some shit where we control the fuckin' school system, where it reflects how we gonna solve our own problems, then niggas ain't gonna relate to school."[147] As this recommendation from dead prez suggests, in addition to changes made in programs of study, some raptivists proposed community control of public schools as a way to prevent the whitewashing of young black minds. "[O]nce we can control, you know, not in a negative way, but just supervise what's going into the heads of our kids, then we can have unity and become an economic strength," proposed Ice Cube. "And once you become an economic strength here, you got no problems, no more problems."[148] Chuck D even insisted that alongside a pro-black curriculum facilitated by community control over neighborhood schools, the public educational system should prepare black students for the job market. (In an interesting line of argumentation Chuck D conflated the opposing educational philosophies of Booker T. Washington and W. E. B. Du Bois.)[149] While Ice Cube and Chuck D made the case for revamping public education to attain economic self-sufficiency and, in turn, liberation for blacks in the United States, Wise Intelligent of Poor Righteous Teachers took the issue a step further. Wise Intelligent maintained that freedom for African America is freedom from ignorance and, like his cultural nationalist predecessors, believed that knowledge is *the* key to black liberation. In his estimation, revolution is dependent upon the support and maintenance of independent Afrocentric schools. "The only way we're going to [effect] change en masse is by establishing black schools with black curriculums."[150]

Like the artist-activists of the Black Arts movement, rap nationalists considered it their duty to both inspire and cultivate a racial consciousness among young black folk, to promote a sense of race pride constantly put in jeopardy by white cultural hegemony in mass media, popular culture, and public educational systems. They were, in fact, "standing in for the state."[151] Despite their limitations, rap nationalists provided a counterideology to white supremacy, a system of knowledge that was both race and class conscious. Sister Souljah bore witness to this fact in *Essence* magazine. For African American youth during the late 1980's/early 1990's, raptivists' effort was both meaningful and transformative.

> I think hip hop is a blessing because the Poor Righteous Teachers, Brand Nubian, and KRS-One have actually been *the* educational system for Black kids, in place of the so-called educational system that is entirely financed by the American government. And in the absence of the voice of young people in hip hop, we would have even more chaos than we have today.[152]

While Sister Souljah's enthusiasm for raptivism was justifiable, it is important to question exactly what *kind* of order was being imposed upon this so-called chaos. If it was the intention of raptivists to, as Inspectah Deck of Wu-Tang Clan asserted, "kick the truth to the young black youth," what is the truth they were teaching?[153]

4

Ladies First?

Defining Manhood in the Golden Age of Rap Nationalism

During a 2001 interview at his Brooklyn, New York, home, hip-hop journalist Kevin Powell recounted his experiences as a student activist at Rutgers University in the mid- to late 1980's. "I think that the thing I got from that period in the 1980's was definitely heightened consciousness," he recalled. Black students were mobilizing around the anti-apartheid movement, Jesse Jackson's presidential campaigns—even the rise in popularity of Nation of Islam Minister Louis Farrakhan—all of which inspired the future founder/chairperson of HipHop Speaks (a community forum that uses hip-hop culture to increase political awareness among young blacks and Latinos) to become a political science major. Yet, on that Monday afternoon in November, Powell was frank about his burgeoning race consciousness: "It definitely further entrenched me in patriarchy, without question. It was all about the men." As a young man, Powell's nationalist politics affirmed his sense of masculinity: "Certain things get passed down from generations, and one of the stories that got passed down was Stokely Carmichael saying the only position for black women was prone. I remember us [thinking] 'Yeah, it's true.' We're like nineteen or twenty years old and had not been introduced to progressive black feminist thinking at all. No kind of feminist thinking."[1] In retrospect Powell regrets marginalizing the concerns of women in Rutgers' black student organization. "[W]henever women in our African Student Congress would question the behavior and attitudes of men, I would scream, 'We don't have time for them damn lesbian issues!'"[2]

As Powell demonstrates, the hip-hop generation's construction of a counterhegemonic discourse to white supremacy—be it at colleges or on compact discs—did not preclude the incorporation of a sexual politics that parallels bourgeois notions of male domination. Speech, lead rapper of the Grammy Award–winning Arrested Development, is one notable exception. On the group's debut album *3 Years 5 Months & 2 Days in the Life of . . .*, he challenges traditional sexual divisions of labor by declaring that childcare is collective community work that should be done by women *and* men and by instructing black men to "raise your fist but also raise your children." Speech also contests the limitations of his gendered identity by confessing vulnerability in love ("you're making me weak and it's scary") and imagining long-term heterosexual relationships that are reciprocal, not hierarchical ("maybe I could be the U for U and U could be the U for me too.") Despite the progressive gender politics of Arrested Development, the vast majority of raptivists during the golden age of rap nationalism inherited the masculinist discourse of their black nationalist predecessors—especially its emphasis on the reclamation of black manhood. For instance, Jeru the Damaja resurrected the theme of black nationalism as a politics of (ex)slave resistance and translated what he perceived to be the systematic destruction of African America in terms of black male castration, a disengendered status he likened to invisibility or death. In his 1995 song "Frustrated Nigga" Jeru rationalizes that being "victimized / circumcised / by the lies / of the system / is equivalent to being non-existent." In prophesizing a black insurrection (read: the remasculation of the black man), he promises to break the chains of his mental enslavement and reclaim his rightful place at the head of the strong black nation. "You shall now bear witness / to a new breed of nigga," he presages.

> This nigga is smarter
> than the nigga of times past
> this nigga is the nigga of the future
> this nigga will emancipate
> himself from the title nigga
> and restore his title as king.

"So beware," he warns, "the frustrated nigga."[3]

As previously discussed, the race politics of American black nationalism have been historically and intimately tied to issues of gender and sexuality, and the golden age of rap nationalism did not deviate from that tradition. In the power-brokering politics of the Hip-Hop Nation, race and class were not the only stocks being bought and sold on the market—

rap nationalists also traded upon their shares of gender and sexuality. As writer Russell A. Potter reveals, at times the politicking of rap artists "matches Rush Limbaugh in its emphasis on the centrality of black male authority for moral redemption."[4] In this sense black nationalist politics, once again, became less about a politics of liberation than about a politics of substitution, an appropriation of a male role cast in the gender play of hegemonic masculinity. Those rap artists who appeared to be most radical on issues of race were, in reality, extremely conservative when it came to issues of gender and sexuality. In fact, the embodied-social politics of rap music in the late 1980's/early 1990's was reminiscent of the sexual politicking of such Black Power notables as Eldridge Cleaver, Stokely Carmichael, and H. Rap Brown—it was profound, as well as profane—and it stands as the postmodern revisioning of black nationalism as a politics of masculine protest.

From Eunuchs to Endangered Species: Black Nationalism as a Politics of Masculine Protest Revisited

> I heard payback's a muthafuckin' nigga . . .
> —Ice Cube, "The Nigga You Love to Hate"

Ice Cube opens the second track on his transitional LP *AmeriKKKa's Most Wanted* with a simple, yet clever, twist on a vernacular expression. By changing its gendered modifier and adding an expletive, he turned a benign declaration ("payback is a bitch") into a declarative threat: "I heard payback's a muthafuckin' nigga." It is a warning of the possibilities of collective defiance, steeped in the kind of indirection that is reminiscent of David Walker's *Appeal* or the use of eschatology in slave religion. From the preaching of Nat Turner to the teachings of Elijah Muhammad, many black nationalist texts are framed by the type of vengeful thinking reflected in Ice Cube's imagining of an (ex)slave revolt: "just think if niggas decide to retaliate."[5] As we have seen, the recurring theme of violent resistance is a staple of black nationalism, and it is a persistent subject of Ice Cube's work as a "gangstAfronationalist." While it may be provocative, the theme of violent resistance is also rooted in an identity politics that, by its very nature, involves a rigid and hierarchical gender order that dictates—and, therefore, limits—the configuration of power and empowerment.

After his break with gangsta rap pioneers Niggaz With Attitude, Ice Cube moved his act from Los Angeles to New York City, where he joined ranks with Public Enemy's production team, the Bomb Squad, and, under the influence of Chuck D, began crafting his neonationalist politics. The result was *Amerikkka's Most Wanted*, an LP that combines the macho posturing of West Coast "gangsta" rap (e.g., exaggerated tales of sexual conquests and of the violent acquisition of money) with the masculinist discourse of East Coast raptivism (e.g., endorsing conventional gender/sexual roles and a more equal distribution of money). Whether this transition is seen as a political awakening or a brilliant strategy for marketing "unmitigated black rage prepackaged for . . . cathartic or voyeuristic convenience,"[6] Ice Cube's first solo effort demonstrated how black nationalism as an embodied-social politics is dependent not only on performative blackness (e.g., ghettocentricity) but also on performative masculinity. As Ice Cube, O'Shea Jackson's race/gender/class identification was that of "nigga," an identity that affiliated him with an imagined community of black men who were hardcore: fearless, aggressive men who often expressed themselves in violent ways—in fact, at times, the more violent, the more "authentic." For the self-proclaimed "nigga" vulnerability is not an option, and is an emotional state reserved for their "feminine" counterparts—the gender-inclusive "bitches." Women and gay men were held in contempt by Ice Cube in *Amerikkka's Most Wanted*.[7] For instance, while he claimed to "love black women with a passion,"[8] fictional violence against women is more prevalent on *Amerikkka's Most Wanted* than any expression of affection, from his declaration that he is a "bitchkillah" in "The Nigga Ya Love to Hate" to the misogynistic "You Can't Fade Me," a venomous mother's-baby-father's-maybe tale that concludes with a murderous fantasy: "Damn, why did I let her live / after that I should have got the gat / and bust and rushed and ill'd and peel'd the cap." Ice Cube's lyrics demonstrate the flip side of a liberatory politics based on race and gender rationales. "[T]he problem with unmitigated black rage," relays author/journalist Joan Morgan, is that "[i]t grabs white people by the jugular with one hand, and strangles black folks with the other."[9]

This hypermasculine gender politicking is rampant among rap nationalists. While there has been a lot of hype about rap music's sexism, misogyny, and homophobia, hardly any critics have placed this issue within its proper context: the social-political struggle for the remasculation of black men. To truly understand and appreciate the subtle distinction between pro-male celebration and antifemale sentiments (without assuming the position of an apologist), it is necessary to assess the sexual politics of hip-hop culture within the masculinist tradition of black cultural politics and political culture. A few scholars, like Jeffrey Louis Decker, Michael Eric Dyson, Robin D. G. Kelley, and Barbara Ransby and Tracye Matthews, have acknowledged these continuities. For example, in a brilliant essay that places male rap artists' machismo/masochism within the context of black vernacular culture, Kelley argues that issues of sex and violence tend to converge in communities among men whose limited access to resources jeopardizes their claim to a gendered position of power: "[I]n a world where male public powerlessness is often turned inward on women and children, misogyny and stories of sexual conflict are very old examples of the 'price' of being baaad."[10] In this manner, the hip-hop generation's reclamation of black nationalist-masculinist discourse becomes somewhat predictable. For a sense of masculine dispossession was particularly recognizable in the gendered pronouncements of—and privileging of heteronormativity among—raptivists during the golden age of rap nationalism, and these sentiments represent both continuity and discontinuity with the classical and modern periods of black nationalism.

During the post–Civil Rights, post–Black Power era, in communities where the majority of male children were raised in female-headed households, masses were imprisoned, more were under- or unemployed, and too many died a premature and violent death, the reclamation of black manhood reemerged as the primary issue on the political agenda. Despite the fact that a multitude of African American families were in the care of "abandoned and abused young black women"[11] who tended to be "over-arrested, over-indicted, under-defended and over-sentenced"[12] and for whom AIDS was increasingly becoming the leading cause of death, a perceived crisis of masculinity once again seized the spotlight in the black public arena as Eldridge Cleaver's Black Eunuch became an "endangered species." This situation speaks directly to the perilous ways in which nationalisms in general are invented and institutionalized, and is particularly consistent with the tradition of black nationalist thought, which since the nineteenth century has evolved as a politics of masculine protest. It is within this context that rap nationalist Ice Cube was able to audaciously, albeit naively, suggest to freedom fighter and feminist Angela Davis the retrograde argument that black men's struggle takes precedence over that of black women, and Afrocentric rap artists like the Jungle

Brothers confidently recycled the retrogressive idea that "with every great man there's a woman behind him."[13]

For young black men in search of what it meant to be a man in the late 1980's/early 1990's postindustrial economy, the political philosophy of black nationalism was particularly attractive. With the ability to provide being central to the heteronormative definition of masculinity and in the midst of declining opportunities for gainful employment, rap nationalism became an outlet for black males' frustrations over their compromised sense of masculinity. In black nationalist thought, masculinity is defined as not-femininity; and, as we have seen, black nationalism is an embodied-social politics that, more often than not, sanctions the subordination of the feminine, which is symbolized by women and gay men. (Lesbians rarely figure into the work of rap nationalists—or in the sexual politics of rap artists in general, despite the lyrical presence of pornographic heterosexist same-sex fantasies—because they do not present the same kind of threat to the conceptualization of hegemonic masculinity posed by heterosexual women or gay men.) And yet, in the Hip-Hop Nation it was not only men who bought into concepts of male power and powerlessness; female rap artists also engaged in the antiwoman/antigay discourse that characterized rap music's sexual politics. Public Enemy's Sister Souljah, for example, defined black liberation in masculinist terms when she exclaimed, "Every brother and sister has got to be a soldier in the war against the black man."[14] Thus it is important to examine the role of female artists, not only as pro-woman advocates but also as champions of masculinist constructions of gender identity. For, as historian Tricia Rose writes, doing so "allows us to make sense of the contradictory modes of resistance in women rappers' work."[15]

In the Hip-Hop Nation, raptivists propagated the Madonna/whore dichotomization of women: cultural nationalist/Nation of Islam–inspired tributes to the black woman as the "mother of civilization" coexisted alongside profane narratives reminiscent of a Cleaver/Carmichael depiction of black women as hypersexual creatures in control of a dangerous, yet delicious, "pussy power." The sexually explicit lyrics of rap nationalists were a direct descendant of the raunchy poetry of artists/activists of the Black Power movement. Note the x-rated verse of H. Rap Brown in *Die Nigger Die* (which is even more scandalous because it is akin to a "yo mamma" joke): "I fucked your mama / Till she went blind / Her breath smells bad / But she sure can grind / I fucked your mama / For a solid hour / Baby came out / Screaming, Black Power."[16] Like their Black Power predecessors, rap nationalists were no strangers to prurient prose. Raptivists like Public Enemy, Boogie Down Productions, Brand Nubian, and Jeru the Damaja all celebrated the virtues of black womanhood and, at one point or another, bragged about their sexual exploits with women, or their ability to "mack." In fact, Public Enemy appropriated "Brothers Gonna Work It Out," a song title on *Apocalypse 91 . . . The Enemy Strikes Back*, from the sound track for the classic blaxploitation film *The Mack*, which featured a pimp as its protagonist. And in a manner reminiscent of Stokely Carmichael's now infamous declaration, Ice Cube once argued that the only position for women in "a man's world" is that of sexual service: "Women they good for nothin', naw maybe one thing / to serve needs to my ding-a-ling."[17] This kind of sexual politics may appear to be incongruous with nationalist values. But as self-proclaimed "pimp" Too Short (who is not a raptivist) has attempted to explain, the "pimp attitude" is less about the exploitation of women than it is about the remasculation of black men: "To me, it's positive, it's not really about degrading women, it's about the black man. It's almost like the Muslims. Being a Muslim is like keeping your mind straight. The mack thing is about keepin' your mind correct. It's a self-esteem thing if you ask me."[18]

While hip-hop scholar William Eric Perkins argues that this comparison is "sheer folly," it is not as ridiculous as it may seem. The assertion of male power in the sex industry and in the public sphere both depend on the legislation of black women's sexuality and involve a politic predicated upon women's complicity in their own subjugation. Furthermore the extraordinary popularity of the pimp as folk hero during black nationalist moments in both the 1970's and the 1990's suggests that both the pimp and the protester represent a potent response to a perceived sense of male powerlessness as it is translated into a politics of masculine protest. In fact, during the late 1960's and '70s, the sensational ideals of pimp narratives—in both literature (e.g., Iceberg Slim's *Pimp: The Story of My Life*) and film (e.g., *The Mack*)—converged with those of their black nationalist peers. For example, in Iceberg Slim's seminal best-selling 1969 novel *Pimp*, he describes pimping as (infra)politics, a tool with which black men are able to challenge white hegemony. Slim's cinematic counterparts in blaxploitation films like *The Mack* in 1973 and *Dolemite* in 1975 also "stick it to The Man," engaging in what philosopher of African America Tommy L. Lott deems a politics of self-defense against the urban reality of police brutality and Hollywood's (sur)reality of black male emasculation.[19] Or as the closing line of Melvin Van Peebles's pioneering

1971 film *Sweet Sweetback's Baadasssss Song* warned, "Watch out. A baadasssss nigger is coming back to collect some dues." Therefore, it is no coincidence that Iceberg Slim expressed great respect for the Black Panthers' Eldridge Cleaver, whom he deemed "miraculous," and Huey Newton, whom he described as "beautiful,"[20] or that Newton, in turn, praised the politics of *Sweetback* as the "first truly revolutionary Black film."[21] In this context, it is also not surprising that, almost thirty years later, former rap nationalist Ice Cube announced that he would produce and star in a film documenting the life of Iceberg Slim.

Not all black nationalists romanticized the pimp. Black Arts movement pioneer Larry Neal denounced the "Brother Pimp" ("yeah, motherfucker, you ain't shit. / you just another kind of slave master") and contended, in a patriarchal manner, that "a man does not allow his women to go down / on sick white beasts." As an alternative—and in a manner that was no less problematic than that of his Black Panther counterparts—Neal encouraged pimps to "JOIN THE STRUGGLE / FOR REAL MANHOOD / become a new kind of pimp. yeah, brother, pimp for the / revolution."[22]

It's a Man's World: Defining Women's Roles in the Hip-Hop Nation

While outrageous, the appeal of the pimp to black nationalists in the 1970's and 1990's is consistent with the gender and sexual politics of the Black Power and hip-hop movements. Even classical black nationalists like Alexander Crummell, W. E. B. Du Bois, and Marcus Garvey coveted sovereignty over and, therefore, promoted surveillance of black women's sexuality—because, as previously discussed, in nationalist circles a woman's power lies in her ability to (re)produce the nation. In fact, among raptivists and Black Power activists, procreation was perceived to be the primary role of women in the struggle for black liberation. With rap nationalists this standpoint is exemplified by the Jungle Brothers' 1989 song "Black Woman." "Love," they explained, is "the woman's weapon." "Her womb is the chamber that produces life / Her breast provides the nutrition for growth." That same year Monie Love, like her Native Tongues brothers, celebrated her childbearing capabilities and embraced a sexual division of labor in the ironically titled "Ladies First." "We are the ones that give birth / to the new generation of prophets," she pronounced, "because it's ladies first." Not to be outdone by their Afro-centric peers, X-Clan's resident goddess of fertility, Isis, described her revolutionary power in conventional terms. "I am a self coming forth / a creature bearing life, a renaissance, a rebirth." Even Queen Latifah, who is hailed by many rap scholars as a feminist-nationalist, propagated a masculinist position on female subordination. Despite her strong voice and imposing cult-nat stature, Latifah revamped the campaign for separate spheres endorsed by her nineteenth- and twentieth-century black nationalist sisters when she identified her role in the hip-hop movement as "secondary but necessary to reproduce."[23]

Public Enemy's Sister Souljah was one of the only female raptivists who did not wholeheartedly support this rhetoric. The same woman who declared the reclamation of black manhood the primary struggle of the Hip-Hop Nation paradoxically challenged men who believed in female subordination: "I'll never keep quiet, so don't even try it / Sit in the back row, I won't buy it / Necessary but secondary, that's your insecurity."[24] Sister Souljah imagined a way for women to maintain their gender identity and assume leadership positions in the political arena, unwittingly using the moral suasion argument originated by many nineteenth-century female suffragists. "I think that feeling has to be put back into the movement, whether it's hip hop or politics," she claimed in 1991. "That emotional side comes from women, so we have to be included in the leadership in order to impact and shape the ways things are going to move forward."[25] Sister Souljah's public pronouncements were so incongruous that cultural critic Jeffrey Louis Decker suspected she was a pawn, her presence in Public Enemy a ploy to evade charges of sexism.[26] Decker's assessment is debatable, but there is no question that, despite her inconsistencies, Souljah's outspokenness on the conventional gender standards of rap nationalists was rare.

It is tempting to criticize female raptivists for participating in a gender politics that reinforces women's subjugation; however, their unwillingness to publicly castigate their male peers reflects a double bind that has haunted black women freedom fighters since the nineteenth century: when faced with the prospect of counterposing race with gender, black women have historically put race first. During the post–Civil Rights, post–Black Power era, when hip-hop music reigned as one of the premier forums for black politicking, the silence of female artists and journalists (and sometimes even scholars) was largely due to their refusal to be used in the antirap propaganda machine. For example, scholar Tricia Rose notes that Salt of the hip-hop trio Salt 'N' Pepa was the only woman in the industry who went on record and challenged 2 Live Crew during the 1989–1990 media frenzy surrounding the Miami-based rap group's controversial "obscene" lyrics. Others may have found 2 Live Crew objectionable, Rose writes, but many female rappers did not want to join the chorus of voices protesting the infamous group "because they were acutely aware of the dominant discursive context within which their responses would be reproduced," namely, that they were "being used as a political baton to beat male rappers over the head."[27]

Female rap artists were not the only women in hip-hop culture who carried this burden of silence. In 1994 journalist dream hampton aptly articulated the experience of many hip-hop aficionadas in her "Confessions of a Hip-Hop Critic." "I find myself in the uncomfortable and precarious position of defending great poets like Tupac, Snoop Doggy Dogg, and Kool G Rap when outsiders want to reduce them to monster misogynists and murderers," she writes. "Because I love rap music . . . I've recognized and struggled to reconcile the genius and passion of my brothers—even when it meant betraying my most fundamental politics. I'm in the same position I imagine I would have assumed had my peers been the eloquently sexist Ishmael Reed or genius/woman-beater Miles Davis."[28] (It is also important to note that fear of violent reprisal is another reason some women were disinclined to challenge sexism and misogyny in rap music. This concern was amplified in 1991 when Dr. Dre of N.W.A. publicly assaulted Dee Barnes in a Los Angeles night club in retaliation for what he perceived to be an unflattering segment aired on her television program *Pump It Up*.) These women's reluctance to speak out against sexism in rap music, and the rationale behind their silence, is not remarkable because it is reminiscent of a long tradition of black women's participation in the public sphere. What *is* surprising, though, is that this gender dynamic continues to exist in the post–second wave feminist era.

Even after women of color revolutionized feminist theory and politics during the 1970's and '80s, a history of racism in the women's movement has tainted black women's associations with "feminism."[29] And, as black lesbian-feminist Barbara Smith reveals, because feminism threatens the very foundation of intraracial, intergender interaction, black men have been instrumental in cultivating myths that reinforce black women's fears about the women's movement.[30] Consequently, during the early 1990's the conservatives' antirap campaign combined with female rap artists' rejection of "feminism" and conspired to reinforce a discourse of male dominance in the hip-hop movement. This retrogressive development of events brings to mind the period directly following the publication of the 1965 Moynihan Report when women in the Black Power movement felt compelled to support female subordination in response to representations of black women as castrators of black men. When confronted with the proposition of critiquing sexism in black America or racism in white America, raptivists like Queen Latifah of the Native Tongues coalition, Isis of X-Clan, and Sister Souljah of Public Enemy had but one option before them; and it was an option that echoed forth from times past: race first.

The embracing of a traditional sexual division of labor by male and female rap nationalists—even in the postfeminist era—is not as shocking as it may seem given hip-hop's primary audience; as Nelson George argues, the rap music scene is more than merely male centered. It reflects a solipsism that is suggestive of an underlying desire for male affection and attention. "There was, and remains, a homoerotic quality to hip hop culture," he writes, "one nurtured in gangs and jails, that makes women seem, aside from sex, often nonessential."[31] The return to "tradition" that characterized the lyrical narratives involving a gendered discourse in rap nationalism appears to have been motivated by a number of factors. Taking for granted the most obvious reasoning (that male domination is a cultural value in mainstream and African America), its reappearance in rap music was partly a result of black men's anxiety over their aggrieved sense of masculinity. It reveals an underlying fear of women inspired by an inability to live up to traditional standards of manhood in a postindustrial economy.[32] Simply put, the sexism prevalent in the Hip-Hop Nation signifies male bonding over disappearing economic opportunities.

At the 1994 congressional hearings convened to target violence and sexism in rap music, historian Robin Kelley urged critics to keep the real issues of sexism in perspective. Unlike the wage gap or sexual harassment in the workplace, profane rap lyrics do not represent the most dangerous manifestations of sexism in American culture, he testified.[33] While Kelley advocated equal rights for women in American social, political, and economic life, most raptivists argued that in the context of African America, women had more than their fair share of gender rights and privileges. In fact, the viewpoint of nationalists in the Black Power and hip-hop movements was that "The Black Woman Is Already Liberated."[34] Be they the matriarchs of Daniel Patrick Moynihan's imagination or the "Amazons" of Eldridge Cleaver's fantasy, artists and activists in both periods pronounced black women guilty of being a dominant and domineering force in black communities. "Historically, Afro-American women have had to be the economic mainstays of the family," Black Arts movement theorist Larry Neal justified in a 1968 essay. "The oppressor allowed them to have jobs while at the same time limiting the economic mobility of the black man. Very often, therefore, the woman's aspirations and values are closely tied to those of the white power structure and not to those of her man."[35] Over thirty years later, in a manner strikingly similar to Neal's, members of the Hip-Hop Nation employed this line of argumentation as an explanation for what they perceived to be the contentious state of gender relations in black America; and like their Black Power predecessors, they subscribed to the notion that black women were a pawn in a conspiratorial plot to maintain white supremacy over black people, particularly black men, in the United States.

According to music executive Bill Stephney, who in his post–Public Enemy postyouth became the founder of Families Organized for Liberty and Action and a member of the National Fatherhood Initiative,[36] social programs sponsored by the government after the Civil Rights movement created favorable socioeconomic conditions for black women at the expense of black men. Stephney took particular exception to government aid to women and children, which he believed not only ignores the fact that black men also experience poverty but also strengthens what he perceived to be a matriarchal family and community structure in African America. While Stephney considered gender equality an important political issue, he declared that a politics of black female empowerment—be it via social programming or feminism—is redundant: "How much more power do [women] need in the black community?" he queried. "If we look at issues of mortality, life expectancy, employment, family structure, executive income, black women are above black men on every level in every standard and statistic." After establishing the argument that local and federal governments purposely created economic disparity (and, therefore, a power differential) between black women and black men, Stephney concluded that rap music evolved as a response to the systemic devaluation black men experience within their families and communities—or, as he articulated, "Hip-hop wanted to be a soundtrack for this marginalization."[37] Writer and activist Kevin Powell also believed hip-hop culture was a response to the increasing estrangement of black men from their families and communities. And like Stephney, he subscribed to the notion that black women received certain privileges denied black men. "Hip-hop was created by black and Latino men, who were left out of the advancements of the Civil Rights movement," he contended. "Black women were allowed to advance in a certain way that a lot of black men were not. Not to say [women] had it better than us," Powell assured, "but black men represent a certain type of threat that black women don't represent to this white power structure. That's why hip-hop was very male-centered. For a lot of us working-class cats it was the one space where we're visible, where we could say whatever we want and be free."[38]

This assessment of the social and economic dispossession of black male youth during the 1970's and '80s provides a contextual understanding of a song like Public Enemy's "Sophisticated Bitch," which— along with "She Watch Channel Zero?!"—led some cultural critics to label the group "misogynist." While its hostile condemnation of black women somewhat tarnished their reputation as rap nationalism's pioneers, according to journalist Nelson George, "Sophisticated Bitch" spoke to an "uncomfortable truth" about black professional women: it "was a benchmark," he writes, "in that the critique wasn't about money alone but the class differences between an upwardly mobile woman and a working-class man."[39] However "uncomfortable" (or inaccurate) this revelation may be, it reflects a sense of male powerlessness not only in the economic realm but within the sexual domain as well, suggesting a more literal interpretation of the concept of "pussy power." Kevin Powell bears witness to the fact that fear is a significant motivation behind black male aggression—particularly fear of black women, "of their mouths, of their bodies, of their attitudes, of their hurts, of their fear of us black men."[40] Therefore, like that old hip-hop proverb "never trust a big butt and a smile," Public Enemy's sexual politics may indicate that, as Tricia Rose articulates, "many men are hostile toward women because the fulfillment of male heterosexual desire is significantly checked by women's capacity for sexual rejection and/or manipulation of men."[41]

Stephney's, Powell's, and George's statements intimate that the threat to black masculinity was made even more perilous by black women's historic participation in the workforce. Therefore, in a curious way, hip-hop provided a safe space, a nurturing place, for those young men who felt under attack from The (white) Man and black woman. "These brothers are mad at a whole bunch of folks," not just women, Stephney stated assuredly. "It's safer to get into the discussion of black male anger against white cops, the white corrections system and the government in general," he claimed, while discussions of their anger toward women, black and white, are "like the third rail." Since Stephney understood the sexual politics of rap artists to be indicative of their declining status in local and national arenas, he regretted that their artistic expression "winds up being reduced to [accusations that] black men are misogynist," for he believed this to be a one-dimensional reading of a multifaceted experience. "There are some black men, I assume, who are misogynist, just as there are some black women who are antimale. But there is a specific condition that needs to be ameliorated that these young brothers have been talking about."[42] That condition: the systematic emasculation of black men, instigated by the government and ministrated by black women.

Thus, like their predecessors in the 1960's and '70s, a significant number of rap nationalists portrayed black women as an accessory to the crime of their systemic oppression. For example, Tricia Rose argues that when Ice Cube identifies himself as "the bitch-killah / cop-killah" in "The Nigga Ya Love to Hate," he alludes to an affiliation between black women and "state authority figures" in the "disempowerment and oppression" of black men.[43] When coupled with "You Can't Fade Me" and "I'm Only Out for One Thing," Ice Cube's narratives in *AmeriKKKa's Most Wanted* "are obviously symptomatic of underlying anxieties about the consequences of sexual desire."[44] Similarly, in a manner that contradicts his humanist standpoint, KRS-One delivered two chilling antiwoman songs dealing with sexual exploit(ation)s on his 1992 album *Sex and Violence*. In "13 and Good," KRS boasts about a sexual escapade with a minor. She may have been thirteen years old, he says, "but she was good." And then there's "Say Gal," a song written in response to a number of highly publicized celebrity rape cases in late 1991–early 1992, including that of heavyweight boxing champion Mike Tyson. "All you see in the newspapers nowadays is nuff gal talk 'bout them been raped and them been molested and them been feel up and them been all sexed up," he prefaces in the song's opening line. "Say Gal" absolves public figures of any responsibility for acts of sexual violence and instead holds women accountable for their style of dress and behavior. This line of self-defense, a classic rationale in U.S. rape culture, is evidence of male sexual frustration and reveals an underlying sense of subordination—male panic even—in the realm of sex and (hetero)sexuality. In his lyrical interrogation, KRS-One posits that if women don't want "sex," they should not dress provocatively. "Don't tell me you can wear what you want," he anticipates, "'cause nowadays a most dem gal a dressin' like a slut."[45]

It is important to note that not all rap nationalists supported a reactionary sexual politics. Mutulu Olugbala (M-1) of dead prez repudiated sexism in rap music. "I think it's fucked up," he exclaimed. "And I think it's not just on sisters to represent that for sisters, I think the brothers should represent that. And we don't. We be frontin' on it, saying 'Put it on the backburner.' And it's not right."[46] Even those artists—like Public Enemy, KRS-One, and Ice Cube—who at times exhibited outright and outrageous misogyny at other times displayed more liberal gender politics. For example, when questioned in 2002 about the prevalent image of underdressed, hypersexual women in rap music videos, Chuck D responded, "Being a heterosexual man, artistically, I never have a problem. Exploitation-wise, I have a problem."[47] As this statement demonstrates, the relationship between raptivism and sexism was a conflicted one, and the desire to challenge sexism in rap music was often just as conflicted. "The last thing any of us want is for another man to question how we treat women," admits Kevin Powell. "Aren't we, black men, the endangered species, anyhow?"[48] Reluctance aside, the presence of retrogressive gender politics in rap nationalism did not represent an entirely hopeless scenario for women in the hip-hop movement; for unlike the activists of the Black Power movement who argued that women should be "off the front lines and in the home," many raptivists could imagine a role for women in the masculinist struggle for black liberation . . . as long as their "gender identity as *women* is effaced."[49] Sister Souljah explicates that delicate balance in a 1991 interview with hip-hop documentarians James G. Spady and Joseph D. Eure: "[A] lot of times when you're a sister in a leadership position you always have to deal with someone saying, 'you're manly or masculine.' Or somebody thinking because you're a leader you're a lesbian. My thing is the last thing on earth I would ever be is a lesbian, because I love black people, and I love black men of course."[50]

Punks Jump Up to Get Beat Down: The Politics of (Homo)Sexuality during the Golden Age of Rap Nationalism

Sister Souljah's homophobic pronouncement exposes yet another problematic relationship between gender and sexuality in the neonationalist politics of rap music. It was acceptable for women to assume leadership positions in the Hip-Hop Nation—as long as they were not lesbians (whom she portrays, much like her Black Power predecessors, as race traitors). Although this may be a step forward for heterosexual women, for lesbians and gay men there was no role in the hip-hop movement. When Marlon Riggs reaffirmed black gay cultural politics in his 1989 film *Tongues Untied*, asserting that "black men loving black men is the revolutionary act of our times," he demonstrated that black nationalism as a politics of masculine protest is not necessarily dependent upon heterosexism. Nevertheless, the rap nationalist position on "black men loving black men" contradicted Riggs's point of view and is probably best characterized by a lyric in Brand Nubian's 1992 song "Pass the Gat," when Sadat X threatens to "shoot a faggot in the back for actin' like that."[51] The antigay sentiment expressed by raptivists ranged from homophobic insinuations to outright threats of violence and appeared in the lyrics of Public Enemy, X-Clan, Poor Righteous Teachers, and Ice Cube, to name a few. And although there was no articulated politics around the policing of black gay sexuality as there was for black heterosexual women in the Hip-Hop Nation, it is quite clear that the existence of a gay male population within black communities jeopardized the construction of black nationalism as a politics of masculine protest. "I can't be the rapper in hip hop that stands up for the gay cause," explained Bay Area raptivist Paris. "It's not something I agree with, if you get down to it."[52] Aside from the obvious reason for his avowal, Paris's aversion to homosexuality was probably due, in part, to the fact that, for most rap nationalists, same-sex intercourse between men represents the effeminization of black manhood. As Ice Cube maintained, "I'm a man / and ain't nobody humpin' me."[53] Among rap nationalists homosexual relationships were perceived to have little value in the struggle for the reclamation of black manhood. Sexual intercourse between men, however, is another story.

In the struggle for remasculation among rap nationalists, there was a conspicuous anxiety around homoeroticism between men—an anxiety that, more often than not, was reflected in a fear of being penetrated, or sexually violated. The sense of uneasiness around penetration expressed by various presumably heterosexual but decidedly hypermasculine politicized rap artists is not surprising because in a racist, capitalist, patriarchal society penetration is associated with submission. However, what is striking is just how grave that fear is. In Grandmaster Flash and the Furious Five's pioneering political rap "The Message," it is not just the cumulative effects of stagflation that present the most danger to black manhood in the postmodern period. In Melle Mel's lyrical drama the threat to black masculinity is more intimate; it is the experience of sexual exploitation—

a jailhouse rape—not social or economic violence that drives the protagonist to a self-inflicted death:

> Now your manhood is took and you're a nametag
> spent the next few years as an undercover fag
> being used and abused to serve like hell
> till one day you were found hung dead in a cell.[54]

According to this urban tale, poverty may be a bitch, but death is preferable to homosexuality.

Rap nationalists inherited some of their homophobic ideology from Black Power advocates, who rationalized their antigay sentiment in cultural nationalist terms that deemed homosexuality symptomatic of white supremacy in black America and/or in conspiratorial terms that implicated homosexuals in the genocide of black people. This rhetorical practice extended through the 1970's and into the '80s, as exemplified in the text of a flyer publicizing the First National Plenary Conference on Self-Determination held in New York City in December 1981: "Homosexuality does not produce children"; it does not, the flyer continues, "birth new warriors for liberation." And because of the reproductive incapabilities of homosexuals, the organizers conclude that the "practice of homosexuality is an accelerating threat to our survival as a people and as a nation."[55]

Chuck D's early homophobic remarks stand as an example of the "changing same" of the sexual politics of black nationalism and the oral/written texts on (anti)homosexuality. In 1987 Public Enemy's lead lyricist pronounced to *New Musical Express* (NME), a British rock magazine, "there's no room in the black race for gays." In response to being labeled antigay, he defended himself by invoking the rhetoric of reproduction ("I just said gays don't do nothing for our race") and by characterizing homosexuality as an example of the whitewashing of black America: "if they're gay, they're not holding to their responsibility to hold the community together, they're meshing and assimilating into white culture and definitely confusing the black situation even more."[56] Chuck D was not the only raptivist making remarks reminiscent of those made by their counterparts of the 1960's and '70s, for like Eldridge Cleaver, Brother J of X-Clan characterized homosexuality as a "sickness" when he insisted that he is not "a freak or an addict or a F-A-double-G-O-to-the-T."[57]

By the time Chuck D wrote *Fight the Power: Rap, Race, and Reality*, however, his position on homosexuality shifted to one that signaled, if not acceptance, at least tolerance. In his recollection of the Million Man March, Chuck D remarks that "[e]ven Black gay men were there," and acknowledges that "a Black man who happens to be a homosexual still has to deal with the racist aspects of being a Black man in this society." Chuck D recognizes that black gay men are susceptible to a double jeopardy—racism and homophobia—but issues a warning: race first. "A Black man is a Black man," he writes, "not because of his character, but because of his visual characteristics. . . . Young Black men and women should first know that they're Black men or women and be informed with the bullshit that's going to be thrown at them just on the level of their Blackness."[58] Bay Area raptivist Paris also suggested that homophobia is low on the list of priorities for African American men. "We're getting killed, our women being raped," he told journalist Farai Chideya. "Considering that we are on a collision course for destruction, the issue of homophobia is trivial." However, Paris reluctantly added that, unlike some of his peers, he does not condone antigay violence. "As far as beating people down, I'm not into that. To each his or her own."[59]

In spite of their homophobia, or perhaps because of it, rap nationalists tended to use same-sex intercourse as a rhetorical device—utilizing it not as an expression of desire but to illustrate acts of violence and humiliation, thus revealing a new twist on the old theme. As we have seen, the masculinist discourse of black nationalism is articulated through a language of violence; black nationalist theorists have used violence, or the threat of violence, to purge an emasculated sense of (male) self. From the eschatological rhetoric of David Walker's *Appeal to the Colored Citizens of the World* (1829) and Henry Highland Garnet's *Address to the Slaves of the United States of America* (1848) to the militant imaging of the Universal Negro Improvement Association and the Black Panther Party, black nationalists have endorsed violence as a weapon in the war against the personal/political castration of black men. The post–Civil Rights era was no exception. However, among rap nationalists the theme of violence was utilized in new and disheartening ways, particularly when framed as a method of social/sexual control.

Like Melle Mel, many raptivists exhibited their fear of emasculation through a preoccupation with rape, a preoccupation that centered upon the act of penetration; therefore they utilized the metaphor of same-sex intercourse as a signifier for disempowerment. For instance, in Ice Cube's

"No Vaseline," male-on-male rape is mediated as punishment in the form of sexual terrorization ("The villain does get fucked with no Vaseline") and is also a euphemism for economic exploitation ("gang-banged by your manager, fellah / gettin' money out yo' ass / like a muthafuckin ready teller").[60] Within this context, pain negates pleasure. In "No Vaseline" it is imperative that the sex act be described with brutality (e.g. "rippin' your asshole apart")—there must be no implication of (homo)sexual gratification—because for Ice Cube, as with many of his contemporaries in both nationalist and nonnationalist circles, penetration represented the ultimate form of emasculation.

Regardless of its vulgarity, "No Vaseline" was a postmodern manifestation of a tradition of race/gender politics that dates back to the early nineteenth century and was heir to a stylized sexual politics that dates back to the mid-twentieth. In this song, Eldridge Cleaver's Black Eunuch meets Ice Cube's Endangered Species. Like the Black Eunuchs' castigation of the Infidel in *Soul on Ice*, Ice Cube's "No Vaseline" is ultimately a call to black manhood. Embedded in his vicious attack is a test of loyalty to a narrowly defined race/gender identity—that of "nigga." Those who betray that race *and* gender identity are punished and exiled, threatened with castration. Or in Ice Cube's words, "I'm a cut them balls, 'cause I heard you like givin' up the draw[er]s."[61]

Despite Ice Cube's warning against homoeroticism, there are instances, albeit rare instances, in rap nationalists' narratives when it was considered acceptable to commit "homosexual" acts. Most raptivists did not find it acceptable to receive penetration from another man, but, under certain circumstances, it was acceptable to penetrate another man. The line between acceptable and nonacceptable sexual intercourse with a man—that moment when Ice Cube could say "I'd rather fuck you"[62] without being categorized, even by his own standards, as a "faggot"— was determined by whether or not the act could be translated as an act of empowerment. For example, according to Ice Cube's reasoning, it is not okay to "bend over for the goddamn cracker" but it *is* okay to "fuck them like they fuck us."[63]

This declaration bears witness to a keen statement made by Michele Wallace over twenty years ago in *Black Macho and the Myth of the Superwoman*. In her critique of the macho posturing of the Black Power leadership, Wallace exposed the irony of a politics based upon race/gender rationales. She argued that if you follow the logic of men like Eldridge Cleaver in *Soul on Ice*, "if *a black man were doing the fucking* and the one being fucked were a white man, the black male homosexual would be just as good a revolutionary as a black heterosexual male, if not a better one."[64] And yet, however reasonable this deduction may be, at no point in time has a prominent black nationalist theorist self-identified as a homosexual. To be clear, despite Ice Cube's use of same-sex intercourse as a metaphor, he did not confuse his desire—the desire for revenge—with pleasure; otherwise penetration, even when framed in violent terms, could become associated with gayness/homosexuality. Clarity on this issue is crucial, because according to black nationalist discourse, homosexuality is the antithesis of black masculinity. It is, in the struggle for the reclamation of black manhood, counterrevolutionary. After all, as Ice Cube warns on *Death Certificate*, "True niggas ain't gay."[65]

As an embodied-social politics, one that is rooted in what bell hooks deemed an "'it's-a-dick-thing' version of masculinity"[66] and that has a history of reducing race relations to a cockfight between black and white men, it is not surprising that the most common form of homophobic expression among raptivists was the use of antigay language to describe white men. Despite their empowered position as "The Man," white men were often characterized by rap nationalists as lacking real masculinity. Labeled "faggots" by Poor Righteous Teachers,[67] "sissies" by X-Clan,[68] and "punks" by Kam,[69] white men were considered weak, unable or unwilling to challenge black men one on one. This hypothesis was tested by Ice Cube in his description of the Rodney King incident on his postrebellion release *The Predator* and confirmed as he describes the LAPD as "faggots with guns and badges."[70] Under these circumstances male raptivists transferred their emasculated status to white men, utilizing a sexualized language to describe white exploitation of black people, particularly black men. Ice Cube's "Horny Li'l Devil" is a case in point.

In "Horny Li'l Devil" Ice Cube delivers an intense and interesting reading of the political economy of race and racism, one that (once again) privileged his gender identity and used penetration as a rhetorical device. This time, penetration symbolizes economic and/or social violence. "Horny li'l devil must be an F-A-G," he announces, "tryin' to fuck me out my land and my manhood / got me broke eatin' Spam and canned goods."[71] Despite his position among the truly disadvantaged (read: black men), Ice Cube demanded recognition in a way that confirmed the fact that his race/gender status and esteem were dependent upon his (hetero)sexuality: "My ass is a virgin," he insisted. "You may have fucked them Indians / but you can't surge in me." In "Horny Li'l Devil," Ice

Cube defines and denies white male desire for hegemony with lyrics that are simultaneously literal and figural. It was his express intention to invert dominant race/sex constructions: he maintained that it is not black men and women who are sexually depraved, but white men. According to Ice Cube's lyrical narrative, African America bears an historical imprint, marked by an uncivilized people. "The devil is a savage mutha-fucka / that's why I'm lighter than the average brother," he explained. "'Cause you raped our women and we felt it / but it'll never happen again if I can help it." Therefore, Ice Cube portrayed white men not only as deviants but also as sadomasochists—"horny li'l devil[s]"—who gain sexual gratification through domination.

Ice Cube's "Horny Li'l Devil" is remarkable because it provides a glimpse into the social psychology of black nationalism in the United States, as well as an insight into its dynamics as a form of race/gender politicking. Because Ice Cube's politics were figured by a fixed race *and* gender *and* class *and* sexual identity, his concept of liberation was also determined by that identity. For Ice Cube, power was defined in terms of violence and the execution of violence was perceived as empowerment, as demonstrated in his warning to the "Horny Li'l Devil": "when I'm on top I won't be fuckin' ya / I'd rather put a buck[shot] in ya." Like his nineteenth-century predecessors, Ice Cube demanded his manhood rights and claimed his (naturalized) role as provider and protector; yet in a manner reminiscent of Black Power rhetoricians, he did it in a language that would not be misunderstood:

> Li'l devil can't fuck me out my pay
> 'cause horny li'l devil true niggas ain't gay
> and you can't play with my Yo-Yo
> and definitely can't play with me
> you fuckin' homo.[72]

Conclusion: When the Secular and Sacred Collide . . .

Although extremely sensational, the sexual politics of rap nationalists was, in all actuality, an extension of a centuries-old tradition of black male politicking that has never been restrained in, or apologetic for, its desire for male power. While many critics, both black and white, have made rap artists the poster boys for sexism and misogyny, it is quite clear that the masculinist discourse of rap music is not an anomaly, and that it has its roots in institutions that are prominently located within American communities. The "most nefarious expression of sexism and misogyny" in American society, particularly in black American communities, is in the "nuclear family, religious communities and educational institutions,"[73] Michael Eric Dyson argues, sites in which antiwoman attitudes and behaviors are "nurtured and rationalized."[74]

One of these sites—religious communities—will be the focus of the next chapter, demonstrating that the "'it's-a-dick-thing' version of masculinity" is not limited to the secular world. From Ethiopianism to eschatology, biblical figuralism is central to the construction of black nationalism as a politics of masculine protest, particularly as a politics of (ex)slave/masculinist/violent resistance.

5

Representin' God

*Masculinity and the Use of
the Bible in Rap Nationalism*

On the Digable Planets' 1994 single "Dial 7 (Axioms of Creamy Spies)," Sara Webb, a featured vocalist, demystifies white power and dismisses social constructions of white supremacy with one short line: "The Man ain't shit." Webb takes her cultural cues from urban, black, working-class communities and denounces the representative of white domination—"The Man"—thus expelling him from his center of power. According to her verse, he is a devil ("your tongue is forked, we know") whose days of deception ("your double-dealin' is scoped") and conspiring ("The Man's game is peeped") against the disempowered black masses are over ("It's Nation Time, Nation Time"). Racially conscious brothers and sisters, the "creamy spies," inspired and informed by the teachings of Elijah Muhammad ("we are sun, moon and star"), have revealed white folks' true nature and the righteous legacy of blacks: "We are God's sequel." Armed with knowledge and an arsenal ("we all got pieces"), they are "ready to put in work"—to mobilize and organize— black folks at the "ghetto-level" to take control over their lives through a nationalist agenda and a black united front: "We can make life phatter / together / not divided."[1]

The perspective expressed by Sara Webb is an archetypical example of the kinds of cultural critiques advanced by rap politicos during the golden age of rap nationalism. Among those artists who used rap music as a forum for politicking, black nationalism shaped their political position and, with few exceptions, the teachings of Elijah Muhammad informed their nationalist perspective. For example, in his controversial 1989 release *The Devil Made Me Do It*, militant Oakland-based raptivist Paris traces his black nationalist roots to the 1940's and the founding of the

Temple of Islam, which would later become known as the Nation of Islam. In "Brutal," Paris, who at the time was a self-proclaimed member of the Nation, describes the legacy of black nationalism as beginning with W. D. Fard, founder of the Nation of Islam, and being preserved by Elijah Muhammad and Malcolm X, who in turn inspired the Black Panther Party. According to Paris, this tradition of "intelligent Black men" continued in the post–Black Power era with the Honorable Minister Louis Farrakhan and through men like himself, rap artists who were dedicated to producing music "to spark a revolutionary mind-set" in the black nation.[2] As he declares, his mission is both sacred and secular: "Best believe I won't stop / teachin' science in step with Farrakhan / drop a dope bomb, word to Islam / peace my brothers up on it 'cause I'm / black and now you know I'm brutal."[3]

Paris's outline of the history of black nationalism is characteristic of the androcentric historical narratives put forth by raptivists in the hip-hop movement. The politics of the Nation of Islam under the leadership of Farrakhan and through the memory of Malcolm X reawakened the consciousness of black youth and informed the politicization of rap music that began in the late 1980's with artists like Boogie Down Productions and Public Enemy. In a manner that truly speaks to the dearth of black leadership in the post–Civil Rights/post–Black Power era, Louis Farrakhan's extraordinary rise in popularity as a public figure during the mid- to late 1980's occurred despite his lack of any salient political platform. His provocative style of race politicking and articulation of black rage were enough to capture the attention of a generation of black youth frustrated with postindustrial urban landscapes arrested by de facto racial segregation and economic abandonment. "Minister Farrakhan is the link and the reason that we all understand that we do have this one thing in common, and this mission to be self-sufficient in America or in the rest of the world," proclaimed Public Enemy front man Chuck D.[4] His bandmates Flava Flav and Sister Souljah, as well as other rap nationalists like Ice Cube, Paris, Brand Nubian, and Wise Intelligent of Poor Righteous Teachers, have also acknowledged Farrakhan as an inspiration for the development of their political standpoint. In 1991 Public Enemy's resident trickster Flava Flav, who claimed to be a former member of the Nation of Islam, celebrated the virtues of his spiritual mentor. "[A]ll praise is due to Minister Farrakhan for teaching us the way of perfection which is the direction, cause there was a big mistake but he made the correction."[5]

As previously discussed, among black nationalists hero worship is not an isolated phenomenon but an inherited one; and more often than not, this type of invocation is a "production of exemplary masculinity."[6] Marcus Garvey admired Booker T. Washington, while Malcolm X and Farrakhan revered their spiritual father, Elijah Muhammad. In turn, during the Black Power era self-proclaimed "sons of Malcolm"—be they revolutionary nationalists like the Black Panther Party or cultural nationalists like the US Organization—cultivated a masculinist memory of (the Nation of Islam) Malcolm X. Twenty years later, as the focus of black nationalist politics shifted from the emasculated black man to the black man as "endangered species," the children of the Civil Rights/Black Power generation, through their celebration of Louis Farrakhan, once again demonstrated that the production of exemplary masculinity is fundamental to framing black nationalism as a politics of masculine protest. It is not surprising, then, that this consortium of rap artists merged elements of masculine discourse and biblical allusion so familiar to the tradition of black nationalism, with one significant difference. During the golden age of rap nationalism, Christianity no longer held center stage as the dominant theological structure of black liberatory philosophy—Islam gained prominence with a prophetic promise of the rise of the "Asiatic Black Man."

Until the foundation of the Moorish-American Science Temple in 1913 and the formation of the Temple of Islam in the 1930's, black nationalist theology was rooted exclusively in the gospel of Christianity. The Temple of Islam would soon become the Nation of Islam, and after the disappearance of founder W. D. Fard in 1934, its leadership responsibilities were assumed by Elijah Muhammad, whose interpretation of the Islamic faith would, in turn, inspire three contemporary religious sects/organizations: the Nation of Islam, led by Louis Farrakhan; the Lost Found Nation of Islam, led by Silis Muhammad; and the Five Percent Nation of Islam (also known as the Nation of Gods and Earths), originated by Clarence 13X. Two of these groups—the Nation of Islam and the Five Percent Nation—are significant to the study of rap nationalism.

While the origins of both the Nation of Islam and the Five Percent Nation of Islam are rooted in the teachings of Elijah Muhammad, the organizations developed somewhat different ideologies. Constant themes among Five Percenters are generally consistent with those of the Nation of Islam: the characterization of all black men as "gods" and the white man as the "devil," the argument that God is not a "mystery" god in heaven, and the condemnation of Christianity as the white man's religion.

What distinguishes the Five Percent Nation from the Nation of Islam is its emphasis on the tenet that only five percent of the population—the "Five Percenters"—knows God (Allah); these poor righteous teachers believe they are on a mission to spread their knowledge to the black majority, who do not know their real exalted identity as black Asiatics. Despite Nation of Islam leader Louis Farrakhan's pervasive influence on the politics of the hip-hop movement, there were more rappers who claimed to be members of the Five Percent Nation. East Coast artists such as Poor Righteous Teachers, Brand Nubian, Rakim, King Sun, and Doodlebug of Digable Planets were self-proclaimed Five Percenters, while West Coast artists Paris, Kam, and MC Ren (formally of N.W.A.) were among the few rap nationalists who were in the Nation of Islam. This disparity can probably be attributed to the strict code of conduct the Nation of Islam demands of its members—they must adhere to a one-meal-a-day restricted diet and are not allowed drink, smoke, or fornicate. The Five Percent Nation, on the other hand, offered believers similar religious doctrines without the forbidding restrictions.[7]

What began in the early twentieth century with the Moorish-American Science Temple and the Temple of Islam, then, continued to shift the parameters of black liberatory theology during the late twentieth century, as Muslim influences from the Nation of Islam and the Five Percent Nation of Islam informed the nationalist perspectives manifest within the lyrics of groups like Public Enemy, Boogie Down Productions, Poor Righteous Teachers, and artists like Ice Cube and Paris. Yet despite this adaptation, the ideations of rap nationalists were reminiscent of those expressed in slave spirituals and in black nationalist publications of the nineteenth century, both of which were informed by Christianity. One of the more obvious explanations for this continuity is that it is due to the perduring importance of scripture in African American culture.

Despite their Muslim influences, raptivists maintained the black nationalist-masculinist tradition by using the Bible as a (re)source of power and knowledge. By relying on the Bible as an authoritative text, black nationalist strategists claim the "final word" by providential design; and in a politics of substitution, the Bible works precisely because, as philologist Erich Auerbach noted, it is "tyrannical." "[I]t excludes all other claims," he explains. "All other scenes, issues, and ordinances have no right to appear independently of it, and it is promised that all of them, the history of mankind, will be given their due place within its frame, will be subordinated to it."[8] When nineteenth- and twentieth-century black nationalists invoked God as a god of the oppressed and black Americans as His chosen ones, they not only reconstructed "blackness," elevating it to a valued and sacred state, but their words functioned "rhetorically as ritual incantations that reciprocally summon God and . . . 'invite us to make ourselves over in the image of the imagery.'"[9] As a result, black liberation—and, by extension, masculinist appropriation—becomes divinely ordained.

This kind of biblical interpretation reveals the "changing same" of black nationalist theology and exemplifies the cultural and political continuity that constitutes the black nationalist tradition. It is especially significant because, among raptivists, the Bible itself was a contested issue. For example, KRS-One put forth a provocative argument before an assembly at Northwestern University in the spring of 1991 when he claimed that the King James version of the Bible was rewritten for immoral purposes. Because the word "holy" applies to objects that are divine, he reasoned, the KJV by definition could not be referred to as the "Holy Bible." "King James was a madman," he said. "He was a complete lunatic. One day he wanted to have sex with his daughter. In the original Bible it said you couldn't, so he ripped it out. He got his homeboy Aristotle to edit it up, and this is what you got: the authorized King James Version of the Bible." In an alternative argument, Poor Righteous Teachers' Wise Intelligent contended that the history of the Bible has been misrepresented, declaring that it is, in fact, a testament of the African Diaspora. "We've been deceived into believing that the Bible represents some Western culture or Western philosophy or religion. We've been deceived into thinking the Bible is 'the white man's book' when in actually it's your book, your history book."[10] Despite raptivists' disclaimers—and consistently shifting hermeneutics and (con)textual forms—the Bible was a constant that has continued to provide a framework for the philosophy of black nationalism.

The sacred text of Christianity proved to be a mainstay in post–Civil Rights African American culture, yet Christianity itself came under fire, particularly among young black men. As Black Muslims grew increasingly popular among raptivists, Christianity became the object of criticism, skepticism, ridicule, and contempt. Raptivists overwhelmingly perceived black Christians to be accommodationists and their religion to be conciliatory and compromising; both judgments were reminiscent of critiques launched by Black Power activists toward the Civil Rights generation, as exemplified by the "quotable" Maulana Karenga, who mocked,

"My brother told me Jesus didn't really get crucified, niggers begged him to death."[11] In fact, it was the philosophical and political tensions between mainstream black churches and Black Power advocates during the late 1960's that prompted theologian James Cone to question, "Is Black Power . . . compatible with the Christian faith, or are we dealing with two utterly divergent perspectives?"[12] While his seminal text, *Black Theology and Black Power* (1969), was an attempt to answer affirmatively and to reconcile the two entities, thirty years later rap nationalists would answer emphatically: Christianity and Black Power are diametrically opposed. According to the rationale of artists in the Hip-Hop Nation, it was necessary to embrace a religious tradition dedicated to the transformation of a national black consciousness and conducive to the construction of a strong black nation.

"If Your Slavemaster Wasn't a Christian . . .": *Rap Nationalism and the Rejection of Christianity*

In his 1992 song "The Real Holy Place," KRS-One of Boogie Down Productions issues an indictment of Christianity. He characterizes its practitioners as hypocrites, labels its testament a "dead book," and, perhaps most importantly, declares its mission the subjugation of people of color—particularly Americans of African descent. "If your slavemaster wasn't a Christian you wouldn't be a Christian / your whole culture is missin'," he informs the postmodern descendants of slaves.[13] This judgment of Christianity as the "slavemaster's religion" represented a consensus of sorts among raptivists and stands as an example of how black nationalist thought has continued to be framed as a politics of (ex)slave resistance. According to most rap nationalists, the contemporary incarnation of the so-called slave mentality was most readily recognized among black Christians. Yet this aversion to Christians and Christianity was the result of misconceptions and misinformation influenced by the ideologies of the Nation of Islam. It is a position raptivists adopted from their heroes, their model(s) of strong and militant black manhood, the Ministers Malcolm X and Louis Farrakhan, and therefore indirectly inherited from the teachings of their spiritual (grand)father, the Honorable Elijah Muhammad.

Throughout his career as the leader of the most successful non-Christian black religious movement in the history of the United States, the Nation of Islam's "Messenger of Allah" made his opinion on Christianity quite clear. Elijah Muhammad held white Christians directly responsible for the trials and tribulations of African America, tracing black degradation from the northern ghettos of contemporary America to the southern plantations of antebellum America. As a child, this son of a Baptist minister listened to his grandfather, also a preacher, tell tales of enslavement and of the ways in which Christianity was used to pacify those in bondage.[14] These stories, in addition to his experiences with racial terrorism in the turn-of-century South and his spiritual conversion through Detroit's Temple of Islam in 1931, informed Muhammad's position on Christianity and convinced him that it "is a religion organized and backed by the devils for the purpose of making slaves of black mankind."[15] Therefore Muhammad insisted that only through Islam, the true religion of the "Blackman in America," could the ex-slave reclaim his manhood and the "so-called Negro" gain knowledge of himself as the "Original Man," or the "first and last, maker and owner of the universe."[16]

Rap nationalists also maintained that throughout American history white men manipulated Christianity to justify the horrific institution of slavery and consequent black subjugation; or as cultural nationalist Maulana Karenga testified over twenty years earlier, "They taught us Christianity so we could be like Jesus—crucified."[17] In fact, the primary perception that prejudiced the Hip-Hop Nation's critique of black Christianity was the belief that it is the "slavemaster's religion." Among rap-tivists, African Americans' adoption of Christianity was interpreted as a sign of black accommodation and submission to white power, not only in the religious sphere but in the political sphere as well. This reading of Christianity was appealing to a generation of black youth disillusioned with what they felt was the black church's abandonment of a social agenda.[18] Growing up in a post–Civil Rights era marked by a return to political conservatism by most mainstream independent African American denominations, most rap nationalists argued that the black church lacked relevancy—that it was unable or unwilling to confront the white power structure—and that the practice of black Christian theology was incapable of inspiring black liberatory thought among its believers.

Rap nationalists' critique of the "black church" began with an assessment of black preachers, whom they characterized as carnal and corrupt. As Killah Priest articulates in "B.I.B.L.E. (Basic Instructions Before Leaving Earth)," his youthful days in church were spent bearing witness to more than the glory of God:

> I went to church since birth
> but it wasn't worth the loot
> that I was payin'
> plus the prayin'
> I didn't like stayin'
> 'cause of busybodies
> and dizzy hotties
> that the preacher had souped up with lies
> had me cooped up
> lookin' at loot, butt, and thighs.[19]

Yet more than the sexual exploitation of women, many rap nationalists accused black ministers of economically exploiting black communities. As Public Enemy satirized, "You spend a buck in the 80's—whatcha get is a preacher."[20] During a period when many blacks were working-class, underemployed, or unemployed, this behavior was considered reprehensible—even in a youth culture obsessed with conspicuous consumption. The alleged profiteering of black ministers was the reason Ice Cube claimed to support the Nation of Islam, because, as he stated, "heaven ain't just wealth."[21] In "When I Get to Heaven" Ice Cube situates the corruption of the "black church" in opposition to what he perceived to be the righteousness of the Nation of Islam—despite existing evidence of Elijah Muhammad's extramarital affairs and material wealth.[22] Ice Cube assures his listening audience that the Nation is "much more than bow ties and bean pies." He then positions it as the vehicle for black liberation ("Elijah's got a plan"), and its leaders, unlike black Christian ministers, as uncompromising in the face of white oppression: "Got the white man screamin' / 'Damn that Farrakhan.'"[23]

Although the purported greed of black clergymen and their congregations was frequently referred to by rap nationalists, by far the most frequently cited criticism of black Christians was their focus on the afterlife. In the Hip-Hop Nation, Christianity was on trial: instead of being concerned with the obstacles of this world, black Christians were charged with fantasizing about freedom in the next. Black nationalist rappers denounced Christianity as a belief system that diverts attention from concrete reality and, therefore, inhibits the expression of social discontent. The tone of their critical assessment was comparable to Nation of Islam ministers like raptivist hero extraordinaire Malcolm X, who in 1954 castigated black Christians for their gullibility: "The white man has taught us to shout and sing and pray until we *die*, to wait until *death*, for some dreamy heaven-in-the-hereafter, when we're *dead*, while this white man has his milk and honey in the streets paved with golden dollars here on *this* earth!"[24] Over thirty years later, Malcolm X's philosophical progeny recorded their disaffection with the next generation of churchgoers. Grand Puba of Brand Nubian spoke of the black church as a "Soul Controller" in a lyric that implicates local city planning in a national government conspiracy:

> Now brothers say, "Why you dis' the church like [that]?"
> 'cause if the church was good for us it wouldn't be on every block
> of our neighborhood
> just like the liquor store [it] just ain't no good.[25]

In "Fishin' 4 Religion," Grammy Award–winning rap group Arrested Development's lead lyricist, Speech, also documents his disapproval with the black church. He accuses Baptist ministers of pacifying their congregations and discouraging them from challenging the oppressive conditions that define African America. To illustrate his point Speech tells the story of a woman who appeals to her pastor for guidance and he, in turn, counsels her to pray so she "can see the pearly gates of white." Taking the pastor's advice, the woman "prays 'n prays 'n prays 'n prays 'n prays 'n prays, 'n prays 'n prays" . . . but for the wrong results. "There's nothing wrong with prayin' / it's what she's askin'," he explains. Because "what you pray for God will give / to be able to cope in this world we live." Speech is mindful to note that his grammar lesson is not just an issue of semantics. "The word 'cope' and the word 'change' is directly opposite not the same / She should have been praying to change her woes / but pastor said pray to cope with those."

Not unlike Marxist theorists who deem religion the "opiate of the masses," Speech holds black Baptist ministers accountable for collaborating with white supremacy and maintaining the status quo. He labels them silent conspirators in black oppression ("they're praising a God that watches you weep / and doesn't want you to do a damn thing about it"); and, according to his evaluation, their effectiveness has not escaped the attention of the state: "The government is happy with most Baptist churches / 'cause they don't do a damn thing to try to nurture / brothers and sisters in the revolution / Baptist teaches dying is the only solution." Speech preferred a more proactive approach to spiritual awareness and political activism than that offered by the post–Civil Rights generation of Christian preachers because, as he argues, "passiveness causes others to pass us by." So like many other rap nationalists, Speech renounced the "black church" in search of a religious organization that would address his needs and concerns for black people in the United States. He was, in his own words, "Fishin' 4 Religion."[26]

Many raptivists argued that the conciliatory religiosity of the "black church" not only was a result of opportunistic black ministers but also was endemic to Christianity, or, as Chuck D insisted, black youth "can't be blamed for searching for other religious avenues when the religious avenues in the past have failed us and have been hypocritical."[27] The same year that Arrested Development went in search of a liberatory theology, Lord Jamar of Brand Nubian unwittingly affirmed feminist Audre Lorde's statement, "the master's tools will never dismantle the master's house,"[28] when he portrayed Christianity as a diversionary tool of the "master" classes in Brand Nubian's "Ain't No Mystery." "Bloodsuckers of the poor wanna keep your wealth / keep you slaves / so you don't misbehave / you'll never know the truth till you're dead in your grave." Like his Afrocentric colleague Speech, Lord Jamar contended that Christianity transposed righteous anger into passivity and, thus, kept black folks from their true nature. "Me and my people been lost for over 400 years and done tried this mystery God," he states, "and all we got was hard times, hunger and nakedness." And in a style reminiscent of fellow Black Muslim Malcolm X, this Five Percenter was suspicious of mainstream Christian theology's separation of the spiritual and the temporal. "Beaten and killed by the ones who say look to the sky for your piece of the pie / They didn't wanna tell you that God's within the Self."[29]

So many rap nationalists, like their Black Muslim and Black Power forerunners, believed it necessary to abandon Christian theology because, according to their estimates, it is not organic to the black nation. As a product of the "rich slavemakers of the world"[30] and the "bloodsuckers of the poor,"[31] they insisted that Christianity is harmful to the psychological and material well-being of black communities, particularly, as Ice Cube maintains, after "400 years of gettin' our ass kicked / by so-called Christians and Catholics."[32] Yet as Black Arts movement theorist Larry Neal articulated in 1970, the position on Christianity put forth by Black Power artists and activists—and, by extension, their neonationalist progeny—was out of touch with the communities they sought to serve. "A life-style exists among black folk that is totally at odds with the attitudes of nationalist intellectuals who instead of denigrating the religion of much of the national black body should be trying to understand the influence—past and present—of the black church," he wrote. "In short, these intellectuals often look down on their mothers and fathers whose spiritual legacy gave birth to the very struggle we all claim to support."[33] Indictments of Christianity as the "white man's religion" or the "slavemaster's religion" work under the misguided supposition that black Americans, once introduced to Christianity, passively accepted white supremacists' interpretations. KRS-One, for example, identified slaves' adoption of Christianity as the beginning of the end of a dynamic African consciousness. "You wanna know how we screwed up from the beginnin'," KRS-One interrogates, "we accepted our oppressors' religion / so in the case of slavery it ain't hard / 'cause it's right in the eyes of their God."[34] Statements like these and their underlying assumptions were based on raptivists' ignorance of slave theology and of the black nationalist tradition, an ignorance that is informed and reinforced by masculinist historical studies of the slave experience.

This flawed representation of slave religiosity is not unique to rap's neonationalists. It was a perspective shared by their black nationalist predecessors dating back to the nineteenth century and a characterization rampant among many social scientists trained to study the slave experience in the United States, leaving few in the position to defend slave intelligence. "The slaves were uneducated, by Western standards, but they were not fools," religious studies scholar Gayraud Wilmore writes in *Black Religion and Black Radicalism*.

> They were fully aware that the God who demanded their devotion and the spirit that infused their secret meetings and possessed their souls and bodies in the ecstasy of worship, was not the God of the slavemaster, with his whip and gun, nor the God of the plantation preacher, with his segregated services and unctuous injunction to humility and obedience.[35]

Despite Wilmore's protest, as we have seen, misrepresentations of slave behavior in popular culture and academic studies have had a significant impact on the historical memory of black nationalists and, consequently, their writings on the legacy of slavery in the United States. As historian of *Slave Culture* Sterling Stuckey observes, nineteenth-century calls for militant black manhood—from David Walker's *Appeal* to Martin Delany's "Political Destiny"—illustrate a strong tendency in the tradition of U.S.

black nationalism to "exaggerate the degree of acquiescence to oppression by the Black masses."[36] Effeminate stereotypes of the slave personality as submissive and/or accommodating, in effect, contributed to the shaping of black nationalist thought as a politics of (ex)slave/masculinist/violent resistance. Yet, primary sources reveal that regardless of nineteenth- and twentieth-century black nationalist assertions about the character and value of slave culture, their philosophies and worldviews were much closer to their slave brethren's than they presumed.

While black nationalists in the Black Power and hip-hop movements cited slaves' acceptance of Christian doctrines as evidence of their submission to white oppression, the work of scholars like Gayraud Wilmore (1973) and Lawrence Levine (1977), shows that those slaves who accepted Christianity as a formal structure of religion "simply refused to be uncritical recipients of a religion defined and controlled by white intermediaries and interpreters."[37] According to Stuckey, whose collection of work stands as a testimony to slave ingenuity, slaves blended European religions with African cosmologies. Christianity, he concludes, served as a "protective exterior" for complex African principles and practices.[38] (In the spirit of conjunctive thinking, Stuckey also argues that there is little doubt that Christianity "contributed in large measure to a spirit of patience which militated against open rebellion among the bondsmen."[39]) While slaveowners' theology stressed deference and obedience, slave bards transformed Christianity in ways that made it more compatible with their experience as Africans in America. For example, during the 1791 slave revolt in Haiti, voodoo priest Joseph Boukman made it clear to his followers that their god contradicted that of their slavemasters: "Our god who is good to us orders us to revenge our wrongs," he insisted.[40] However, scouring records of slave insurrections for evidence of the radical potential of Christianity is superfluous. Legendary theologian Howard Thurman argued that one need only look at the spirituals to witness liberatory theology at work in slave religion: "The existence of these songs is in itself a monument to one of the most striking instances on record in which a people forged a weapon of offense and defense out of a psychological shackle," he determines. "By some amazing but vastly creative spiritual insight the slave undertook the redemption of a religion that the master had profaned in his midst."[41]

With this new slave theology the seeds of a protonationalist consciousness were sown. The subversive constitution of slave culture fostered critiques of the slavocracy and its religious contradictions that are surprisingly similar to those professed almost two hundred years later during the golden age of rap nationalism. In fact, three common themes that characterize black nationalist theology, regardless of time and space, free/slave status, or religious background, are (1) the belief in moral superiority (for example, the characterization of blacks as "gods" and whites as "devils"), (2) the belief that God is a god of the oppressed and that black folks are God's chosen ones, and (3) the belief in divine retribution.

"White Man's Got a God Complex":
Deities, Devils, and the Identity Politics of Black Nationalism

> Where is our God, the God that represents us
> the God that looks like me, the God that I can trust?
> —KRS-One, "Higher Level"

In his 1991 song "The Eye Opener" KRS-One narrates a story about an African American attempting to come into political and spiritual consciousness and the barriers s/he faces on the road to discovery, in particular, the church and the Bible. According to KRS-One the church has served to rationalize the capitalist exploitation of people of color, while the Bible has been used as a tool of white supremacy, rewritten for the express purpose of disempowering black folks. Like his raptivist peers, KRS-One was particularly concerned with representations of biblical figures, men like Jesus, Abraham, and Noah, pivotal characters in the Christian story, whom he claimed are black according to modern-day (American) racial standards.

> Jesus Christ, Jesus Christ, Jesus Christ was BLACK
> read and study and know thyself because this too is a fact
> Abraham, Noah and King Solomon and John the Baptist was
>   BLACK
> The Europeans rewrote the Bible and they use it as a fact.[42]

The focus of hip-hop dialectics on the whitewashing of biblical history typically centered on the (Christian) son of God, Jesus Christ. The depiction of Jesus as racially white in icons, portraits, and popular culture antagonized rap nationalists most, because for Christians (the majority of religious practitioners in the United States), he is the physical manifestation of God, and his life and teachings are the essence of Christianity. In light of this fact, rap nationalists insisted that white supremacist indoctrination through visual representations of the son of God leave negative psychological impressions that retard black spirituality and facilitate a mass inferiority complex among African Americans. KRS-One confronts this issue in "The Eye Opener," assessing the damage that contemporary biblical imagery wreaks on black consciousness and tracing its logic:

> Ya pick [the Bible] up and learn it and try to see the light
> but everyone you read about happens to be white
> so when Jesus is white and his father is Jah
> then Jah must be white the white man is better.

Following this line of racial argumentation KRS-One deduces that if Jesus, the son of God, is white, then God Himself must be white; and if God is white, it stands to reason that whites are superior and deserve to maintain their position of dominance in the world—white power is, thus, divinely ordained. KRS-One challenges this conception, identifies it as a manifestation of white cultural hegemony, and labels those responsible for this imaging as agents of the Antichrist: "This is the work of Satan, egotistical / and negatively psychological."

That whites would manipulate the word of God in their attempts to justify the economic exploitation and social subordination of black people ("You know, it was the church that made every man see / the black man's supposed to be in slavery") suggests to KRS-One their irredeemability. After exposing white participation in black subjugation through the interrelated structures of race, class, and religion, he dismisses halfhearted repentance over historical discrimination in the religious sphere and extends a final warning to the white public. According to scripture, he states, it is divine revelation that God will return—"and when He comes back He'll come blacker than black / blacker than blacker than blacker than black."[43]

KRS-One's "The Eye Opener" is an efficacious example of the presence of moral superiority in the black nationalist-masculinist tradition, for it shows how rap nationalists situated representations of "white" as the Antichrist in opposition to the characterization of "black" as godhead. Among black nationalists this redefinition of oppositional dichotomies of race was considered essential to the psychological liberation of black people from the cultural domination of white supremacy, also known as a Negro/nigga-to-black conversion of consciousness. The godfathers of rap music, the Last Poets, demonstrate this methodology in a 1971 lyrical composition called "Opposites" as spoken word artist Alafia Pudim exploits the power of moral persuasion in an attempt to purge internalized racism.

> Understand that black is true and false is white
> understand that black is right and white is wrong
> understand that white is weak and black is strong
> understand that whiteness is suffocation and blackness a deep
>   breath
> understand that black is life and white is death.[44]

Rap nationalists, like cultural nationalists in the late 1960's and early 70's, also used this strategy to decolonize the minds of African Americans from overwhelming portrayals of black people as intellectually, morally, and culturally inferior. And, as previously discussed, they were passionate about their mission to "kick the truth to the young black youth,"[45] to provide the spark that would generate both psychological and spiritual transformation. For example, in 1991 Wise Intelligent insisted that it was his duty as a Poor Righteous Teacher to restore the mentality of contemporary black America to its preslavery state—and he did so using biblical imaging. "[T]he poor have been living a savage way of life here in the wilderness of North America," he maintained. "So what we're trying to do is bring those black people back to the state of mind in which they once possessed, which was the highest state of mind ever known to any living species on the planet or in the universe."[46]

One of the ways that raptivists sought to effect this change is by asserting their belief in moral superiority, a belief configured by a politics of substitution and manifested in a strict, dualistic ideology rooted in racial essentialism. In black nationalist thought "white" and "black" are conceived of as being biologically, diametrically opposed entities; and ideologues tend to use the logic of white power by inverting it. They assume and transpose one of the conceptual categories characteristic of Western thought— i.e., white/black—and its inherent value judgment of good and evil. The most obvious manifestation of this dogma can be recognized in the demonization of whites and the deification of blacks in the work of black nationalist theorists and artists/activists, a theme most associated in the popular imagination with the writings and rhetoric of the Nation of Islam.

When Malcolm X entered the public realm of black politics as the national spokesman for the Nation of Islam in 1963, his presence and ensuing popularity marked the beginning of a shift in black political consciousness in the midst of the modern Civil Rights movement. Working within the framework of Elijah Muhammad's teachings, his exposé of the white man as "the devil" and the black man, the "Original Man," as a "god" was culturally revolutionary and gained him tremendous respect among many urban blacks who considered him a fearless leader. "It was necessary and revolutionary for the Muslims to come saying the white man is the devil because the 'Negro' thought he was 'God,'" recalled US Organization founder Maulana Karenga.[47] While the power of this revelation should not be underestimated, neither the demonization of whites nor the deification of blacks originated with Malcolm X and the teachings of Elijah Muhammad, contrary to popular belief. This ideology of black moral supremacy fit squarely within a tradition of black nationalism that had begun more than a hundred years before the founding of the Nation of Islam with the publication of David Walker's *Appeal to the Colored Citizens of the World*.

In 1829 David Walker wrote that white people were the "natural enemies" of people of color and that their history had been one of continual perpetuations of evil. "The whites have always been an unjust, jealous, unmerciful, avaricious and blood-thirsty set of beings, always seeking after power and authority," he observes in the *Appeal*. "In fine, we view them all over Europe, together with what were scattered about in Asia and Africa, as heathens, and we see them acting more like devils than accountable men."[48]

As emphatic as Walker's indictment of Europeans and European Americans was, most early black nationalists tended to identify whites as devils through their actions and environment, suggesting that a shift in consciousness could lead to spiritual rebirth. (Consequently, this interpretation directly affected the issue of conflict resolution: that is, nineteenth-century black nationalists considered reconciliation an alternative to retribution.) Twentieth-century black nationalists, though, were more inclined to attribute white behavior to nature. In "Freedom or Death," Wise Intelligent of Poor Righteous Teachers assesses the physical and spiritual deprivation experienced by blacks and executed by whites in a manner similar to Walker's condemnation of the historic activities of Europeans. However, Wise Intelligent imputed white people's demeanor to biological difference, regarding the "Caucazoid" race as inherently evil: "I believe that your nature is that of the devil / and very wicked."[49] This essentialist view is the equivalent of damnation, for it necessitates violence as the solution to the "Negro problem"—or, as the Minister Louis Farrakhan declared, "You cannot reform a devil. All the prophets tried and failed. You have to kill the devil."[50]

Whether their primary point of reference is the Nation of Islam or the Nation of Gods and Earths, rap nationalists' characterization of the white race as "devils" was a direct adaptation of the teachings of Elijah Muhammad. The Nation of Islam's "demonogony"[51] is rooted in the story of a mad scientist named Yakub who supposedly grafted the white race from the "original," or "Asiatic," black man. This pseudoscientific theory of racial formation was embraced by rap nationalists like former Ice Cube protégé Kam in his 1995 song "Keep tha Peace." A self-proclaimed member of the Nation, Kam presented organizational doctrine as a way to explain the roots of black-on-black crime and gang violence in America's inner cities: "I'm really not knowin' who to blame or fault / for this tension / I mention this gump / Yakub's cavey / the blue-eyed punk / playin' both sides against each other / now that's the real mutha[fuckah]."[52] While exposing the present-day evil-doings of a mad scientists' progeny may be an inventive way to account for social problems in post–Civil Rights African America, the Yakub creation story also informed black nationalist rappers' advocacy of violent resistance. In 1990 Grand Puba of Brand Nubian announced that his calling was to bring enlightenment to black people and an end to white domination.

> This time black man we takin' no shorts
> we can't be used as a tool nor as a slave
> Here comes the god to send the devil right back to his cave. . . .
> We're gonna drop the bomb on the Yakub crew.[53]

The identification of white folks as the devil was one of the more sensational features of Nation of Islam–inspired rap nationalism. However, a more significant revelation that the teachings of Elijah Muhammad reintroduced to post–Civil Rights black youth was the idea that black people have inherited a righteous legacy as God's chosen ones—that is, that they represent God. In the oral and literary texts of traditional black nationalists, this belief is most apparent in the emphasis placed on the figural prophecy of Ethiopianism. However, Black Muslims, especially those of the Five Percent, claim a more direct connection to God. There is democratization of deity in the biblical hermeneutics of the teachings of Elijah Muhammad, and believers regard all black men as gods.[54] In their revision and retention of the masculinist discourse of black nationalism, raptivists like KRS-One remade themselves over in the image of *the* Maker: "Don't call me nigga . . . call me God / 'cause that's what the Black Man is."[55] Rap nationalists who embraced Muhammad's "Supreme Wisdom" insisted that the Christian concept of a "mystery God"—that is, a detached superhuman entity who commands the heavens—is yet another example of the devil's tricknology, of his never-ending attempts at mental enslavement to keep black people thinking about the "pie in the sky" instead of their hell on earth. Therefore rap nationalists, like Five Percenter Grand Puba, embarked upon their mission to inform black folks of their true birthright: "I didn't come to conceal it, I come to reveal it / the true and living God which is Son of Man."[56]

Representin' God: Ethiopianism and a Conjuring (Political) Culture of Black Nationalism

> [R]epresentin' Allah
> and I'm raw
> 'cause I'm God   —Paris, "It's Real"

Religious studies scholar Theophus Smith's award-winning book, *Conjuring Culture: Biblical Formations of Black America* (1994), explains the often codified meaning behind the veil of black religious experiences and the significance of scripture to Christian and non-Christian African American religious communities. The Bible, he writes, is a "conjure book" used by slaves and slave descendants to create a theology that invokes God as a god of the oppressed. Black religion should be understood as a form of "conjuring culture," he argues, the purpose of which is to summon God for black liberation. Smith's conceptualization of the function of religion in black communities is particularly true in the case of the religious-political tradition of black nationalism and is especially accurate when one considers the black literary-religious tradition of Ethiopianism.

From slave spirituals to rap music, the oral and literary texts of black nationalists have employed a number of biblical themes, but none is as significant as the figural prophecy of Ethiopianism, a tradition based on Psalms 68:31: "Princes shall come out of Egypt, Ethiopia shall soon stretch out her hands unto God." The Ethiopia configuration traces the black legacy from enslavement to liberation, and for some, to a destiny of black supremacy. (It is important to take note that in Ethiopianism, Egypt no longer represents a site of civilization but is instead a symbol of oppression.) Ethiopianism is "God-conjuring"[57] that signifies upon white readings of past and present racial hierarchies and imparts righteous meaning to a history of black enslavement and exploitation through claims of divine providence. "In summary, Ethiopianism may be defined as the effort of the English-speaking black or African person to view his past enslavement and present cultural dependency in terms of the broader history of civilization," instructs Wilson Moses, historian of U.S. black nationalism. "It expresses the belief that the tragic racial experience has profound historical value, that it has endowed the African with moral superiority and made him a seer."[58]

Although they may not recognize its origins, black nationalists' gnosticism has its roots in slave religion. This fact is evidenced in slaves' utilization of the Bible, particularly their employment of Old Testament imagery in the spirituals. In slave theology, God was a god of the oppressed, and blacks, like the children of Israel, were his chosen people. Many scholars of slave religiosity have determined that a chief function of slave religion was to maintain a spiritual and material link between the fate of the enslaved in biblical Egypt and those in postbiblical America. "The most persistent single image the slave songs contain is that of the chosen people," affirms cultural studies scholar Lawrence Levine. "The vast majority of the spirituals identify the singers as 'de people dat is born of God,' 'We are the people of God,' 'we are de people of de Lord.'"[59] The leading figures in black spirituals were those who were liberated by God—Joshua, Daniel, and particularly Moses and the children of Israel—and as the lines of the following spiritual demonstrate, the reason is clear: "My Lord delivered Daniel / My Lord delivered Daniel / My Lord delivered Daniel / Why can't He deliver me?"[60] Although partial to the Old Testament, slave theology also circumvented slaveowners' interpretations of the New Testament by envisioning Jesus as a warrior engaged in personal combat with the Devil, further demonstrating their need to create a theology that stressed divine revelation and the liberation of oppressed people.

The deliberate selection of biblical stories in the spirituals stands as historical documentation of slave consciousness. "The similarity of these

tales to the situation of the slaves is too clear for them not to see it,"
Levine confirms, "too clear for us to believe that the songs had no worldly
content for blacks in bondage."[61] With this awareness, it becomes clear
that the "conjuring culture" of nineteenth- and twentieth-century black
nationalists has been, directly or indirectly, inherited from the "conjuring
culture" of their slave ancestors—particularly their conceptualization of
liberation by providential design and the belief that "Ethiopia shall soon
stretch out her hands unto God."

Theophus Smith, however, argues that scholars of black religious
and/or political experiences should recognize Ethiopianism as more than
a passive imagining of prophecy, "that is, as a visionary prediction of the
coming emancipation." Instead, he believes, it is generative and should
be understood as "prophetic incantation" or "religious expression in-
tending to induce, summon, or conjure the divine for the realization of
some emancipatory future."[62] The spirit behind the "conjuring culture"
of black nationalism is reflected both in the use of the Bible to project
God as a god of the oppressed and in the use of biblical typology to elu-
cidate black historical experiences. At issue is the construction of a positive self-concept, or a (re)valuation of a collective black identity, because as Smith explains, "when a community or people designates its pa-
tron god or deities it simultaneously constitutes or reconstitutes its
collective identity."[63] This claiming—this "incantatory naming"—is as
evident in the tendency of slaves to idealize Moses as it is apparent in the
tendency of black nationalists from David Walker to the Hebrew Israelites to identify with those he liberated. Yet, considering time and
place, perhaps its most notorious manifestation was during what historians have deemed the "nadir" of black American history, when one of
black nationalism's most militant advocates declared in 1898 that "God
is a Negro."

At the eve of the twentieth century Bishop Henry McNeil Turner of the
African Methodist Church prefigured Elijah Muhammad's conceptualization of blacks as a "nation of gods"[64] with his proclamation, "God is
a Negro." In a manner uncharacteristic of a period dominated by the accommodationist politics of Booker T. Washington, Turner argued most
defiantly that black people had the same prerogative to claim God as
whites. "We have as much right biblically and otherwise to believe that
God is a Negro, as you buckra or white people have to believe that God
is a fine looking, symmetrical and ornamented white man." Mocking
dominant notions of aesthetic beauty, Turner challenged white suprema-

cist imaginings of God as "a white-skinned, blue-eyed, straight-haired, projecting nosed, compressed lipped and finely robed *white* gentleman sitting upon a throne somewhere in the heavens." Nevertheless, he recognized that his dissenting voice was but one among many—both white and black—that sustained the prevailing belief among Christians that God is white. After assessing the impact of this bias on African American self-esteem, Bishop Turner concluded that emigration was the only means by which the race could gain respect as human beings, for "as long as we remain among the whites, the Negro will believe that the devil is black and that he (the Negro) favors the devil, and that God is white and that he (the Negro) bears no resemblance to Him."[65]

Like Bishop Henry McNeil Turner, black nationalist theorists in the twentieth century expressed an overwhelming concern that depictions of God as a white man had an emasculating effect on the manhood of the race. Marcus Garvey, who was called the "Black Moses," challenged portrayals of a white God in Christian iconography. So George Alexander McGuire, chaplain-general of the Universal Negro Improvement Association and founder of the African Orthodox Church (in the United States), insisted in 1924 that blacks throughout the Diaspora destroy all visual representations of a white Madonna and a white Christ and worship instead a black Madonna and a black Christ. They too participated in "incantatory naming" in an effort to conjure God against racial terrorism and employed biblical typology to infuse meaning into black pain and suffering. The Ethiopia and Egypt configurations are also quite conspicuous in the lyrics of rap nationalists. In KRS-One's 1989 rap classic "Why Is That?" he surveys the genealogy of biblical figures and takes a systematic approach to proving the racial heritage of such holy men as Abraham, Noah, and Moses. His case for "Egyptocentrism"[66] was based upon a common reasoning among twentieth-century black nationalists: because the geographical area in which biblical events occurred is within the current boundaries of Africa, by American standards of racial classification all Christian apostles were black. Or as the Reverend Albert B. Cleage, Jr., of the Shrine of the Black Madonna concluded over twenty years earlier, "In America, one drop of black makes you black. So by American law, God is black."[67]

KRS-One began his painstaking, methodical examination of biblical bloodlines with Shem. "Genesis Chapter 11 verse 10 / explains the genealogy of Shem / Shem was a black man in Africa / If you repeat this fact they can't laugh at ya." By first revealing Shem as a "black man in

Africa," KRS-One establishes him as the patriarch of a line of consequential and influential biblical characters whose descendants range from Abraham and Isaac to Jacob and Moses. Abraham, progenitor of the Hebrews, figures prominently in black nationalist theology because of the connection drawn between the experiences of African America and the plight of the Israelites in Egypt. So in "Why Is That?" when KRS-One asserts that Abraham, "being a descendant of Shem / which is a fact / means Abraham too was black," he confirms the black nationalist belief that African Americans have inherited the legacy of the children of Israel as God's chosen people. KRS-One continues to substantiate this belief by tracing the lineage of Abraham's descendants: "Abraham was the father of Isaac / Isaac was the father of Jacob / Jacob had 12 sons, for real / and these were the Children of Israel."

In the process of illustrating the racial heritage of men like Shem, Abraham, and Jacob, KRS-One attacks the logic of white supremacist interpretations of the curse of Ham. The ethnocentric reading of the curse of Ham began around the sixteenth century as an attempt by British travelers in Africa to explain the darker skin color of the continent's inhabitants. It was then transported to British North America by colonists and used as a justification for racialized slavery during the late seventeenth century, when the peculiar institution was becoming legally defined, and again in the early nineteenth century due to the rise of abolitionism.[68] KRS-One's lyrical composition contradicted the use of the curse of Ham as a rationalization of black exploitation. He argues that Ham's punishment could not have been his blackness, because Ham—like his brother Shem—was already black.

Ham's descendants, the Egyptians, were thus also black; and one of those descendants was Moses, Hebrew prophet and deliverer of the children of Israel. The "T'cha" thus teaches:

> According to Genesis Chapter 10, Egyptians descended from Ham
> 600 years later, my brother read up
> Moses was born in Egypt
> in this era black Egyptians weren't right
> they enslaved black Israelites
> Moses had to be of the black race
> because he spent 40 years in Pharaoh's place
> He passed as the Pharaoh's grandson
> so he had to look just like 'em.[69]

The conclusion of KRS-One's rap sermon has a conspiratorial tone, implicating white institutions—particularly churches and schools—in a plot to conceal the truth from African Americans in an attempt to keep them subjugated. "Yes my brothers and sisters take this song / Go, correct the wrong / Information we get today is just wack / but ask yourself, why is that?"[70] From "Why Is That?" to "The Eye Opener" KRS-One warns white people to beware their sins against people of color, particularly those who were guilty of misrepresenting God. White supremacy may reign in America, but a higher power reigns in the heavens, he testifies. KRS-One's exegesis demonstrates the power and persistence of the legacy of slave theology. With its emphasis on God as a god of the oppressed who will return to liberate his children in bondage, the "conjuring culture" of black nationalist theology resurfaced in the last part of the twentieth century, impressing upon slave descendants that a time will come when "Ethiopia shall soon stretch out her hands unto God."

The race/gender politicking of black nationalism necessitates not only a dramatic but also a violent solution to the historic dispossession of the nation's manhood. In an embodied-social politics, the boundaries between good and evil are naturalized just as the boundaries between black and white are simultaneously historicized and essentialized. Farrakhan's solution—"You cannot reform a devil . . . you have to kill the devil"—thus becomes virtually inevitable, perhaps even logical. Consequently, black nationalists' use of the eschaton is not surprising, for it symbolizes the final battle in the war between god(s) and the devil(s). The concept of divine retribution is a prevalent theme in the writings and oratory of nineteenth- and twentieth-century black nationalists, because it represents a moment in which black manhood is finally and eternally redeemed. Or in the words of Poor Righteous Teacher Wise Intelligent, "The future is like the Bible states the dark races will regain power once and for all. That's the bottom line."[71]

"Every Dog Must Have Its Day": Divine Retribution and Redemption for God's Chosen Ones

> Grand Verbalizer, what time is it?
> I dwell among the mortals, the time is in the verse . . .
> —X-Clan, "Grand Verbalizer, What Time Is It?"

Many black nationalist jeremiads interpreted the latter part of Psalms 68:31—"Ethiopia shall soon stretch out her hands unto God"—as a prefiguration of the apocalypse story of the New Testament.[72] Although usually presented as a warning rather than a certainty, as Theophus Smith clarifies in *Conjuring Culture*, black eschatology can be conciliatory, like Martin Luther King's "I Have a Dream" speech, or catastrophic, like the writings of black nationalist Ethiopianists. "[The] catastrophic view of the *eschaton* has a long history," he writes, "spanning biblical apocalypticism and slave religion and extending into the twentieth century in various forms and permutations—some religious or mystical; some political, revolutionary, or ideological, and some romantic, fashionable or popularist."[73] Among black nationalists, the eschaton is the culmination of masculinist phallic/ies and hi(s)stories, its significance being that in its wake lies the reclamation of manhood. It is the ultimate transcendence of white (male) power, for the spoils of this holy war include the right to patriarchal power and privilege in the post-Armageddon black nation. Therefore it is the final example of the ways in which black nationalism is framed as a politics of (ex)slave/masculinist/violent resistance, for as Killah Priest of the Wu-Tang Clan affirms, according to the "B.I.B.L.E. (Basic Instructions Before Leaving Earth)" its ending is predetermined: it's judgment day, a day when "the first shall be last / and the last shall be first."[74]

The concepts of divine providence and divine retribution are dependent upon the "incantatory naming" of God as a god of the oppressed and predicated on the nationalist belief that blacks have inherited a righteous legacy as God's chosen ones. Just as the cultural practice of "God-conjuring" linked twentieth-century black nationalists to their slave predecessors, the eschaton exemplifies another continuity in the black nationalist tradition that has its roots in slave religiosity. In fact, the presence of an apocalyptic vision in slave religion is probably the most convincing historical evidence that betrays the hidden transcript of slaves' "conjuring culture" and contradicts black nationalists' presumption of a so-called slave mentality. As fugitive slave Charles Ball testified in 1837, the belief in divine retribution is at the core of slave theology: "The idea of revolution in the conditions of whites and blacks, is the corner-stone of the religion of the latter. . . . Heaven will be no heaven to him if he is not avenged of his enemies."[75] In 1860 William Craft, another ex-slave, also verified the existence of prophetic incantation within the religious expression of the enslaved: "there is . . . great consolation in knowing that God is just, and will not let the oppressor of the weak, and the spoiler of the virtuous escape unpunished here and hereafter. I believe a similar retribution to that which destroyed Sodom is hanging over the slave-holders."[76]

Like many slaves, nineteenth- and twentieth-century black nationalist theorists took psychic comfort in their belief in divine retribution, making it one of the more prevalent themes in their oral and literary works. For instance, the nineteenth century witnessed two of the most fiery doomsayers in the history of black nationalism with the pioneering publications of David Walker and Henry Highland Garnet. In his controversial *Address*, which advocated slave insurrection as a strategy of abolitionism, ex-slave Garnet justified his position on violent resistance to enslavement and exhorted slaves to tell their masters "in a language which they cannot misunderstand . . . of a future judgment, and of the righteous retributions of an indignant God."[77] Or as David Walker aptly stated in the *Appeal*, a document that was devoted almost completely to the idea of divine retribution, "'Every dog must have its day,' the American's is coming to an end."[78]

Rap nationalists both adopted and transformed the apocalyptic vision characteristic among classical black nationalists. Finding no contradiction between violence and the gospel of Christ, these artists advocated freedom "by any means necessary." Like their slave forefathers and mothers, raptivists envisioned their God as a warrior God who both exacts and sanctions vengeance upon white America for their sins against His chosen ones. For instance, in "When I Get to Heaven" gangstAfronationalist Ice Cube sermonizes,

> The same white man that threw me in the slammer
> he bombed a church in Alabama
> So if I cocked the hammer God won't mind
> if I have to kill the human swine
> 'cause God is a killer from the start
> why you think Noah had to build his Ark?[79]

Ice Cube's neocivilizationist peers Poor Righteous Teachers also subscribed to the characterization of God as a persecutor of those who defy and exploit His word. In "Each One, Teach One" Wise Intelligent sardonically warns whites, "Bear witness to He, the builder and destroyer / and all you negative snakes, I hate it for ya."[80]

The belief in the potential of God and His prophets toward violence that is apparent in the cultural production of slaves and the literary work of nineteenth-century Ethiopianists appealed to a post–Civil Rights generation angered by the widespread denial of racial justice in a period characterized by intense economic polarization between the "haves" of a white minority and the "have-nots" of a black majority. As problems of destitution and deprivation, unemployment and underemployment, and substandard and nonexistent housing plagued blacks in the inner cities of major metropolitan areas, many in African America—from cultural workers to academics—held the white power structure and its collaborators responsible for increasingly impoverished living conditions. Therefore the New Testament prophecy of "the last shall be the first, and the first shall be the last" was attractive to rap music's neonationalists because of its promise of black redemption and divine retribution for the crimes of white America. "When it comes to Armageddon, me I'm gettin' mine," promises Chuck D: "Here I am, turn it over [Uncle] Sam."[81]

Raptivists were also attracted to black eschatology because it was a homeopathic approach to framing black nationalism as a politics of (ex)slave/masculinist/violent resistance. In the conjuring cultural politics of black nationalists, the apocalyptic figuration functioned as the "use of dis-ease to cure disease"[82]—or as the cure for an affliction among black nationalists that may be diagnosed as the wounded male ego. Violence, or the threat of violence, was prescribed by black nationalist theorists to purge an emasculated sense of (male) self cultivated by social, political, and economic dispossession in both the public and private spheres. And rap's neonationalists learned early that violence—real or surreal—earned them the respect (or at least the attention) of white America, for as Ice Cube explains in his 1992 post–Los Angeles rebellion release "When Will They Shoot," "If I say no violence, devil / you won't respect mine / Fuck the dumb shit, and get my Tech-9."[83] Raptivists like Ice Cube concluded that violent times demand violent measures; and in the pursuit of manly respect, divine retribution was perceived to be the "sacred" solution to a secular problem. In fact, in a manner that exemplified the integral role of the Bible in (and, therefore, the hybridity of) Nation of Islam theology, rap nationalists from Nation of Islam member Paris to N.O.I. supporters Public Enemy embraced the Old Testament revelation of "an eye for an eye." Or as Chuck D warns in *Fear of a Black Planet*, as part of the "Revolutionary Generation" he gets "exact on a track / It's an eye for an eye, tooth for a tooth."[84] So much like their nineteenth- and twentieth-century predecessors, rap nationalists interpreted the Book of Revelation as a biblical sign of the righteousness of violent resistance. Armageddon was envisioned as a race war between the god(s) and the devil(s), or between black men and white. This blending of an embodied-social politics with gnosticism among raptivists was borrowed from the master of post–Civil Rights "homeopathic" black nationalist-masculinist discourse: the Honorable Minister Louis Farrakhan.

Take, for instance, West Coast rap nationalist Kam's *Made in America*. On "Intro," the first track of his 1995 release, this Nation of Islam member introduces his listening audience to the firebrand politicking of his spiritual father by utilizing one of Farrakhan's lectures as a sonic source. In the speech Kam excerpts, the Nation of Islam leader executes the type of critical assault against white America that his black admirers grew to love and expect from him. Yet what is most interesting about this sample is how Kam exploits the power of rap music as a "cultural recycling center"[85] through his appropriation of Farrakhan's words. "Intro" becomes a form of possession—a type of ownership and incarnation—for Kam employs Farrakhan as a symbol: he is the voice of disaffected and defiant black manhood. Part of the genius of "Intro" is that Kam simultaneously engages in hero worship and demonstrates the appeal of the teachings of Elijah Muhammad for a post–Civil Rights generation of politically, economically, and socially disenfranchised black men: "Young brothers are tired of this crap," Kam declares, using Farrakhan as a medium. "They're tired of you feedin' them this weak . . . religion and this faggot God. They want a real God. A God that can bring justice and judgment down."[86]

This sample clearly illustrates the fact that "it's-a-dick-thing" politicking knows no boundaries between the sacred and the secular. Although it may be a startling revelation, Farrakhan's assessment was correct: the hip-hop generation was in search of a hypermasculine (heterosexual) and vengeful God as well as a liberation theology that was willing to deliver Him. It is this kind of recognition, along with his no-holds-barred style of preaching and his ability to tap into masculine sensibilities, that garnered Farrakhan the reverence of even the most irreverent of post–Civil Rights/post–Black Power black youth. "The Minister said white people respect what they fear," related Chuck D, "and they fear and respect us, respecting ourselves."[87] A year later, Chuck D remained faithful to Farrakhan as he defended the Nation of Islam in a *Spin* interview. "The NOI gets a lot of bad ink," he affirmed, "but what is white America going to say for an organization that builds strong black men? Fuck what the white man thinks."[88] The promise to cultivate an awe-inspiring, uncompromising standard for black manhood also inspired Ice Cube to profess that the "best place for a young Black male is the Nation of Islam."[89]

Farrakhan's raptivist protégés, from Kam to Chuck D and Ice Cube, reveal the power of homeopathic strategies in black nationalist discourse. The apocalyptic vision of black nationalist theology is seductive, frankly, because it fulfills revenge fantasies for many African Americans. Or as Public Enemy's Sister Souljah articulates in her rendition of "The Hate That Hate Produced," "If my survival means your total destruction / then so be it. . . . They say two wrongs don't make it right/But it damn sure makes it even."[90] But as political scientist E. U. Essien-Udom indicates, the lure of black eschatology can be entrapping because the desire for vengeance has a tendency to make black nationalists shortsighted and narrow-minded. "The nationalists tend to become preoccupied with the means of overcoming their sense of powerlessness," he states, "but in their preoccupation with the means, the end of building up black power appears to become less important because it seems either unattainable or utopian. Hence, they call upon superhuman or divine intervention for its realization."[91]

It is important to take note of Essien-Udom's suggestion that although black nationalist eschatology may impart a temporary sense of empowerment to its believers, it can also be disempowering. Black nationalists' obsession with the process of empowerment causes them to overemphasize—or overestimate—white power in black lives. For instance, black nationalist calls for divine intervention inadvertently bestow upon white (men) an aura of invincibility; by investing white men with supernatural powers, many black nationalists then conclude that only the omnipotence of God can destroy white domination. Yet although this reliance upon divine intervention may appear pacifist, it is not a sign of total resignation to the will of God. In the conjunctive tradition of black folk culture, the apocalyptic vision of black nationalists also facilitates empowerment precisely because it legitimizes black rage. Black nationalist theology functions as a medium through which to inspire believers to take control over their lives: God, not "The Man," is the supreme being, and through God's will black Americans, His chosen people, are to fulfill biblical prophecy by destroying white civilization and its bastardized form of Christianity.

Conclusion: Critically (Re)thinking the White Man's Religion

> God created man and man created hip hop.
> —Ras Kass, "Soul on Ice"

While most rap nationalists did not recognize the rich tradition of black liberatory Christianity that began in the early nineteenth century with the development of a distinct, protonationalist gnosticism in southern slave communities and in the conception of black nationalist thought in northern free communities, it is clear that Christian theology is not incompatible with radical political philosophies. Speech of Arrested Development was one of very few raptivists who, although critical of mainstream African American Christian denominations, recognized their revolutionary past *and* conservative present. "Back during slavery, the black church was so powerful. Reverend Nat Turner came out of the black church. The white slave masters had to watch over the church sessions because they were so organizational and had a uniting type of power to them. I believe it was because of those strong ties in the black church that we're alive today," he told a *Washington Post* reporter in 1992. Yet after paying respect to the historical role of the church in black spiritual and political life, Speech considered its declining significance in post–Civil Rights African America.

> [T]oday, the black church is one of the few black businesses that black people fully support, it's one of the very few black entities that black people go to, and yet, with all that power and influence they could potentially have, they don't—to me and to many other black youth—don't address any issues that are real. I mean concrete issues. They talk about abstract. Heaven.[92]

Speech was not the only post–Civil Rights black nationalist to provide a balanced and valid critique of black Christians. In the midst of charges by Black Power rhetoricians that Christianity was a "white religion," his cultural nationalist predecessor Larry Neal argued that, instead of promoting conversion to "African and Eastern religions," community organizers and social theorists should encourage black churches to incorporate a theology of liberation. "The revolutionary black churchman must take the implicit values of Christianity and shape them according to the cultural needs of his people." It is imperative for black clergymen to join the political effort to change the consciousness of black people, Neal insisted, because they had an organic advantage in black communities: "He can do this better than most activists because he commands a base of operations, while most activists, however pertinent their ideas, don't control anything."[93] Albert B. Cleage, Jr., founder of the Shrine of the Black Madonna, agreed that the church was the most efficacious space for organizing and challenged those who labeled Christianity "whitey's religious bag."[94] "[T]hose who believe in the Movement but who do not believe in the Christian Church . . . do not understand that the Movement is the Christian Church in the 20th century and that the Christian Church cannot truly be the church until it also becomes the Movement."[95]

As Neal and Cleage suggest, Christianity is a mainstay of black culture in the United States. And despite a conservative shift in the post–Civil Rights era, the "black church" continues to be one of the most viable centers of social and political organization in African America. Therefore, no matter the religious affiliation, it is important to invalidate the common and totalizing misconceptions of Christianity as the "white man's religion" or the "slavemaster's religion" advanced by Black Power advocates and their hip-hop descendants. The three common themes that characterize black nationalist theology, regardless of historical period or religious doctrine—the belief in black moral superiority, the belief that God is a god of the oppressed and that black folks are God's chosen ones, and the belief in divine retribution—bear witness to the fact that the philosophy of late-twentieth-century rap nationalists was not far removed from that put forth by early-nineteenth-century free black and slave nationalists. Even allowing for changes in historical context and their impact on content, the only truly significant factor separating the former from the latter was a contemporary lack of knowledge about the theory and practice of classical black nationalism. The fundamental principles did not change. This is probably due to the fact that racism and racial terrorism continued to be a constant in American social, political, and economic life: although its dynamics changed, the structure remained.

6

Be True to the Game

Final Reflections on the Politics and Practices of the Hip-Hop Nation

In a June 1996 interview with noted Bay Area DJ and community activist Davey D, Boots Riley of the revolutionary nationalist rap group The Coup described the demise of the golden age of rap nationalism. Gangsta rap superseded political rap because it was more in tune with the culture and consciousness of black youth. "Rappers have to be in touch with their communities no matter what type of raps you do otherwise people won't relate," he maintained. Both genres could interpret the material realities of the truly disadvantaged, but according to Riley, the raptivist lacked the support of a movement. Hardcore rap artists lyrically sketched postindustrial urban landscapes that were devastated by declining economic opportunities and a concomitant burgeoning drug trade. These circumstances thus provided a mobilizing force—or as Riley articulated, the "movement"—behind gangsta rap. "The drug game . . . has directly impacted lives and for so many it's been positive in the sense that it earned people some money. Hence gangsta rap has a home." Political rap groups, on the other hand, "offered solutions only through listening," Riley reasoned. "They weren't part of a movement. So they died out when people saw that their lives were not changing."[1]

Though somewhat provocative and undeniably reductive, Boots Riley's implication of gangsta rap in the downfall of rap nationalism is commonplace among hip-hop artists, activists, and scholars. Many believe this shift was the unfortunate, if not inevitable, result of a dialogical relationship between racial representations, racist perceptions, and the commercial imperative. "A careful reading of the rap industry might suggest the pliability of capital and the extent to which a politically engaged culture such as hip-hop can most easily be put to the service of dominant ideologies," writes music theory scholar Adam Krims.[2] To put this in laypersons' terms, it is the price rap artists paid for "keepin' it surreal."[3] Some hip-hop observers describe this revolution in rap music as yet another example of the risk of situating black culture as a product in a (white) buyers' market, while others ascribe more nefarious motives. Hip-hop journalist and activist Kevin Powell alleged that strategists in the music industry masterminded the declining significance of race music in the mid-1990's. "Hip-hop was re-directed after Public Enemy," he asserted. Powell punctuated his point by referring to Public Enemy's call to action anthem "Fight the Power." "I really believe that the powers that be were like, 'Elvis was a hero to most, but he never meant shit to me? No way we're going to have that.' They would rather have the gangsta, the thug, the baller, shot-caller, because that's safe."[4] Rap nationalist pioneer Chuck D concurred and contended that the "niggativity" of gangsta rap "became a scapegoat" for many white Americans, that is, an exoneration of social inequality and a justification for oppressive conditions like the criminalization of black youth and police brutality.[5]

Whether the impetus was commercial or conspiratorial, it is clear that the introduction of gangsta rap and its influence on the commodification of hip-hop music brought an end to the golden age of rap nationalism. Hip-hop's analysts may not agree about what forces were responsible for this transformation. But in retrospect they do agree that in the absence of a social movement, raptivism could not sustain itself as a form of cultural politics or function separate and apart from formal political culture. Music executive Bill Stephney assessed the limitations of rap nationalism's "politics of symbolism"[6] as he reflected during a 2002 interview upon his days with Public Enemy. Articulating discontent and encouraging pro-black styles and sensibilities were not enough, he insisted, because "we had nothing to constructively flow that anger into. We were telling kids they should wear African medallions and twist their hair and look natural. Fine. But you must also create institutions where they can comfortably go."[7] Boots Riley also invoked Public Enemy in his critique of the hip-hop movement and its stylized expression of black nationalist politics. "Public Enemy inspired me. I remember I bought their first album just because they had on berets and they were in the basement. I remember thinking, 'This is the shit,'" he said.

> Unfortunately, when they and X-Clan came out, a lot of people started wearing African medallions and stuff, but there wasn't a material move-

ment to go along with that. Political music, to be viable, has to have a movement to go along with it. If you're wearing the clothes and memorizing the lyrics, but you go home and you don't have anything in the refrigerator, you're gonna say, "This music doesn't have anything to do with the material world."[8]

As we have seen, a number of cultural critics also have questioned the viability of rap music as a site of resistance. Although there is no shortage of scholars that indiscriminately celebrate the politics of rap music, Michael Eric Dyson (1993), Nelson George (1998), Bakari Kitwana (2002), and Paul Gilroy (1992), to name a few, some have been quite outspoken about the constraints and capabilities of the Hip-Hop Nation. But perhaps no one has been as inflexible about the liberatory potential of cultural production as political scientist Adolph Reed, Jr. Reed is unambiguous: he has no patience with rap music "posing as politics" nor does he partake in "progressives' current romance with youth culture and cultural politics in general"—because, he concludes, "[c]ultural production can reflect and perhaps support a political movement; it can never generate or substitute for one. There is no politics worthy of the name that does not work to shape the official institutions of public authority that govern and channel people's lives. Anything else is playacting."[9]

Reed is right. Political practices—grassroots and electoral—are necessary to effectively challenge the state-sanctioned domestic terrorism targeting black communities at the turn of the twenty-first century. Problems such as the "War on Drugs," welfare reform, the "three strikes" law, and the increasing gentrification of urban areas will not be solved by the "Prophets of Rage." Nevertheless, it is important to acknowledge the burden of articulating and addressing social issues placed upon rappers in general and rap nationalists in specific by hip-hop fans, black baby boomers, and the mainstream media. Those expectations speak volumes about a void in black political leadership as well as to a collective confusion over the black political agenda during the post–Civil Rights era.

"Prophets of Rage" or Leaders of the New School?
Defining the Role of the Rap Nationalist

This rap shit is a motherfucker. —Mutulu Olugbala, 2002

With rap music's ever increasing influence in the public sphere, much has been said and written about the role and responsibility of hip-hop artists in African America, particularly those exhibiting any social consciousness. In fact, this issue became an explosive point of contention in October 2003—ten years after the beginning of the end of the golden age of rap nationalism—during a conference held in Chicago and hosted by the Field Museum's Center for Cultural Understanding and Change. Organized by anthropologist Raymond Codrington, the "Hip Hop and Social Change" conference was an ambitious and groundbreaking venture that sought to encourage "dialogue about what civil activism means, what politics means, and what participation means in the context of hip-hop."[10] The rap session brought together diverse elements—practitioners, scholars, students, community organizers, and activists from various nations, including the United States, Brazil, Tanzania, and South Africa—to facilitate discussions about the global and local use of hip-hop culture as a mechanism for political empowerment. James Bernard, founding editor of the hip-hop magazines *The Source* and *XXL*, was recruited to participate in a conversation about the political future of rap music. In an interview published prior to the event, he spoke very highly of the conference's potential to cultivate political agency among those who engage hip-hop's cultural practices. "We want to build an infrastructure," he proclaimed. "We hope to develop a platform on the issues. We're trying to create a political community in hip-hop, and this conference is emblematic and part of that at the same time."[11]

The proceedings that followed were informative and stimulating, incorporating symposiums on hip-hop culture and politics as well as workshops featuring dance, spoken word, and grassroots organizing. One interesting development of the two-day affair was the rampant use of the black-white paradigm of race, particularly among African American attendees. The multiracial and international discussants and audience members consistently debated the status of nonblacks and non-Americans in hip-hop culture. This issue caused tempers to flare (and brought gender dynamics to the surface) during the question-and-answer period for a panel titled "Hip Hop in the U.S. and Abroad," as a black male audience member questioned a Latino panelists' legitimacy after she challenged the American hip-hop community to raise its standards for production and consumption. (Incidentally, she was a former member of pioneering breakdancing group the Rock Steady Crew.) While this confrontation provided interesting insight into the racial, national, and gender discourses that inform perceptions of authority and authenticity in hip-hop culture, no moment was as provocative or revealing of the contemporary import of hip-hop culture as the events that unfolded at the conference's keynote address.

Black Star's Talib Kweli and Mos Def were invited to conclude the weekend's activities, presumably by talking about the political promise of hip-hop culture from the perspective of the musical artist. Both rappers articulated the joys and frustrations of being identified as "conscious" rappers. Kweli kicked off the evening by applauding the students and activists that "use hip-hop music as the soundtrack of their lives." He was optimistic, affirmative, and counted his blessings for the opportunities that hip-hop has provided him. He said he felt particularly fortunate to be able to perform at concerts sponsored by the Black August Hip-Hop Collective, an offshoot of the Malcolm X Grassroots Movement that uses rap music as a tool for disseminating information about political prisoners in the United States.[12] Kweli informed audience members, which conference officials estimated at over nine hundred, that he has participated in Black August's annual cultural exchange to Cuba since its inception in 1998 and that he went with the group to South Africa for the United Nation's World Conference on Racism at Durban in 2001. "Those two trips had more impact on my life than traveling to promote my music," he pronounced.

Mos Def followed Kweli's lead and began by expressing an appreciation for the social significance of rap music. The beauty of hip-hop culture, he asserted, is that it "provides a sense of imagination" to real life. He also acknowledged the influence of rap music on the world stage. "Hip-hop has a lot of power," he testified, because "it speaks to the frustrations of the marginalized." Things began to go awry, however, when Mos Def addressed the presumption that he and other rappers should be both champion and spokesperson for the less fortunate in black communities. "There is a lot of scrutiny put on an entire genre of music," he explained. "It's not the artist's responsibility to be a leader. It's the artist's responsibility to be honest with him or herself. To be true to his or her own reality." Mos Def vehemently rejected the public's expectations that rap artists be organic intellectuals or (post)modern-day race men and women. "In the real world, we just people with ideas," he said, quoting dead prez lyricist M-1. "I have no ambition to be a politician. I don't even vote. I have no intention to vote."

These comments and others evoked a passionate response from a number of people attending the presentation. One man, who claimed he had been on death row for seventeen years, took particular offense at Mos Def's statements. During the question-and-answer session, he loudly and repeatedly insisted that rap artists should be held accountable for the welfare of black communities. When rebuffed, he attacked and threatened not only Mos Def but also other audience members. Chaos and confusion ensued for over an hour. The accuser was eventually escorted out of the Field Museum by security guards, but not before Mos Def responded in his defense, "Me and Kweli is working-class dudes in a billion-dollar industry. We got bills," he justified. "The problems we have is way, way, way deeper than hip-hop."

The controversy in Chicago betrays a continuing sense of desperation among those who are concerned with the present and future of African America. "When you ask these people to come speak on panels, you're asking people who are fundamentally artists," clarified attorney-activist Baye Adofo almost two years prior to the "Hip Hop and Social Change" conference. "Mos Def is an artist. Stic [of dead prez] is an artist. Talib is an artist. To ask them to be national spokespeople on racism in America and they're young, [have] no organizing background and they want to rap, it's unfair."[13] And yet, regardless of whether or not it is reasonable, the fact that intelligent, responsible, civic-minded black people were seriously looking to creative artists for solutions to social, political, and economic problems evidences the growing pains of a people who are living in the shadow of gains made by the Civil Rights movement. Because their lyrics are deemed "conscious" by hip-hop aficionados, Mos Def and Talib Kweli were glaringly reminded on that cold, rainy night in October of the pressure to (politically) perform. "Members of the hip-hop generation do not want to be seen as self-righteous because they don't want to be pigeon-holed into something they can't live up to," remarked conference panelist Bakari Kitwana, author-activist and former executive editor of *The Source* magazine. "But what we need to understand is that what it means to 'be political' goes well beyond electoral politics, it goes from the barber shop to the church."[14] While cultural critics go back and forth over the efficacy of expanding the definition of "political," it is important to bear in mind that—despite scholarly debates—there are many people outside of the academy who fail to differentiate between cultural politics and political culture. "Fans may perceive them as spokespersons, and rappers really do voice sentiments that don't get voiced," reported James Bernard. "But the fact that people are now questioning the political significance of rappers shows the dearth of leadership in the grass-roots arena."[15]

The unfortunate degeneration of traditional modes of black politicking, the rising popularity and politicization of hip-hop culture, and the coincidental occurrence of nationally publicized, racially motivated incidents in Bensonhurst, Howard Beach, and Los Angeles are all forces that conspired to catapult rap artists onto the public stage in the late 1980's/early 1990's. "We bought into it—Public Enemy, KRS-One—we wound up being de facto teachers and professors, because of a loss of any real relevant leadership," recounts Bill Stephney. And yet, according to Stephney, the edutainers of the Hip-Hop Nation suffered a price for accepting this role: "You have folks who are looking for some sort of political awakening, who see more in the group than maybe there should be," he attested. "That put a lot of pressure on the group, it put a lot of pressure on Chuck. He went from being a dope, fly emcee to being the second coming of Dr. King. It wound up being unfair."[16]

Fair or not, politicized rap artists were (and are) constantly called to represent the race in black and white America. In the late 1980's/early 1990's the media regularly approached rap artists as though they were experts on the mood of black youth—especially after the acquittal in the Rodney King police brutality case against the Los Angeles Police Department. KRS One expressed his frustrations over the post-riots media frenzy in 1992. "Funny how they pick rappers like me rather than pick our black leaders," he stated. "After the Rodney King verdict, and after the beating, when all this was going down, no one asked Louis Farrakhan or Kwame Toure. Nobody asked black elders what they think should be done." KRS-One felt this disregard for black political personalities indicated the ways in which African Americans were not taken seriously in the United States. "We are respected as a race of entertainers. We're like the court jesters of the world—as a race!"[17] Chuck D was similarly frustrated by the media's fixation on black celebrities during that period of racial crisis. "In any other country they don't look at the athletes and entertainers to explain the state of their people," he protested. "They ask rappers like myself the state of the Black situation. I say, 'The people you need to be asking you're afraid of.' Ask Ben Chavis, Minister Farrakhan, Kwame Toure, Al Sharpton, deal with them."[18]

Despite their objections, rap nationalists were making a strong impression on the mainstream American public and were deemed the organic intellectuals of post–Civil Rights African America by many scholars, hip-hop aficionados, and media pundits who looked to them as more than the officiators of a nation-state of mind. When asked to comment upon a *USA Today* survey that found that rap artists and Civil Rights leaders were equally revered by those arrested in the Los Angeles riots, KRS-One was forthcoming: "The black leaders are not revolutionary enough," he concluded. "Kids want to hear fuck America. Rappers talk about what's real; that's why people love us."[19] In fact, at the height of the golden age of rap nationalism, the media's perception and projection of rap artists was so immoderate that a number of journalists went so far as to ask rap nationalists like Chuck D and KRS-One if they would consider a career as an elected official. KRS-One explained to *Rolling Stone* reporter Alan Light why—for him—this was not an option. "Any black man running for political office in this country is a fool, because this country has done nothing but try to destroy the black man."[20] KRS-One, who once proclaimed that he did not vote but has since endorsed the "Rock the Vote" campaign, further clarified his position on electoral politics in another interview. "I can't do nothing in this government," he stated. "We have more than 300 black mayors in America, major cities, major states. Still ain't got no juice. I got more juice as a rap artist than I would as a mayor."[21]

While miscalculated, this statement certainly speaks to the disenfranchisement and disillusionment of young blacks at the turn of the twenty-first century. The political sense and sensibility of the post–Civil Rights generation may have been somewhat misguided, but there were lessons to be learned from the stumbling blocks of their predecessors, particularly concerning the definition and desirability of black leadership. "We're a nation of millions, it's not about having *one Black leader*," Chuck D theorized. "It's about having a cabinet of leaders who are able to drop their tags and badges when they come in the community and represent a united force of different philosophies when they're dealing with the outside. Whether it's Minister Farrakhan, Jesse Jackson, Ben Chavis, or Cornel West." The Public Enemy front man encouraged political intervention and embraced the Black Power motto "Unity without Uniformity." "If you're looking for a leader, be one. As long as we're united and standing in the same pattern of what progresses us as a people, that is what's important."[22] Six years later, during the melee at the "Hip Hop and Social Change" conference, Mos Def echoed Chuck D's standpoint and argued that the absence of black leaders has become a scapegoat for the lack of personal agency. "The idea of leadership takes responsibility away from the individual," Mos Def pronounced in his own defense. "I have a problem with the notion of black leadership. I think everyone has potential for leadership within themselves. I'm not waiting for another Malcolm or another Martin. That day is over. Self-preservation is the primary law of nature."

Perhaps Mos Def's conclusion signifies the spirit of *The New H.N.I.C.*, that is, what hip-hop observer Todd Boyd describes as the tendency toward individualism emblematic of a generation coming of age during and coming to terms with the postintegration era. Or perhaps Chuck D and Mos Def's critique of the concept of leadership was motivated, in part, by self-interest; for it is apparent that many raptivists found public expectations overwhelming, not just because of their lack of experience in social activism or formal training in sociology but also because of the constraints of being a commercial artist. The pressure to move units took its toll on those who had a clear and sophisticated grasp of political issues. The "stakes is high" for raptivists, writes hip-hop journalist Jeff Chang, because it is only by remaining competitive in the marketplace that artists, regardless of genre, keep their corporate sponsorship. Chang highlights the dilemma facing post–golden age artist Talib Kweli, who feels compelled to please both his fans and his record company. "Kweli worries that being pigeonholed as political will prevent him from being promoted to mass audiences. Indeed, to be a 'political rapper' in the music industry these days is to be condemned to preach to a very small choir."[23]

Regardless of what is behind raptivists' consideration, one thing is for sure: the crisis in black leadership that haunted post–Civil Rights African America resulted in an inordinate amount of critical attention for rap's neonationalists. For example, when asked to compare the hip-hop movement to the Black Panther Party for a 1993 article that appeared in *Rap Pages* magazine, former party member Paul Coates was full of praise for the music ("It's rebellious, it's raw and it's this generations' voice against oppression") and cautiously optimistic about its composers. "The question is whether [rappers] perform as well on the stage of life as they do on the performance stage."[24] That someone intimately familiar with political activism would pose this question indicates just how powerful and dynamic the presence of raptivists was in the public imagination. Furthermore, the constant comparison of rap nationalism to the Civil Rights and Black Power movements suggests a fundamental misunderstanding of and lack of clarity about political methodology among some artists, activists, and intellectuals. For instance, it is both excessive and unreasonable to propose, as many were doing during the late 1980's/early 1990's, that any rapper was more significant for contemporary African America than the legacy of Martin Luther King, Jr. For while cultural critics like Todd Boyd would like to believe that rap artists "represent the vanguard," Talib Kweli's concern about marketing and promotion exposes the fundamental flaw of locating creative artists at the forefront of any social movement.[25] Or as Arrested Development's vocalist Aerle Taree rationalized to a reporter after the group was invited to lecture at Northeastern Illinois University's Center for Inner-City Studies, "We can't be leaders of movements, because there is a whole bunch of politics you have to deal with in this business."[26]

And yet it is clear that rap artists, irrespective of genre, are in a unique position vis-à-vis the public sphere. As a manager of the rap nationalist group dead prez, Rosa Clemente understands how rappers are handicapped by the recording industry. But as a hip-hop activist and organizer for the Black August project, she challenged raptivists to do more. "In a perfect world, it would be great to have no leaders," she consents.

> It would be great to have collective leadership and consensus. But we don't live in that type of world. We live in a hierarchical society, a capitalistic society. People are going look for a leader. They are looking for the next Farrakhan, the next person speaking truth to power. And for a lot of young cats, that is the hip-hop artist.[27]

Unfortunately, with few exceptions, those artists are not political activists. Chuck D has been involved in various public service projects and organizations, including the "Rock the Vote" campaign, the National Urban League, the National Alliance of African-American Athletes, Campaign for National Peace, and the Partnership for a Drug-Free America. He has also worked with the "Free Mumia" campaign and the Black August Hip-Hop Collective. One of the few rap nationalists who has had hands-on political experience is dead prez lyricist M-1. M-1 has been a community organizer with the International People's Democratic Uhuru Movement since the early 1990's. However, he confessed that his involvement with the organization significantly decreased after he received a recording contract because it is difficult to be both a movement organizer and a cultural worker—or as he articulated, "This rap shit is a motherfucker."[28]

Will the Real Revolutionaries Please Stand Up?
Raptivism vs. Activism in the Hip-Hop Movement

> U.S. government is waging a war against our people. It's a battle for
> our minds. We have to battle back. One of the chief weapons we
> can use is hip-hop. —Mutulu Olugbala, 2003

So what is the role and responsibility of the politicized rap artist at the turn of the century? Edutainment is one of the most reasonable functions of raptivism. In hindsight, rap nationalist pioneer Chuck D proclaims that the method to his madness was to "get some light out there. If it happens to come through the culture, then so be it."[29] His strategy worked. In a 1988 interview published by the *Washington Post* Chuck D described the feedback he received from black working-class youth who had never been exposed to black nationalist heroes like Marcus Garvey, Malcolm X, or Bobby Scale before listening to Public Enemy. "They hear it in the songs and then they go do research on their own," he stated. "We get letters all the time, so now we send out a bibliography. Curiosity has been sparked."[30] Chuck D's account is a microcosm of the personal transformations inspired by the hip-hop movement during the late 1980's/early 1990's. Although hip-hop journalist Nelson George argues that, thus far, rap music has had "surprisingly little concrete long-term impact on African-American politics," he does acknowledge that raptivists played an integral part in the consciousness raising and political education of the hip-hop generation. "Chuck D once said he hoped Public Enemy would spawn thousands of black leaders. To the degree that his band opened the eyes of its listeners to political thought, Chuck D and his crew have probably affected many more young people than that."[31] Kevin Powell also evokes Chuck D's pronouncement and insists that the talent of rap artists was not in being leaders but in breeding them. "I realize in retrospect that I was one of those leaders Chuck helped to create," he declared.[32]

Because they understand the limitations of commercial artists and the arduousness of grassroots organizing, hip-hop activists tend to convey a more realistic perspective on the political knowledge and know-how of rappers. "People have outlandish expectations," Clemente verified. "We can't just expect that because you've become famous, you've become political. If you didn't have it before, you're not going to have it after you win a Grammy." Clemente believes that, much like their noncelebrity counterparts, rap artists need to be instructed in the art of political science. "I don't like the expectations that artists should have their political ideology straight," she said. "Something has to happen to hopefully change that person to become a more sophisticated thinker."[33] The U.S. Hip Hop Ambassador Toni Blackman echoed this sentiment because, as she maintained, "If there is such a thing as a 'conscious' rapper, then there must be such a thing as an 'unconscious' rapper."[34] Like his female counterparts, artist-activist M-1 reasons that rap artists are in need of leadership training: "Hip-hop isn't revolutionary in and of itself. Hip-hop has never had political education," he said. "Hip-hop speaks from the heart from a people looking for a voice and searching for something to say."[35] Because the vast majority of rappers lack experience and expertise, hip-hop activists define rap artists' role in the hip-hop movement in terms of their ability to motivate—not mobilize. "The activism needs to be directed toward the people in the communities and neighborhoods, and I think that artists have the responsibility to help sustain that," stated Ras Baraka. "They don't have to begin it or articulate it, but they have a responsibility to help sustain it and to popularize it, to bring it to people's homes and their neighborhoods and their cars. They can do that. They can show up, represent, make it popular."[36] Kevin Powell's seasoning as an industry insider informed his take on the political potential of rap nationalists like Chuck D, Talib Kweli, and Common. They are "interpreters of the times," he asserted, much like their predecessors Billie Holiday, Marvin Gaye, and Nina Simone.[37]

While this type of cultural work is valuable, Baye Adofo advised that it is important to make the distinction between artist and activist: "Nina Simone was phenomenal, but she wasn't Angela Davis."[38] Adofo took care to recognize the fact that, unlike their predecessors in the 1960's and '70s, rap nationalists made artistic contributions that were not supported by a political movement. Yet because artists were mistakenly identified as activists during and after the golden age of rap nationalism, the presence of black freedom fighters in the post–Civil Rights period was underestimated by scholars, journalists, and laypersons. "The organizers in our communities, they don't receive the same recognition," explained Adofo. "We haven't figured out a way to manipulate the media, that's one part of it. Another part of it is because the artists really aren't doing that much—they're just singing. So on one level they're not as threatening."[39] The obsession with celebrity culture and the confounding of fact and fiction proved frustrating for some community organizers and activists. "That de-emphasizes the work that people like me do because we're not in the public eye like that," said Powell. "It's not as sexy to be an activist. So the struggle we have is to try to make it sexy."[40]

Many of these organizers and activists agree that hip-hop is the key to seducing black youth into becoming more politically engaged in their communities. "The outreach of hip-hop is hard to beat," admitted Adofo. "I'm not sure that right now there is a more effective way of reaching young people. It is the most effective way of communicating ideas to a large amount of people."[41] Baraka—whose 2002 campaign for councilman-at-large in Newark was supported by rap artists like Mos Def, Talib Kweli, and Lauryn Hill, hip-hop activists like Kevin Powell, April Silver, and Toni Blackman, and rap music mogul Russell Simmons—bears witness to the influence of hip-hop culture. "Hip-hop is at the forefront of an international cultural revolution," he testified. "I've been many places around the world and seen hip-hop music in action and the effect that it has on youth. It has a lot of potential."[42] Fellow son of the Black Power movement, Fred Hampton, Jr., concurred. As the chairman of the Prisoners of Conscious Committee, an organization whose interests include the prison industrial complex and police harassment and brutality, Hampton considers hip-hop culture to be an indispensable tool for disseminating political information to and stimulating political action in black communities. So he recruited dead prez artists M-1 and Sticman to be the group's "Minister of Culture" and "Minister of Health," respectively. "Minister Huey P. Newton said [that] in the fight for power we have to recognize that power is the ability to define phenomena and make it act in the desired manner. Hip-hop is phenomenal. We want to define this phenomenon and make it work in the interest of the people."[43]

With this objective in mind, in the late 1990's these members of the hip-hop generation and others set out to make the hip-hop movement a reality; their intention: to harness the power of hip-hop's cultural currency, using it as a resource to inspire and inform black and Latino youth. In fact, Baye Adofo and Ras Baraka were instrumental in organizing the first National Hip-Hop Political Convention held June 16–19, 2004, in Newark, New Jersey, to develop leadership among and articulate a political agenda for the hip-hop generation. Around two thousand delegates—each of whom had to register fifty voters—attended. "The ones who are going to [effect change] are the ones who are on the front lines in these organizations, like Baye, who have grown up with hip-hop, but who are not necessarily artists," clarified Talib Kweli.

It's going to be the hip-hop generation but it ain't going to be hip-hop artists, because hip-hop artists by nature are followers. "MC" means "move the crowd," but in order to move the crowd you've got to go where the crowd is. We need to raise leaders, and there are leaders who were raised in hip-hop, but they're just now finding their voice, or just now growing to the age where they can take power and do things. I'm blessed by history to know some of these people, because those are the people who are really going to change shit. And the music is going to be their fuel. It's going to be their tool to change shit.[44]

Two groups that Kweli has worked with either directly or indirectly are the Black August Hip-Hop Collective and HipHop Speaks, both of which exemplify the space where raptivism meets activism in the Hip-Hop Nation. HipHop Speaks, cofounded by Kevin Powell and April Silver in April 2001, is a public forum based in New York City that uses emcee battles to attract black and Latino youth to panels that focus on questions and concerns deemed important to the hip-hop generation. The "town hall meetings" have covered subjects such as public education, women in hip-hop and female empowerment, manhood and fatherhood, and the "War against Terrorism" and have included panelists like hip-hop activists Ras Baraka, Toni Blackman, and Rosa Clemente, hip-hop artists KRS-One, Mos Def, and DJ Kuttin Kandi, and cultural producers Asha Bandele and Jeffrey Wright. In addition to moderating topical discussions, the organizers of HipHop Speaks distribute brochures with information on HIV and AIDS, domestic violence, the prison industrial complex, and alternative education.

Like HipHop Speaks, the Black August Hip-Hop Collective employs hip-hop culture to promote and popularize political awareness about the internal and external affairs of African America. Inspired by Nehanda Abiodun, a former Black Power activist and current political exile in Cuba, the Black August project began in 1998 as a way to galvanize the hip-hop generation around American foreign and domestic policies, specifically the U.S. blockade against Cuba and the political imprisonment of black freedom fighters.[45] Collaboration between Abiodun and members of the Malcolm X Grassroots Movement resulted in a cultural exchange between Cuban rappers and American raptivists, the latter of which perform at annual concerts held in New York City and Havana, Cuba. (The Black August Hip-Hop Collective traveled to Cuba in 1998, 1999, 2000, and 2003. In 2002 they were invited to perform in Brazil.)

As it developed, the hip-hop collective expanded its political campaign to tackle problems like the criminalization of black youth, the prison industrial complex, and human rights violations. "Within hip-hop there is the capacity to build the educational base necessary to develop a movement that is more far-reaching than any one particular issue," professed Black August's principal organizer, Baye Adofo. Attempting to maximize hip-hop's promise, Adofo and his colleagues set out to raise the consciousness not only of its audiences but also of participating rappers. "One thing we try to do is politicize the artist as well, not in a direct way, but through the experience," he explained. "We want it to be a life-changing event."[46] Apparently the plan worked. Raptivists like Common, Talib Kweli, and Mos Def have all, at one time or another, expressed how meaningful and influential the Black August Hip-Hop Collective has been in their lives. But perhaps no journey was more profound than the excursion the group took to South Africa in September 2001 to the U.N. World Conference on Racism, Racial Discrimination, Xenophobia, and Related Intolerance. That year Black Thought of the Roots, The Coup, dead prez, Jeru the Damaja, and Talib Kweli performed five shows in five cities: Durban, Johannesburg, Soweto, Cape Town, and the Cape Flats. The schedule was grueling and the travel challenging. With so many places to see and people to meet, memories of the trip were plentiful. Yet there was one moment that stood out the most for everyone involved.

The hip-hop collective was invited to a press conference to promote Black August and discuss their presence at the U.N. conference. As producers of popular culture, the rappers were used to special treatment, "to being hyped and pampered," but as Kweli described, "there wasn't any room for that at the racism conference, because the issues people were dealing with were way too real." They were about to find out just how real. Without a doubt, the artists were familiar with the spotlight. However, they were not prepared for the drama that was about to unfold. South African journalists and students fired away with a series of hard-hitting questions that were unapologetically straightforward. "They really wanted us to be accountable for some of the things that were happening in the U.S. It turned into a very heated debate," Kweli recalls.[47] Among the highlights of the media frenzy was the story of a young woman who delivered an account of her personal hardships and then wondered aloud how the panelists, both as Americans and as rap artists, could solve her problems. Another attendee was offended by the hypocrisy of American rappers whose lyrics routinely focused on living in poverty when the cost of their jeans exceeded the average monthly wages of black South Africans. Even at its worst, they thought, the American ghetto was no shantytown. "Some of them have a very bad perception of America and Black Americans, what we are able to do and what were are not able to do," remembered Kweli. In his recollection of the press conference, Adofo characterized the event as being reminiscent of a firing squad. "People were looking at them like I want you to fix my problems, you rich American," he said. Although the process was painful, it was also powerful. And, according to Adofo, the outcome was positive. "The press conference was a real unique experience [for the artists], because it let them know how much people depend on them and how much they want them to answer their concerns."[48]

As Adofo intimated, the imbroglio in South Africa was transformative for members of the Black August Hip-Hop Collective. For example, by the end of their tour he noticed a change in Black Thought. The Roots' front man is not widely known for projecting a political standpoint in his lyrics, but he began to incorporate what he was learning into his performances. Talib Kweli was equally inspired by the developments in South Africa. "That experience helped me define my role," he admits. "Because [growing up] I had access to certain resources like food, shelter, and education, I have to use those resources to help my people in general all over the world. If I can't see that after all those trips to all those places, then I'm just a fool."[49] Baye Adofo was pleased with the results of the Black August expedition to the U.N. conference and was hopeful about its provocative possibilities. "We want [the artists] to come back and make songs about that experience, because you can't go back to before you went to South Africa. There's just no way. It's in your DNA now, it's part of your makeup. You can't just turn your back on that."[50] Becoming involved in the peripheral activities of an international forum on racism provided organizers of the Black August Hip-Hop Collective with the opportunity to make a difference in the hip-hop generation by influencing the political awareness of artists already perceived as "conscious" rappers. "Our biggest success in Black August is politicizing artists who then go out and in a very general way politicize other people," Baye Adofo reckoned. "We haven't been as successful in organizing as we have been in getting artists to think about different things."[51]

While some observers may not see its revolutionary potential, the Black August project stands as a good example of the coalition—the compromise—between raptivist and activist. Most importantly, it signifies the future of the hip-hop movement. It is a sign of the times. For the cultural politics of rap music in the post–Civil Rights era revealed a crisis in African America, and as a phenomenon it begs the question, What forms of political consciousness and/or styles of political organizing can the current generation borrow from their predecessors to inform a movement for social change in an increasingly complicated (and global) economic system? The situation is especially acute due to the dismantling of the infrastructure in black communities; and particularly distressing is the decline of those historic spaces that served to cultivate and nurture both the oppositional culture that informed social movements as well as the men and women that would lead those movements. The dire conditions of the black political arena are further compounded by the fact that, as Ras Baraka articulated, "There is a generation of leaders that are in competition with their own kids."[52] According to a number of hip-hop activists and organizers, prominent members of the Civil Rights generation have—more often than not—demonstrated active and passive resistance to the input and innovations of the post–Civil Rights generation. Youth organizers are in a tug of war not only with their elders but also with an increasingly commodified and technological public culture. "How do you develop a movement that can, not only organize folks and get them to congeal on the organic, but also do something that Dr. King, Malcolm, and Public Enemy didn't have to deal with: the distractions of [Black Entertainment Television], of [songs like] "How High," of the *Welcome to Death Row* home video, of mix tapes, of advertising, of *The Source*, of *XXL*?" inquired Bill Stephney. "That didn't exist for any of those folks before us, no competition to fight for the attention of black youth."[53] With all of these conflicting elements at play, it is no wonder hip-hop journalist Jeff Chang concludes that in the hip-hop movement, "the biggest obstacle to societal change may simply be the act of imagining it."[54]

Perhaps new times demand new tactics. If the Hip-Hop Nation is not a movement in the strict sense, it is nevertheless still meaningful. For as scholar George Lipsitz writes, "Culture enables people to rehearse identities, stances and social relations not yet permissible in politics." In fact, Lipsitz deduces, "Popular culture does not just reflect reality, it helps constitute it."[55] This is certainly true for raptivists who, during the golden age of rap nationalism, dared to imagine a world in which blackness was not synonymous with inferiority and African America was not plagued with poverty, police brutality, or the prison industrial complex. As cultural workers, they promised to "Fight the Power" and "Stop the Violence." In doing so, they inspired their rap nationalist successors like M-1 and Sticman of dead prez and Mos Def and Talib Kweli of Black Star, as well as hip-hop activists like Baye Adofo and Kevin Powell. Furthermore, that period in hip-hop history provided a blueprint for the use of rap music as a vehicle to express revolutionary ideals. One need only witness raptivists' cultural nationalist partners in rhyme: Mexi-centric rappers like Aztlan Underground and Aztlan Nation, who demonstrate their commitment to Chicanismo by celebrating "La Raza," claiming heroes like Che Guevara and the Brown Berets, and making it clear that "[w]e didn't cross the border / the border crossed us"; Native American rappers like the panethnic group WithOut Rezervation and Cherokee raptivist Litefoot, who honor traditional culture and the ancestors, tackle contemporary problems like gang violence, and explore issues ranging from genocide to the use of American Indians as team mascots; as well as Maori rappers like Upper Hutt Posse and Samoan rappers like Footsouljahs, who use hip-hop music to reclaim their indigenous language and culture, translate the history of European colonization, and advocate sovereignty for the indigenous peoples of the Pacific Islands.

If the impact of rap nationalism was not immediate, it was definitely far reaching. Maybe its legacy will be the creation of what Lipsitz labels "families of resemblance," that is, raptivism served to "illustrat[e] how diverse populations have had similar although not identical experiences."[56] For one thing is apparent: the counterhegemonic discourse that began with the golden age of rap nationalism, ironically, created a sense of community that transcended racial, gender, and national boundaries. "Hip-hop has united all races," said raptivist KRS-One. "Hip-hop has formed a platform for all people, religions, and occupations to meet on something. We all have a platform to meet on now, due to hip-hop. That, to me, is beyond music. That is just a brilliant, brilliant thing."[57]

Conclusion: Problematizing Black Nationalism as a Liberation Politics

> The struggle for democracy in America is not finished. We have to finish it. —Ras Baraka, 2002

What hip-hop's neonationalism was able to accomplish in terms of its race politics, it has not, thus far, achieved for its gender and sexual politics. The interrogative style of the Hip-Hop Nation has yet to be turned inward in any substantial way to critically assess its masculinist discourse and praxis. "Rap's pedagogy, like the initial stages of all pedagogies of oppressed people, emerges incomplete, contradictory and struggling for coherence," writes political scientist Clarence Lusane.[58] Unfortunately, the phallocentric nationalism of the hip-hop generation extends beyond its musical form and into the realm of activism. "The drawback to being female in political struggle," explained Toni Blackman, is that "gender issues don't get addressed."[59] During a 2002 interview, hip-hop activist Rosa Clemente talked about how, because of her ethnicity and gender, she struggled to be recognized as a legitimate commentator on hip-hop issues. After she published a controversial article critiquing Russell Simmons, Clemente, who identifies as a black Puerto Rican, received hundreds of email responses. Some were positive. Most were negative.

> A lot of it was really nasty messages like, "Who the fuck are you," "You're a fuckin' bitch." Some really ill stuff: "You're not even black. You don't know what it's like to be a black person in America." But the interesting thing is that none of them were talking about my article. It was just like, "Who is this bitch. Who is this woman and how dare she question what Russell Simmons is doing?"[60]

Ras Baraka also confirmed that sexism is "very much prevalent" among hip-hop activists and organizers. Much like during the Civil Rights and Black Power movements, "Men Led, But Women Organized."[61] "I don't think it is as disturbing and crazy as it was thirty years ago in terms of the rhetoric and what people were willing to do to women, but it's still there. That's very clear." Baraka used Sister Souljah as a case in point. As a highly respected advocate for social justice, Sister Souljah founded an African Youth Survival Camp, serves as the executive director of Sean "P-Diddy" Comb's nonprofit organization, Daddy's House Social Programs, Inc., and assisted with community projects initiated by high-profile political personalities like the Reverends Benjamin Chavis and Jesse Jackson. Due to her knowledge and know-how, Baraka believes that Sister Souljah should be recognized as a national leader, but "she's a woman and she's vocal," he said. "Nobody's going to help her do anything."[62]

Not surprisingly, in a male-dominated culture supported by a male-dominated industry, women oftentimes are marginalized and their interests, subordinated. Rosa Clemente bore witness to the struggle of her female counterparts in the hip-hop movement. Clemente disclosed that she is frequently the only woman invited to speak in public forums on hip-hop culture and politics, because most panels on hip-hop activism are exclusively male—and more often than not, exclusively black male. It is a state of affairs that many women in the Hip-Hop Nation find extremely frustrating. "Brothers have to stand up and start speaking truth to power. It's not just up to women," Clemente insisted. "I get tired of always talking about sexism. Brothers should be addressing the issue too, and not on a token level." Clemente feels so strongly about this problem that she has rejected requests to participate in events if she is to be the only female representative. "I don't want to be that one woman who gets all the play," she said. "That's wack."[63]

The gender dynamics of black neonationalism are reminiscent of those that characterized the classical and modern periods. Take, for example, M. Josette Harland's position on sexism among the "new nationalists" of the late 1980's/early 1990's: "There has to be a willingness to discuss racism and sexism in the new movement or else there will be a stalemate and further schisms along gender lines." Harland, who at the time was a member of Spelman University's African Sisterhood Incorporated, seemed to take a strong stance against a monistic approach to race politics. Yet her argument is tempered by the belief that, in revolutionary struggle, race supersedes gender—unless it involves the needs of black men. "[T]he issue of sexism must take its place in line behind other issues that concern Black youths," she explained. "And as some Black people, especially Black men, turn to drug dealing to make ends meet, young politically conscious African-Americans must grapple with the economic realities that confront them."[64] Like their predecessors in the nineteenth and twentieth centuries, many black women in the hip-hop generation submitted to a masculinist discourse. Challenges to sexism were varied and uneven. While women like Clemente publicly confronted the androcentric modes and mores of their peers, some choose to critique their male counterparts behind the scenes and others, not at all. "There's a lot of sisters that are struggling against the sexism," Clemente assured. "You just don't hear about them. I know there are a lot of amazing sisters [out there] doing the work."[65]

Because of the sexual division of labor, some women in the hip-hop movement began to create programs and groups that would concentrate on matters of particular concern to women. For example, during the 2003 Hip-Hop and Social Change conference held at Chicago's Field Museum, self-proclaimed "cultural warrior" Toni Blackman announced that, in addition to being the executive director of the Freestyle Union, she planned to launch an Artist Development Institute to instruct young black women in the art of hip-hop while simultaneously teaching them self-confidence and critical thinking skills. Its mission, she said, "is to make a concentrated effort to provide training and support for emerging female hip-hop artists whose voices, activism and lyrics have been largely unnoticed."[66] Similarly, the Brooklyn-based organization Sista II Sista was created in 1996 to fill what its founders perceived to be a void in hip-hop activism: the "political and personal development" of women of color. The collective runs a freedom school that conducts leadership training, holds workshops that teach youth about peer pressure and self-esteem, and sponsors a community action project targeting violence against women.[67]

Despite these efforts, patriarchal attitudes and sexist practices persist among black neonationalists, a fact of life that may be regrettable but is not unpredictable. Historically, there has been a problematic relationship between the "radical" philosophy and the conservative reality of black nationalism in the United States. Whether explicit or implicit, a gendered code has underlined—and undermined—the very definition of empowerment in the race politics of black nationalism. For as literary scholar Hazel Carby notes, African America has inherited "a rarely questioned notion of masculinity as it is connected to ideas of race and nation."[68] The preoccupation with manhood demonstrated in the oral and literary work of black nationalists, from David Walker to Ice Cube, signifies that there has been a "conceptual and political failure of imagination"[69] at work in black public life. That is, these black men (and many black women) have not even *conceived* a politics of liberation that is not dependent upon a masculinist discourse that incorporates a subordination of the feminine. The desire to attain the power and privilege associated with hegemonic masculinity has haunted black nationalists and, therefore, has limited black nationalism's liberatory potential since its debut on the black political scene in 1829. This covetous style of politicking is most evident in the cry for "manhood rights," or the right to male domination in the public and private spheres, witnessed in David Walker's *Appeal* during the early nineteenth century and at the Million Man March in the late twentieth. In fact, the success of the Million Man March was evidence of the enduring lure of a gendered narrative of the black American experience—and of the continued power of "it's-a-dick-thing" masculinity and masculinist politicking in U.S. black nationalism. Yet any politics based in race/gender rationales has the potential to—indeed will inevitably—both legitimate and replicate hierarchical stratification in social, political, economic, and cultural relations. And it is precisely for this reason that gender studies scholar Anne McClintock warns, "[a]ll nationalisms . . . are dangerous."[70]

One example is the slave metaphor discussed in chapter 2. This symbol is used by many black nationalist ideologues to authorize a politics of violent resistance in their struggle to attain black "manhood rights." But if black nationalists advocate the use of violence to obtain patriarchal order, what is to say they will not also use violence to maintain that order? The theory and praxis of so-called revolutionaries during the Black Power and hip-hop movements provide the most explicit manifestations of employing verbal, physical, and/or sexual violence against men and women, black and white, straight and gay. Whether it be Eldridge Cleaver's rape fantasy/reality or the fatal rivalry between the Panthers and the US Organization,[71] Ice Cube's "Cave Bitch" or Brand Nubian's "Punks Jump Up to Get Beat Down," black nationalists' endorsement of violence is/was not restricted to dismantling the white power structure. That is because their macho "it's-a-dick-thing" politicking knows and respects no boundaries but its own. As an embodied-social politics black nationalism necessitates a strict policing of its race/gender and sexuality borders—at times those borders are also defined by class, color, and generation. And part of that policing includes violence, even if it involves violence against those within the "nation": black women and black (and especially gay) men.

Therefore it is extremely important, as bell hooks argues, to be "seduced by violence no more."[72] To accomplish this involves calling the validity of black nationalism as a liberatory politics into question. Black neonationalists must, as Ice Cube once suggested, "Be True to the Game." Any political ideology that does not incorporate the liberation of *all* black people cannot be legitimately considered a liberation politics. As an embodied-social politics, black nationalism has proven itself to be an ideology and practice concerned primarily with the liberation of black heterosexual men. While its primary objective has always been self-determination, black nationalism has been shaped in profound and unexpected ways by dominant society, particularly in terms of its framing as a politics of masculine protest. To be fair, black nationalists' definitions of manhood and masculinity are at times reflective of dominant culture and at others, reflected in dominant culture. Yet in the end, it makes little difference. The results are the same.

Perhaps radical documentarian Marlon Riggs was onto something when he boldly pronounced that "black men loving black men is the revolutionary act of our times." Once black men—particularly heterosexual black men—begin to address their own gendered oppression, redefine the masculine ideal, and learn to love themselves and their communities without fear or anxiety, they can discover and appreciate the value of freedom. For as black feminist pioneer Toni Cade Bambara wrote in 1970, "It perhaps takes less heart to pick up the gun than to face the task of creating a new identity, a self, perhaps an androgynous self, via commitment to the struggle."[73] Of course, that is easier said than done in a country that values male supremacy while simultaneously undermining black male agency through various forms of institutional racism. Nevertheless, black feminists and queer theorists have exposed the limitations and liabilities of black nationalism as a political standpoint that suppresses the heterogeneity of experiences in African America. Decidedly not all blacks are alike, and racial identity is mediated by factors such as ethnicity, class, gender, sexuality—even region and age. "But too often, and perhaps inescapably, starting from a 'race first' position assumes problematically that group oppression has nearly similar, if not identical, causes, and therefore nearly similar, if not identical, solutions," explains political scientist Dean Robinson. "Such a stance overlooks the fact that black 'interests' converge on some issues, and diverge on others."[74]

Black men and women whose vision of liberation is circumscribed by a gendered discourse that aspires to perpetuate the status quo will continue to be betrayed by their own contradictions. As raptivists during and after the golden age of rap nationalism have shown, black nationalism continues to be handicapped by its own self-consciousness and shortsightedness. When African Americans realize that our power lies not in the subordination of others but in collective and democratic struggle, then we as a people can truly get down to the business of liberation. Until that day arrives, we are still in search of a revolutionary generation. For as spoken word artist Sarah Jones declares in her controversial 1999 hip-hop song, "your revolution will not happen between these thighs."

> Because the real revolution, that's right
> I said the *real* revolution
> I'm talkin' about the revolution
> when it comes
> it's gon' be real.[75]

Notes

NOTES TO CHAPTER ONE

1. Although *Lethal Injection* went platinum, the writing was on the wall for Ice Cube as a rap nationalist. After a five-year hiatus from his solo career, Ice Cube's 1998 single "We Be Clubbin'" from the soundtrack for the movie *The Players Club* signified a shift to more popular and less political tastes.

2. "Raptivist" is being used as a descriptive term for the politicized rap artist. It is not my intention to suggest that any or all rap nationalists were activists or were involved in community or political organizing.

3. In this book the term "Hip-Hop Nation" is used to refer to a cohort of black neonationalist rap artists, although the term is commonly used in reference to hip-hop artists and fans regardless of their political standpoint. Similarly, the term "hip-hop movement" is used in reference to the golden age of rap nationalism and the generation of activists it has inspired (the latter will be discussed in more depth in chapter 5).

4. Jeffrey Louis Decker, "The State of Rap: Time and Place in Hip Hop Nationalism," *Social Texts* (Spring 1993): 60.

5. See Henry Louis Gates, Jr., "2 Live Crew, Decoded," *New York Times*, 19 June 1990; and Henry Louis Gates, Jr., "Rap Music: Don't Knock It If You're Not onto Its 'Lies,'" *New York Herald Tribune*, 20 June 1990.

6. Jon Michael Spencer, "Introduction," *The Emergency of Black and the Emergence of Rap*, Special Issue of *Black Sacred Music: A Journal of Theomusicology* 5, 1 (Spring 1991): 4 (italics my emphasis). For a critique of the apologetic scholarship on the sexism in rap music, see Sonja Peterson-Lewis, "A Feminist Analysis of the Defenses of Obscene Rap Lyrics," *Black Sacred Music* (Spring 1991): 68–79.

7. Among many hip-hop artists and enthusiasts the definitions of "rap" and "hip-hop" have more to do with commercial distinctions than cultural ones. For those hip-hop "heads," commercial artists are labeled "rap" while "underground" artists—artists who are recognized as more "authentic" and/or are believed to preserve and project the music as an art form—are endorsed by the more desired "hip-hop" label. These distinctions are best summed up by KRS-

One's oft-cited statement that "rap is something you do, Hip-Hop is something you live." See KRS-One, "Hip-Hop v. Rap," *Sound of the Police* (Jive, 1993).

8. Chuck D, telephone interview by author, 27 January 2002.

9. David Mills, "The Gangster Rapper: Violent Hero or Negative Role Model?" *The Source*, Summer 1990, 39.

10. Chuck D, interview.

11. Adam Krims, *Rap Music and the Poetics of Identity* (New York: Cambridge University Press, 2000), 8, quoting Jody Berland, "Locating Listening: Technological Space, Popular Music, and Canadian Meditations," in *The Place of Music*, ed. Andrew Leyshon, David Matless, and George Revill (New York: Guilford, 1998), 138.

12. For a more extensive discussion of the social, economic, and political context of rap's development, see Tricia Rose, "'All Aboard the Night Train': Flow, Layering, and Rupture in Post-Industrial New York," in *Black Noise: Rap Music and Black Culture in Contemporary America* (Hanover, NH: Wesleyan University Press, 1994), 21–34. And for a discussion of the impact of Reaganomics on black youth, see Clarence Lusane, "Rap, Race, and Politics," *Race and Class* (Great Britain) 35, 1 (1993): 43.

13. "The Trip to the Bronx," *New York Times*, 6 October 1977, 26.

14. Richard Severo, "Bronx a Symbol of America's Woes," *New York Times*, 6 October 1977, B18.

15. Michael Eric Dyson, *Between God and Gangsta Rap: Bearing Witness to Black Culture* (New York: Oxford University Press, 1996), 177.

16. Ibid. For Dyson's description of rappers as "cultural griots," see Michael Eric Dyson, "Rap Culture, the Church, and American Society," *Sacred Music of the Secular City*, Special Issue of *Black Sacred Music: A Journal of Theomusicology* 6, 1 (Spring 1992): 268.

17. Russell A. Potter, *Spectacular Vernaculars: Hip-Hop and the Politics of Postmodernism* (Albany: State University of New York Press, 1995), 108.

18. Ibid., 18.

19. Ibid., 76.

20. Sheila Rule, "Generation Rap," *New York Times*, 3 April 1994, sec. 6, p. 40.

21. Cornel West, "On Afro-American Popular Music: From Bebop to Rap," *Sacred Music of the Secular City*, Special Issue of *Black Sacred Music: A Journal of Theomusicology* 6, 1 (Spring 1992): 293.

22. This is not to minimize Latino influences on hip-hop culture. As Mandalit del Barco, Juan Flores, and Carlito Rodriguez point out, Puerto Ricans in New York were instrumental in the creation and development of breakdancing and graffiti art. See Mandalit del Barco, "Rap's Latino Sabor," and Juan Flores, "Puerto Rocks: New York Ricans Stake Their Claim," in *Droppin' Science: Critical Essays on Rap Music and Hip Hop Culture*, ed. William Eric Perkins

(Philadelphia: Temple University Press, 1996); and Carlito Rodriguez, "Vamos a Rapiar: Latinos and Hip-Hop Music," *The Source*, March 1998. For the influences of Chicanos on West Coast rap music, see Raegan Kelly, "Hip Hop Chicano: A Separate but Parallel Story," in *it's not about a salary . . . rap, race + resistance in Los Angeles*, ed. Brian Cross (New York: Verso, 1993), 65–76.

23. For a more detailed explanation of the kinds of cultural exchange that occurred between Afro-Americans and Afro-Caribbeans during the early years of rap music's development, see William Eric Perkins's *Droppin' Science* and Dick Hebdige, *Cut 'n' Mix: Culture, Identity and Caribbean Music* (London: Methuen, 1987).

24. George Lipsitz, *Dangerous Crossroads* (New York: Verso, 1994), 32.

25. Nelson George, *Buppies, B-Boys, Baps and Bohos: Notes on a Post-Soul Black Culture* (New York: HarperPerennial, 1994), 95.

26. While many rap artists refer to themselves as "niggas," others, particularly raptivists like Public Enemy and KRS-One, problematize and challenge the use of the word. For a discussion of "nigga" as a race/class/gender identity, see Robin D. G. Kelley, "Kickin' Reality, Kickin' Ballistics: 'Gangsta Rap' and Postindustrial Los Angeles," *Race Rebels: Culture, Politics, and the Black Working Class* (New York: Free Press, 1994), 209–14.

27. "It's urban guerrilla commentary," Chuck D proclaimed. Lyle V. Harris, "Reaching the Hip-Hop Generation," *Atlanta Journal and Constitution*, 7 March 1993, C1.

28. Monica Denise Griffin, "The Rap on Rap Music: The Social Construction of African-American Identity" (Ph.D. diss., University of Virginia, 1998), 43.

29. Michael Eric Dyson, *Making Malcolm: The Myth and Meaning of Malcolm X* (New York: Oxford University Press, 1995), 115.

30. Brother J uses serial killer Jeffrey Dahmer as a symbolic tool to expose cultural representations of whites as civilized (and, therefore, superior), and blacks as savage (and, therefore, inferior). By doing so, he draws a racial connection between himself and Dahmer's victims—most of whom were black gay men. Wittingly or unwittingly, Brother J's pronouncement is an interesting departure from the masculinist tradition of black nationalism, a form of race and gender politicking that virtually requires its adherents to exclude homosexuals from the imagined (black) community.

31. X-Clan, "Fire and Earth (100% Natural)," *Xodus* (Polygram Records, 1992).

32. Benedict Anderson, *Imagined Communities: Reflections on the Origin and Spread of Nationalism* (Thetford, Norfolk: Thetford Press, 1983), 12.

33. Theodore Draper, *The Rediscovery of Black Nationalism* (New York: Viking Press, 1969), 147.

34. William L. Van Deburg, *Modern Black Nationalism: From Marcus Garvey to Louis Farrakhan* (New York: New York University Press, 1997), 1.

35. George Breitman, ed. *Malcolm X Speaks: Selected Speeches and State-ments* (New York: Grove Press, 1965), 10.

36. *Malcolm X Speaks*, 9.

37. Wilson Jeremiah Moses, ed., *Classical Black Nationalism: From the American Revolution to Marcus Garvey* (New York: New York University Press, 1996), 1.

38. Draper, *Rediscovery*, 67.

39. Theodore Draper notes that U.S. black nationalism has taken two pre-dominant forms: e/migrationism and "internal statism." The first genre is exem-plified by organizations that promoted black emigration to Africa or the Caribbean (especially Haiti), the second by those organizations, like the Repub-lic of New Africa, that wanted to establish an independent black nation within the borders of the United States.

40. Paul Gilroy, "It's a Family Affair," in *Black Popular Culture*, ed. Gina Dent (Seattle: Bay Press, 1992), 303.

41. Wahneema Lubiano, "Black Nationalism and Black Common Sense: Policing Ourselves and Others," in *The House That Race Built: Black Ameri-cans, U.S. Terrain*, ed. Wahneema Lubiano (New York: Pantheon Books, 1997), 232.

42. Clyde Halisi and James Mtume, eds., *The Quotable Karenga* (Los Ange-les: US Organization, 1967), 8.

43. Anderson, *Imagined Communities*, 15.

44. Rod Bush, *We Are Not What We Seem: Black Nationalism and Class Struggle in the American Century* (New York: New York University Press, 1999), 49.

45. See Ernest Gellner, *Thought and Change* (Chicago: University of Chicago Press, 1965), 168.

46. Anderson, *Imagined Communities*, 15.

47. *Quotable Karenga*, 6.

48. dead prez, "I'm a African," *Let's Get Free* (Relativity Records, 2000).

49. LeRoi Jones, *Home: Social Essays* (New York: Morrow, 1966), 95.

50. William W. Sales, Jr., *From Civil Rights to Black Liberation: Malcolm X and the Organization of Afro-American Unity* (Boston: South End Press, 1994), 57.

51. *Quotable Karenga*, 3.

52. Wilson Jeremiah Moses, *The Golden Age of Black Nationalism, 1850–1925* (Hamden, CT: Archon Books, 1978), 11.

53. Ibid., 23.

54. Jane Rhodes, *Mary Ann Shadd Cary: The Black Press and Protest in the Nineteenth Century* (Bloomington: Indiana University Press, 1998), 86.

55. Anna Julia Cooper, "Womanhood a Vital Element in the Regeneration and Progress of a Race," in *A Voice from the South* (New York: Oxford Univer-

sity Press, 1988), 30. Like Shadd Cary, Anna Julia Cooper also took exception to the gendered approach of Martin Delany's racial politics.

56. Lubiano, "Black Nationalism and Black Common Sense," 245.

57. Wise Intelligent, telephone interview by author, 28 January 2002.

NOTES TO CHAPTER TWO

1. Harriet Beecher Stowe describes Uncle Tom as having a "gentle, domestic heart." Harriet Beecher Stowe, *Uncle Tom's Cabin* (New York: Bantam Books, 1981), 91.

2. *Glory*, dir. Edward Zwick, Columbia TriStar, 1989.

3. Gail Bederman, *Manliness and Civilization: A Cultural History of Gender and Race in the United States, 1880–1917* (Chicago: University of Chicago Press, 1995), 21.

4. Alfred Adler, *The Individual Psychology of Alfred Adler: A Systematic Presentation in Selections from His Writings* (New York: Basic Books, 1956); quoted in R. W. Connell, *Masculinities* (Berkeley: University of California Press, 1995), 16.

5. Anne McClintock, "'No Longer in a Future Heaven': Gender, Race and Nationalism," in *Dangerous Liaisons: Gender, Nation, and Postcolonial Perspectives*, ed. Anne McClintock, Aamir Mufti, and Ella Shohat (Minneapolis: University of Minnesota Press, 1997), 95. McClintock quotes Algerian anticolonialist and revolutionary theorist Frantz Fanon: "The fantasy of the native is precisely to occupy the master's place." McClintock, 95.

6. Connell, *Masculinities*, 66.

7. Paul Gilroy, *The Black Atlantic: Modernity and Double Consciousness* (Cambridge, MA: Harvard University Press, 1993), 85.

8. Significant works on the masculinist discourse of black (American) nationalism include Wahneema Lubiano, "Black Nationalism and Black Common Sense: Policing Ourselves and Others," in *The House That Race Built: Black Americans, U.S. Terrain*, ed. Wahneema Lubiano (New York: Pantheon Books, 1997), 232–52; Amy Abugo Ongiri, "We Are Family: Black Nationalism, Black Masculinity, and the Black Gay Cultural Imagination," *College Literature* 24, 1 (February 1997): 280–95; Barbara Ransby and Tracye Matthews, "Black Popular Culture and the Transcendence of Patriarchal Illusions," *Race & Class* 35, 1 (July–September 1993): 57–68; and E. Francis White, "Africa on My Mind: Gender, Counter Discourse and African American Nationalism," *Journal of Women's History* 2, 1 (Spring 1990): 73–97.

9. Movement activists and scholars debate whether or not this statement accurately represents Stokely Carmichael's gender politics or those of the Student Nonviolent Coordinating Committee. What is most important for this project, however, is that his declaration is consistent with the masculinist discourse of

American black nationalism: Carmichael's suggestion that the role of women in SNCC was one that necessitated their sexual subordination exemplified the provocative, and often profane, sexual politics of the Black Power movement.

10. Ice Cube, "Horny Little Devil," *Death Certificate* (Priority Records, 1991).

11. Gilroy, *Black Atlantic*, 85.

12. Sociologist R. W. Connell explains the symbiotic relationship between masculine and feminine in *Masculinities*: "The phallus is master-signifier, and femininity is symbolically defined by lack." Connell, 70. In the United States this relationship is complicated by race and class, so that "femininity" in both the nineteenth and twentieth centuries is most associated with middle-class, white, Anglo-Saxon, Protestant women.

13. This ideal of Victorian "manliness" was carried into the early twentieth century by black intellectuals and activists, particularly those in the black elite. American Studies scholar Hazel Carby notes the conscious gender imaging of Alexander Crummell's protégé W. E. B. Du Bois, who deliberately projected manly civility through his demeanor and dress at the turn of the twentieth century. Hazel Carby, *Race Men* (Cambridge, MA: Harvard University Press, 1998), 21.

14. bell hooks, "Feminism Inside: Toward a Black Body Politic," in *Black Male: Representations of Masculinity in Contemporary American Art*, ed. Thelma Golden (New York: Whitney Museum of American Art: Distributed by Harry N. Abrams, 1994), 127.

15. Alexander Crummell, "The Black Woman of the South," in *Destiny and Race: Selected Writings, 1840–1898*, ed. Wilson Jeremiah Moses (Amherst: University of Massachusetts Press, 1992), 214.

16. Ibid., 221.

17. Ibid., 215–16, italics in original.

18. For an explicit example of classical black nationalists' policing of black women's sexuality, see historian Michele Mitchell's analysis of the sexual politics (and in particular, her discussion of the antimiscegenationism) of the Universal Negro Improvement Association. Michele Mitchell, "Adjusting the Race: Gender, Sexuality, and the Question of African-American Destiny, 1877–1930" (Ph.D. diss., Northwestern University, 1998), 307–53.

19. See Gail Bederman, "Remaking Manhood through Race and 'Civilization,'" chap. 1 in *Manliness and Civilization*.

20. Amiri Baraka, *Selected Poetry of Amiri Baraka/LeRoi Jones* (New York: Morrow, 1979), 115, 146.

21. Phillip Brian Harper, *"Are We Not Men": Masculine Anxiety and the Problem of African-American Identity* (New York: Oxford University Press, 1996), 51.

22. Angela Davis, "Reflections on the Black Woman's Role in the Community

of Slaves," in *Words of Fire: An Anthology of African-American Feminist Thought*, ed. Beverly Guy-Sheftall (New York: New Press, 1995), 216.

23. Office of Policy Planning and Research, United States Department of Labor, *The Negro Family: The Case for National Action* (Washington, DC: GPO, March 1965), 29.

24. bell hooks, *Outlaw Culture: Resisting Representations* (New York: Routledge, 1994), 110. In her essay about the perpetuation of rape culture within black communities, titled "Seduced by Violence No More," hooks describes the cultural commodification of a black male identity that is based on the abuse/exploitation of black women, an identity she calls "dick-thing" masculinity.

25. Bobby Seale, *Seize the Time: The Story of the Black Panther Party and Huey P. Newton* (New York: Random House, 1970), 247. Seale cites Eldridge Cleaver as the source of this quote.

26. Eldridge Cleaver, "Pronuciamento," *The Black Panther*, 21 December 1968.

27. bell hooks goes in search of an empowered female sexuality—or, as she named it, "Power to the Pussy"—in *Outlaw Culture*.

28. Connell, *Masculinities*, 111.

29. Huey P. Newton, "Fear and Doubt," *The Black Panther*, 15 May 1967.

30. Eldridge Cleaver, *Soul on Ice* (New York: Dell, 1968), 14. This statement is disturbing for multiple reasons, but in particular because prior to joining the Black Panther Party, Eldridge Cleaver spent nine years in California's Soledad Prison for rape.

31. Ibid., 110.

32. Bederman, *Manliness and Civilization*, 8.

33. Larry Neal, "New Space/New Growth," in *Visions of a Liberated Future: Black Arts Movement Writings*, ed. Larry Neal and Michael Schwartz (New York: Thunder's Mouth Press, 1989), 131.

34. Clyde Halisi and James Mtume, eds., *The Quotable Karenga* (Los Angeles: US Organization, 1967), 21.

35. Imamu Amiri Baraka, *Raise, Race, Rays, Raze: Essays since 1965* (New York: Random House, 1971), 148.

36. Imamu Amiri Baraka, *The Autobiography of LeRoi Jones/Amiri Baraka* (New York: Freundlich Books, 1984), 275.

37. Ibid., 276.

38. V. P. Franklin, *Living Our Stories, Telling Our Truths: Autobiography and the Making of the African-American Intellectual Tradition* (New York: Scribners, 1995), 309–10. For an account of Ella Baker's contributions to the modern Civil Rights movement, see Barbara Ransby, *Ella Baker and the Black Freedom Movement: A Radical Democratic Vision* (Chapel Hill: University of North Carolina Press, 2003). For more on Bayard Rustin, see John D'Emilio, *Lost Prophet: The Life and Times of Bayard Rustin* (New York: Free Press, 2003).

39. For a discussion of the masculinist discourse of black Communists see Robin D. G. Kelley, "'Afric's Sons With Banner Red': African American Communists and the Politics of Culture, 1919–1934," chap. 5 in *Race Rebels: Culture, Politics, and the Black Working Class* (New York: Free Press, 1994).

40. Victor Ullman, *Martin R. Delany: The Beginnings of Black Nationalism* (Boston: Beacon Press, 1971), 10.

41. David Walker, *Appeal to the Colored Citizens of the World, but in Particular, and Very Expressly, to Those of the United States of America* (New York: Hill and Wang, 1965), 27.

42. Ibid., 16.

43. Carby, *Race Men*, 12.

44. Connell, *Masculinities*, 214.

45. The narrative songs of early twentieth-century black railroaders and agricultural workers bear witness to the masculine (con)figuration of John Henry: "If I could hammer / Like John Henry / If I could hammer / Like John Henry / Lawd, I'd be a man / Lawd, I'd be a man." Lawrence Levine, *Black Culture and Black Consciousness: Afro-American Folk Thought from Slavery to Freedom* (New York: Oxford University Press, 1977), 425.

46. Gayraud Wilmore, *Black Religion and Black Radicalism* (Garden City, NY: Anchor Press/Doubleday, 1973), 192.

47. Wilson Jeremiah Moses, ed., *Classical Black Nationalism: From the American Revolution to Marcus Garvey* (New York: New York University Press, 1996), 92.

48. Ibid., 96.

49. Louise Moore, "When Will the Real Black Man Stand Up?" *The Liberator*, May 1966, 6.

50. Gilroy, *Black Atlantic*, 194.

51. Toni Cade Bambara, "On the Issue of Roles," in *The Black Woman: An Anthology*, ed. Toni Cade Bambara (New York: Penguin Books USA, 1970), 102.

52. Cleaver, *Soul on Ice*, 61.

53. Julius Lester, *Look Out, Whitey! Black Power's Gon' Get Your Mamma* (New York: Dial, 1968), 80.

54. Moses, *Classical Black Nationalism*, 246.

55. Malcolm X, "The Ballot or the Bullet," in *Malcolm X Speaks: Selected Speeches and Statements*, ed. George Breitman (New York: Grove Press, 1965), 32.

56. Robert Igriega, "Eldridge for 'Pussy Power,'" *Open City* (Los Angeles), 9 August 1968, 1.

57. Larry Neal, "And Shine Swam On," in *Black Fire: An Anthology of Afro-American Writing*, ed. LeRoi Jones and Larry Neal (New York: Morrow, 1968), 646–47.

58. Amiri Baraka, "Black Art," in *Selected Poetry of Amiri Baraka/LeRoi Jones*, ed. Amiri Baraka (New York: Morrow, 1979), 106.

59. Nikki Giovanni, "The True Import of Present Dialogue, Black vs. Negro (For Peppe, Who Will Ultimately Judge Our Efforts)," in *Black Feeling/Black Talk/Black Judgment* (New York: Morrow Quill Paperbacks, 1979), 19–20.

60. Carby, *Race Men*, 33.

61. bell hooks, *Ain't I a Woman: Black Women and Feminism* (Boston: South End Press, 1981), 20.

62. Philip S. Foner, *The Black Panthers Speak* (Philadelphia: Lippincott, 1970), 62.

63. Sterling Stuckey, ed. *Ideological Origins of Black Nationalism* (Boston: Beacon Press, 1972), 4.

64. LeRoi Jones, *Blues People: The Negro Experience in White America and the Music That Developed from It* (New York: Morrow Quill Paperbacks, 1963), 57.

65. For more on this issue see Lawrence Levine, *Black Culture and Black Consciousness*, 54.

66. Sterling Stuckey, *Going through the Storm: The Influence of African-American Art in History* (New York: Oxford University Press, 1994), 90.

67. Eugene D. Genovese, "The Legacy of Slavery and the Roots of Black Nationalism," in *For a New America: Essays in History and Politics from Studies on the Left, 1959–1967*, ed. James Weinstein and David W. Eakins (New York: Random House, 1970), 413–14.

68. Malcolm X, "With Mrs. Fannie Lou Hamer," in *Malcolm X Speaks*, 115.

69. Eldridge Cleaver, "Psychology: The Black Bible," in *Eldridge Cleaver: Post-Prison Writings and Speeches*, ed. Robert Scheer (New York: Random House, 1969), 20.

70. Wilmore, *Black Religion*, 89.

71. Stuckey, *Ideological Origins*, 172.

72. Ibid., 168.

73. Ibid., 170. Over one hundred years later, the US Organization's Maulana Karenga echoed Garnet's sentiment in a strikingly similar manner: "If we fight we might be killed. But it is better to die as a man than live like a slave." *Quotable Karenga*, 11.

74. Walker, *Appeal*, 25.

75. Ibid., 26.

76. Wilson Jeremiah Moses, *The Golden Age of Black Nationalism, 1850–1925* (Hamden, CT: Archon Books, 1978), 202.

77. Ibid., 183. This statement was made by an unnamed black preacher at the "colored" 1889 National Baptist Convention.

78. James H. Cone, *Black Theology and Black Power* (New York: Seabury Press, 1969), 139.

79. For a more extensive explanation and illustration of the conjuring potential of the Bible, see Theophus H. Smith, *Conjuring Culture: Biblical Formations of Black America* (New York: Oxford University Press, 1994).

80. Albert B. Cleage, Jr., *The Black Messiah* (New York: Sheed and Ward, 1968), 214.

81. Ibid., 224.

82. Eldridge Cleaver, "Stanford Speech," *Post-Prison Writings*, 143.

83. Ibid., 142–43.

84. Igriega, "Eldridge," 6.

85. Kay Lindsay, "Poem," in *The Black Woman*, 17. Many Black Power advocates encouraged women to procreate. However, there was much less discussion of men's responsibility for family planning and for taking care of women and their children, leading black feminist pioneer Toni Cade Bambara to conclude in 1969, "Seems to me the Brother does us all a great disservice by telling [women] to fight the man with the womb. Better to fight with the gun and the mind." Toni Cade Bambara, "The Pill: Genocide or Liberation?" in *The Black Woman*, 167.

86. Evette Pearson, "In White America Today," *The Black Panthers Speak*, 25. Black Power advocates were not the first black nationalists to equate contraception with genocide. In the eugenics era, members of the U.N.I.A. also debated the dangers of birth control. See Mitchell, "Adjusting the Race," 331–44.

87. Mumininas of Committee for Unified NewArk, *Mwanamke Mwananchi (The Nationalist Woman)* (Newark, NJ: Jihad Productions, 1971). Original quote in *The Quotable Karenga*, 20.

88. "Where Does the Contradiction Problem Lie?" *The Black Panther*, 23 August 1969, 22.

89. Evelyn Rogers, "Sisters—Stop Castrating That Black Man!" *The Liberator*, May 1966, 21.

90. Cleaver, *Soul on Ice*, 162.

91. Neal, "The Black Arts Movement," in *Visions*, 76.

92. "Sisters!" *The Black Panther*, 13 September 1969, 12–13.

93. Betty Frank Lomax, "Afro-American Woman: Growth Deferred," *The Liberator*, July 1965, 18.

94. Davis, "Reflections," 216.

95. "The Role of a Black Woman in White Society," *The Liberator*, August 1965, 5.

96. Gloria Bartholomew, "A Black Woman's Thoughts," *The Black Panther*, 28 September 1968, 11.

97. Mumininas of Committee for Unified NewArk, *Mwanamke Mwananchi*, 4.

98. For a discussion of the gender ramifications of cultural nationalists' his-

torical revisionism, see E. Francis White, "Africa on My Mind: Gender, Counter Discourse, and African American Nationalism," *Journal of Women's History* 2, 1 (Spring 1990): 73–97.

99. Cleaver, *Soul on Ice*, 188.

100. Foner, *Black Panthers Speak*, 58.

101. "Bobby Seale Explains Panther Politics: An Interview," in Foner, *Black Panthers Speak*, 86.

102. Cleaver, *Soul on Ice*, 160–61.

103. Religious studies scholar Theophus Smith describes René Girard's concept of the "triangle of desire" as being comprised of three elements: "the subject, the other as model/rival, and the other's objects or assets." Smith, *Conjuring Culture*, 195–96.

104. Kobena Mercer, "Fear of a Black Penis," *Artforum International* 32, 8 (April 1994): 122.

105. Walker, *Appeal*, 9; *Quotable Karenga*, iii; Ice Cube, "Cave Bitch," *Lethal Injection* (Priority Records, 1992).

106. Foner, *Black Panthers Speak*, 59.

107. "In Defense of Self-Defense: An Exclusive Interview with Minister of Defense, Huey P. Newton," *The Black Panther*, 16 March 1968.

108. Foner, *Black Panthers Speak*, 62.

109. Ida Walston, "Check It Out Sister," *The Black Panther*, 27 September 1969, 15.

110. *Eyes on the Prize: America at the Racial Crossroads. Power! 1967–1968*, prod. and dir. Louis Massiah and Terry Kay Rockefeller, Blackside, 1990.

111. Farah Jasmine Griffin, "Conflict and Chorus: Reconsidering Toni Cade's *The Black Woman: An Anthology*," in *Is It Nation Time? Contemporary Essays on Black Power and Black Nationalism*, ed. Eddie S. Glaude, Jr. (Chicago: University of Chicago Press, 2002), 124.

112. Ibid.

113. "A Letter from Huey to Revolutionary Brothers and Sisters," *The Black Panther*, August 1970.

114. For more on this issue see Tracye Matthews, "'No One Ever Asks, What a Man's Place in the Revolution Is': Gender and the Politics of the Black Panther Party, 1966–1971," in *The Black Panther Party Reconsidered*, ed. Charles E. Jones (Baltimore: Black Classic Press, 1998), 267–304.

115. Elaine Brown, *A Taste of Power: A Black Woman's Story* (New York: Pantheon Books, 1992), 440.

116. Kobena Mercer and Isaac Julien, "True Confessions," in *Black Male*, 197–98.

117. Nelson George, *Hip Hop America* (New York: Viking Penguin, 1998), 53.

NOTES TO CHAPTER THREE

1. Public Enemy, "Party for Your Right to Fight," *It Takes a Nation of Millions to Hold Us Back* (Def Jam, 1988).

2. Errol Nazareth, "A Powerful Noise: Public Enemy's Chuck D Has a Lot to Say about Race, Society, and the Media," *Toronto Sun*, Sunday, 3 May 1998, Showcase section.

3. In the summer of 1969 FBI director J. Edgar Hoover declared the Black Panther Party the number one threat to the internal security of the United States, or Public Enemy #1.

4. Public Enemy, "Brothers Gonna Work It Out," *Fear of a Black Planet* (Def Jam, 1990).

5. Public Enemy, "Revolutionary Generation," *Fear of a Black Planet*.

6. Jon Michael Spencer, "Introduction," *The Emergency of Black and the Emergence of Rap*, Special Issue of *Black Sacred Music: A Journal of Theomusicology* 5, 1 (Spring 1991): 5.

7. Garry Mendez, "Inside Out," *Horizon*, December 1999; available at http://www.horizonmag.com/1/lord-jamar.asp. Hip-hop journalist Kevin Powell also spoke of a need for alternative (if not radical) representations of black manhood during the mid-1980's. He described the historical impact of rap pioneers Run-DMC: "These three black males—Run, and DMC and Jam Master Jay—[were] just regular cats, you know. They didn't look like Prince or Michael Jackson or El DeBarge, they looked like regular brothers, which was something that was important to a lot of us in the community." Kevin Powell, interview by author, tape recording, Brooklyn, NY, 12 November 2001.

8. David Mills, "Reality in a New Rapping: Arrested Development, Drawing Raves with a Message of Maturity," *Washington Post*, 19 July 1992, Sunday show section. Many hip-hop nationalists echoed this characterization of R & B music.

9. *Tour of a Black Planet* (Sony Music Entertainment, 1991). Rap nationalists rarely used Dr. Martin Luther King, Jr., as a symbol of rehabilitated black manhood. For those young African Americans who were born in the historical moment immediately following the Civil Rights era, the failings of integration politics and Civil Rights rhetoric—as well as the appropriation and commodification of the memory and meaning of Dr. Martin Luther King, Jr.—conspired to deradicalize King's social justice activism in the popular imagination. Chuck D, however, shows great respect for the Civil Rights leader, which, in a sense, is a revision of the revisionist history embraced and/or created by rap nationalists themselves. In the midst of the 1992 media firestorm surrounding the release of Public Enemy's "By the Time I Get to Arizona" and its accompanying video (to protest the 1990 defeat of the state's King holiday bill), Chuck D told a *Washington Post* reporter that King was becoming increasingly militant when he was assassinated

and may have even become "Martin Luther King Farrakhan." He had white people listening, "understanding you can't be no punk," Chuck D testifies in the 1991 film *Rap's Most Wanted*. "So they took him out." Richard Harrington, "Public Enemy's Twisted Tribute," *Washington Post*, Sunday, 13 May 1992, Sunday show section, p. G1; *Rap's Most Wanted*, prod. Luther Campbell and Tas Salini, dir. Tas Salini, Stepping Stone Productions, 1991.

10. Another reason African Americans continued to exercise marginal political power is that, despite increased political representation—for example, the number of black elected officials grew 5.9 percent from 1970 (1,469) to 1997 (8,656)—blacks remained an underrepresented minority in the American political arena. In 1997 African Americans constituted only 1.7 percent of the total number of all elected officials. See David A. Bositis, *Black Elected Officials: A Statistical Summary, 1993–1997* (Washington, DC: Joint Center for Political and Economic Studies, 1998).

11. Ras Baraka, telephone interview by author, 10 January 2002.

12. For a critical analysis of the transition from protest politics to electoral politics in African America, see Robert C. Smith, *We Have No Leaders: African-Americans in the Post–Civil Rights Era* (New York: State University of New York Press, 1996).

13. Jeff Chang, "'Stakes Is High': Conscious Rap, Neosoul, and the Hip-Hop Generation," *The Nation*, 13/20 January 2003, 20.

14. For more about the effects of a postindustrial economy on the black labor force see William Julius Wilson, *When Work Disappears: The World of the New Urban Poor* (New York: Knopf, 1998); for an interpretation of its effects on the hip-hop generation, specifically West Coast "gangsta" rappers, see Robin D. G. Kelley, "Kickin' Reality, Kickin' Ballistics: 'Gangsta Rap' and Postindustrial Los Angeles," in *Race Rebels: Culture, Politics, and the Black Working Class* (New York: Free Press, 1994), 183–227; Bakari Kitwana, "America's Outcasts: The Employment Crisis," chap. 2 in *The Hip Hop Generation: Young Blacks and the Crisis in African-American Culture* (New York: BasicCivitas Books, 2002); and George Lipsitz, "We Know What Time It Is: Race, Class, and Youth Culture in the Nineties," in *Microphone Fiends: Youth Music and Youth Culture*, ed. Andrew Ross and Tricia Rose (New York: Routledge, 1994), 17–28.

15. Powell, interview.

16. Farai Chideya, "Homophobia: Hip-Hop's Black Eye," in *Step into a World: A Global Anthology of the New Black Literature*, ed. Kevin Powell (New York: Wiley, 2000), 96.

17. Manning Marable, "Race, Identity, and Political Culture," in *Black Popular Culture*, ed. Gina Dent (Seattle: Bay Press, 1992), 292.

18. Michael Small, *Break It Down: The Inside Story from the New Leaders of Rap* (Secaucus, NJ: Carol Publishing, 1992), 48.

19. For valid criticisms of the consciousness movement in hip-hop music, see

Todd Boyd, "Check Yo Self Before You Wreck Yo Self: The Death of Politics in Rap Music and Popular Culture," in *Am I Black Enough for You? Popular Culture from the 'Hood and Beyond* (Bloomington: Indiana University Press, 1997), 38–59; Nelson George, "Capitalist Tool," in *Hip Hop America* (New York: Viking Penguin, 1998), 154–75; Paul Gilroy, "It's a Family Affair," in *Black Popular Culture*, 303–16; and Adolph Reed, Jr., "Posing as Politics: Youth Culture Left Behind?" *Village Voice*, 5 December 1995, 20.

20. George, *Hip Hop America*, 155.

21. For a discussion of international youth's appropriation of hip-hop culture as a forum for political expression, see Clarence Lusane, "Rap, Race, and Politics," in *Race and Class* (Great Britain) 35, 1 (1993): 41–56; and Tony Mitchell, ed., *Global Noise: Rap and Hip Hop Outside the USA* (Middletown, CT: Wesleyan University Press, 2001).

22. Wahneema Lubiano, "Standing in for the State: Black Nationalism and 'Writing' the Black Subject," in *Is It Nation Time? Contemporary Essays on Black Power and Black Nationalism*, ed. Eddie S. Glaude, Jr. (Chicago: University of Chicago Press, 2002), 160.

23. Manning Marable defines "liberal integrationism" as "a strategy of political action that calls for the deconstruction of institutional racism through liberal reforms within the government and the assimilation of Blacks as individuals within all levels of the work force, culture, and society." Marable, "Race, Identity, and Political Culture," 296.

24. Sandra Hollin Flowers, *African American Nationalist Literature of the 1960s: Pens of Fire* (New York: Garland, 1996), 150.

25. Rev. Dr. Calvin O. Butts III, "Rolling Out an Agenda for Rap," in *Rap on Rap: Straight Up Talk on Hip Hop Culture*, ed. Adam Sexton (New York: Dell, 1995), 76.

26. David Hinckley, "Harlem Preacher Taking on Ice-T," *Buffalo News*, 15 July 1993.

27. House Subcommittee on Commerce, Consumer Protection, and Competitiveness of the Committee on Energy and Commerce, *Music Lyrics and Commerce*, 103rd Cong., 2nd sess., 11 February 1994, 15.

28. "Deal May Settle Rosa Parks-Outkast Issue," *Rap News Direct*, 21 December 2003; available from http://www.rapnewsdirect.com/News/2003/12/21/Deal.RosaParks.Outkast/.

29. Rod Bush, *We Are Not What We Seem: Black Nationalism and Class Struggle in the American Century* (New York: New York University Press, 1999), 36.

30. KRS-One, "Free Mumia," *KRS-One* (Jive, 1995).

31. Kierna Mayo Dawsey, "Caught Up in the (Gangsta) Rapture," *The Source*, June 1994, 58–59.

32. Bill Stephney, interview by author, tape recording, New York, NY, 18 January 2002.

33. Sheila Rule, "Generation Rap," *New York Times*, 3 April 1994.

34. Richard Harrington, "Public Enemy's Assault on the Airwaves," *Washington Post*, Sunday, 31 July 1988, Sunday Show section, G1.

35. Ironically, black nationalism reappears in the United States at precisely the moment when it is most vulnerable to compromise—politically and culturally. Gilroy (1992, 1993) and George Lipsitz (1994) both describe the ways in which globalization renders the nation-state, and therefore nationalist politics, obsolete, and outline the hazards of the commercialization of local politics in an international marketplace.

36. Marable, "Race, Identity, and Political Culture," 292.

37. Baraka, interview.

38. Talib Kweli, interview by author, tape recording, Brooklyn, NY, 16 January 2002.

39. Ronald Jemal Stephens reports that as the leader of the Zulu Nation, Afrika Bambaataa (a former member of the Black Spades gang in the Bronx) advocated an antiviolence, antidrug, and anti-alcohol platform to an estimated ten thousand members, including rappers, breakers, graffiti artists, and fans, by promoting "positive images and behaviors." Ronald Jemal Stephens, "The Three Waves of Contemporary Rap Music," *The Emergency of Black and the Emergence of Rap*, 30.

40. According to Jeffrey Louis Decker, Malcolm X's widow Betty Shabazz endorsed Keith LeBlanc's "No Sellout." Jeffrey Louis Decker, "The State of Rap: Time and Place in Hip Hop Nationalism," *Social Texts* 60 (Spring 1993): 57.

41. Run-DMC, "Proud to be Black," *Raising Hell* (Def Jam, 1987).

42. Jon Pareles, "Radical Rap: Of Pride and Prejudice," *New York Times*, 16 December 1990, sec. 2, p. 1.

43. Joseph Eure and James G. Spady, eds., *Nation Conscious Rap* (Brooklyn: PC International Press, 1991), 82.

44. This quote from Spike Lee appears on Public Enemy's official website at www.publicenemy.com.

45. William Eric Perkins, "Nation of Islam Ideology in the Rap of Public Enemy," *Black Sacred Music* 5, 1 (Spring 1991): 47.

46. Gregory Tate, *Flyboy in the Buttermilk: Essays on Contemporary America* (New York: Simon & Schuster, 1992), 122.

47. Powell, interview.

48. Paris, "Back in the Days," *Guerrilla Funk* (Priority Records, 1994); Mills, "Reality in a New Rapping." Speech told *Washington Post* reporter David Mills that Public Enemy's "Rebel without a Pause" sparked his political transformation. "That was the first song that made me really say, 'What is this?' . . . it got

me interested [in politics]. So me and [fellow Arrested Development member] Headliner as friends started to try to learn more about culture and about history, and tried to get more deep into this whole thing Chuck D was talking about."

49. Decker, "The State of Rap," 60. Decker seems to overlook the ascendancy and growing influence of Nation of Islam leader Louis Farrakhan, held in high esteem by Public Enemy's front man Chuck D, during the mid- to late 1980's.

50. Commercially, Public Enemy was an extremely successful group, with three of their six releases going multiplatinum, and the other three gold. They also had four gold singles and a platinum home video.

51. R. Stephens, "The Three Waves," 40.

52. Chuck D and Yusef Jah, *Fight the Power: Rap, Race, and Reality* (New York: Delacorte Press, 1997), 74.

53. Robert Hilburn, "Rap—The Power and the Controversy," *Los Angeles Times*, 4 February 1990, Calendar section, p. 64.

54. Stephney, interview.

55. Ibid.

56. Chuck D and Yusef Jah, *Fight the Power*, 86.

57. Chuck D, telephone interview by author, 27 January 2002.

58. Chuck D and Yusef Jah, *Fight the Power*, 257.

59. Chuck D, interview.

60. Stephney, interview.

61. Chuck D, interview.

62. Stephney, interview.

63. Chuck D and Yusef Jah, *Fight the Power*, 216.

64. Sister Souljah was a replacement of sorts for Professor Griff, who was dismissed in 1989. Griffin sparked a media firestorm by making an allegedly anti-Semitic comment that appeared in the *Washington Times* earlier that year.

65. Harry Allen, "Ballet or Bullet?" *Village Voice*, 19 January 1988, 22.

66. Chuck D and Yusef Jah, *Fight the Power*, 221.

67. Harrington, "Public Enemy's Assault on the Airwaves."

68. Stephney, interview.

69. George Lipsitz, *Dangerous Crossroads* (New York: Verso, 1994), 34.

70. Chuck D, interview.

71. See Dick Hebdige, *Subculture: The Meaning of Style* (London: Methuen, 1982).

72. Death Row Records was once home to multiplatinum-selling, controversial "gangsta" rappers Dr. Dre (formerly of N.W.A.), Snoop Doggy Dogg, and Tupac. Their East Coast rival, Bad Boy Records, was created by producer-turned-rapper Sean "Puffy" Combs and featured the Notorious B.I.G., aka Biggie Smalls.

73. Stephney, interview.

74. See James C. Scott, "A Saturnalia of Power: The First Public Declaration

of the Hidden Transcript," chap. 8 in *Domination and the Arts of Resistance: Hidden Transcripts* (New Haven, CT: Yale University Press, 1990).

75. Chuck D and Yusef Jah, *Fight the Power*, 258.

76. Lipsitz, *Dangerous Crossroads*, 12.

77. Chuck D, interview.

78. Chuck D and Yusef Jah, *Fight the Power*, 27.

79. Ibid., 59.

80. Stephney, interview.

81. Chuck D and Yusef Jah, *Fight the Power*, 25.

82. Public Enemy, "Party for Your Right to Fight," *It Takes a Nation of Millions to Hold Us Back*. The influence of the Nation of Islam on rap nationalists like Public Enemy is discussed in chapter 5.

83. The Black Panther Party is overwhelmingly represented in masculinist ways by rap nationalists, including Public Enemy. However, in a rare case of gender inclusiveness, Chuck D recognizes exiled former Panther Assata Shakur in "Rebel with a Pause," stating that he is a "supporter of [JoAnne] Chesimard." Public Enemy, "Rebel with a Pause," *It Takes a Nation of Millions to Hold Us Back*. Other raptivists that have "A Song for Assata" are Common, on his 2000 release *Like Water for Chocolate*, and Paris, in "Back in the Days" on his 1994 release *Guerrilla Funk*.

84. Decker, "The State of Rap," 65.

85. Eldridge Cleaver, *Soul on Ice* (New York: Dell, 1968), 60.

86. R. W. Connell, *Masculinities* (Berkeley: University of California Press, 1969), 214.

87. Michael Eric Dyson, *Making Malcolm: The Myth and Meaning of Malcolm X* (New York: Oxford University Press, 1996), xi.

88. The term "Malcolmania" was coined by sociologist David Maurrasse. Barbara Ransby and Tracye Matthews, "Black Popular Culture and the Transcendence of Patriarchal Illusions," *Race and Class* 35, 1 (July–September 1993): 67.

89. Roger Catlin, "KRS-One Likes to Do More Rapping Than Talking about Racial Problems," *Hartford Courant*, 12 June 1992.

90. Kenneth Burke, *The Philosophy of Literary Form: Studies in Symbolic Action* (New York: Vintage Books, 1957), 100, quoted in Theophus Smith, *Conjuring Culture: Biblical Formations of Black America* (New York: Oxford University Press, 1994), 58.

91. Ice Cube, "Wicked," *The Predator* (Priority Records, 1992).

92. Russell A. Potter, *Spectacular Vernaculars: Hip-Hop and the Politics of Postmodernism* (Albany: State University of New York Press, 1995), 52; George, *Hip-Hop America*, 45.

93. Powell, interview.

94. Scott Mervis, "Teacher from the Old School: KRS-One Goes Deeper into

the Temple of Hip-Hop on 'Spiritual Minded,'" *Pittsburgh Post-Gazette*, 8 February 2002, Friday Sooner edition.

95. Catlin, "KRS-One Likes to Do More Rapping Than Talking about Racial Problems."

96. Boogie Down Productions, "Necessary," *By All Means Necessary* (RCA Records, 1988).

97. Chris Heim, "Boogie Down Productions' Rap Is Educational," *Chicago Tribune*, 28 September 1990.

98. Boogie Down Productions, "Build and Destroy," *Sex and Violence* (Zomba Recording Corporation, 1992).

99. Ibid.

100. Boogie Down Productions, "The Racist," *Edutainment* (Jive Records, 1990); Boogie Down Productions, "Build and Destroy."

101. Paul Gilroy, *The Black Atlantic: Modernity and Double Consciousness* (Cambridge, MA: Harvard University Press, 1993), 84.

102. R. Stephens, "The Three Waves," 38.

103. Michael Eric Dyson actually used this term to describe the nationalist aesthetic style of Ice Cube, but it is also an appropriate description for the rap nationalism of Paris. Michael Eric Dyson, *Between God and Gangsta Rap: Bearing Witness to Black Culture* (New York: Oxford University Press, 1996), 172. It is this fusion of rap styles that made Ice Cube's transition from "gangsta rap" to nationalist rap and back again to "gangsta" rap both startling and predictable. His ability to move in multiple worlds has proven quite lucrative, even if (seemingly) inconsistent. "He made his best album, *AmeriKKKa's Most Wanted*, in New York, then years later dissed New York in a rambling *Source* interview," Nelson George says of Ice Cube's oppositional, and/or opportunistic, career. "He shaved off the Jheri-curls, co-signed the Nation of Islam ideology of self-help and self-respect, and made a bundle hustling St. Ides malt liquor in the ghetto. He is a bankable Hollywood star who still craves hard-core credibility. Consistency is not Ice Cube's calling card." George, *Hip Hop America*, 138–39.

104. Decker, "The State of Rap," 53.

105. This is not to underestimate the veneration of Louis Farrakhan by rap artists, a phenomenon that will be discussed in more depth in chapter 5. Farrakhan was recognized as a symbol of strong black manhood, but his role for rap nationalists was more one of spiritual father than of folk hero.

106. Historian William Van Deburg effectively divides the nationalist element of the Black Power movement into three distinct categories: Territorial Nationalists, who wanted a separate black nation-state, e.g., the Republic of New Africa; Revolutionary Nationalists, who believed there would be no black liberation in the United States without a political and economic revolution, e.g., the Black Panther Party; and Cultural Nationalists. In actuality, the distinctions between

organizations were not so definitive, but Van Deburg's categorizations are useful for understanding the influences of various Black Power leaders and organizations on the hip-hop movement. William L. Van Deburg, *New Day in Babylon: The Black Power Movement and American Culture, 1965–1975* (Chicago: University of Chicago Press, 1992).

107. Chuck D and Yusef Jah, *Fight the Power*, 258.

108. J. The Sultan, "The Inside Dope—Artist Focus: X-Clan," *The Source*, November/December 1989, 28.

109. Ice Cube, liner notes, *Death Certificate* (Priority Records, 1991).

110. William Eric Perkins, "The Rap Attack: An Introduction," in *Droppin' Science: Critical Essays on Rap Music and Hip Hop Culture* (Philadelphia: Temple University Press, 1996), 4.

111. Chuck D and Yusef Jah, *Fight the Power*, 27.

112. Larry Neal, "And Shine Swam On," in *Black Fire: An Anthology of Afro-American Writing*, ed. LeRoi Jones and Larry Neal (New York: Morrow, 1968), 656.

113. Eddie S. Glaude, Jr., writes that a "politics of transvaluation is best understood as a reassessment of 'blackness.'" Eddie S. Glaude, Jr., "Introduction: Black Power Revisited," in *Is It Nation Time?*, 4.

114. Ice Cube, liner notes, *The Predator*.

115. Harrington, "Public Enemy's Assault on the Airwaves."

116. Greg Braxton, "The Voices of Rap—Politics or Just Music?" *Los Angeles Times*, Sunday, 19 July 1992, Calendar section, p. 7.

117. Rule, "Generation Rap," 40.

118. Ibid.

119. Gilroy, "It's a Family Affair," 305–6.

120. George Lipsitz, *The Possessive Investment in Whiteness* (Philadelphia: Temple University Press, 1998).

121. George, *Hip Hop America*, xiii–xiv.

122. Ibid., xiv.

123. Alan Light, "Wisdom from the Street," *Rolling Stone*, 30 May 1991, 42.

124. Van Deburg, *New Day in Babylon*; Mark Anthony Neal, *What the Music Said: Black Popular Music and Black Public Culture* (New York: Routledge, 1999).

125. Rosa Clemente, telephone interview by author, 9 January 2002.

126. Freestyle Fellowship, "tolerate," *Innercity Griots* (Island Records, 1993).

127. Jeru the Damaja, "Come Clean," *The Sun Rises in the East* (Payday, 1994).

128. Eure and Spady, *Nation Conscious Rap*, 156.

129. Ibid., 202.

130. Ibid., 253.

131. Chuck D attributes the idea of the "killing fields" to Nation of Islam leader Louis Farrakhan. Chuck D and Yusef Jah, *Fight the Power*, 34.

132. Baraka, interview.

133. For a descriptive account of the disparities between American private and public school systems during this period see Jonathan Kozol, *Savage Inequalities: Children in America's Schools* (New York: Crown Publishers, 1991).

134. William W. Sales, Jr., *From Civil Rights to Black Liberation: Malcolm X and the Organization of Afro-American Unity* (Boston: South End Press, 1994), 207.

135. Public Enemy, "Brothers Gonna Work It Out," *Fear of a Black Planet*; Jungle Brothers, "Acknowledge Your Own History," *Done by the Forces of Nature* (Warner Brothers, 1989). It is important to note that this obsession among raptivists over "his story" speaks to how they framed black nationalism as a politics of masculine protest.

136. Boogie Down Productions, "You Must Learn," *Ghetto Music: The Blueprint of Hip Hop* (RCA Records, 1989).

137. dead prez, "They Schools," *Let's Get Free* (Relativity Records, 2000).

138. Paris, *Guerrilla Funk* (Priority Records, 1994).

139. Grand Puba, "Proper Education," *Reel to Reel* (Elektra Entertainment, 1992).

140. Barry Deonarine, "Knowledge Your Own History," *The Source*, November/December 1989, 18.

141. Chuck D and Yusef Jah, *Fight the Power*, 173.

142. Ibid., 174.

143. Grand Puba's "Proper Education," *Reel to Reel*; Kam, "Trust Nobody," *Made in America* (Atlanta Recording Corporation, 1995).

144. Henry Louis Gates, Jr., "The Black Man's Burden," *Black Popular Culture* (Seattle: Bay Press, 1992), 77. Although this quote refers to the constructed nature of social identities, it is extremely applicable to black nationalist theory: "[O]ur social identities represent the way we participate in an historical narrative," Gates writes. "Our histories may be irretrievable, but they invite imaginative reconstruction."

145. Dyson, *Making Malcolm*, 92.

146. Chuck D and Yusef Jah, *Fight the Power*, 203.

147. dead prez, "They Schools."

148. Rule, "Generation Rap."

149. Chuck D and Yusef Jah, *Fight the Power*, 32–36. Chuck D quotes Washington's "Industrial Education for the Negro" and Du Bois's "Talented Tenth" essay, a classic anti-industrial, pro–classical education piece in which Du Bois insists "that the object of all true education is not to make men carpenters, it is to make carpenters men." W. E. B. Du Bois, "The Talented Tenth," in *The Negro*

Problem: A Series of Articles by Representative American Negroes of To-day (Miami, FL: Mnemosyne Publishing, 1969), 63.

150. Wise Intelligent, telephone interview by author, 28 January 2002.

151. African American studies scholar Wahneema Lubiano discusses the way the literary tradition of U.S. black nationalism functions as both an opposition to and a substitution for American social, political, economic, and cultural institutions. Wahneema Lubiano, "Standing in for the State: Black Nationalism and 'Writing' the Black Subject," in *Is it Nation Time?*, 156–64.

152. Gordon Chambers, "Souljah's Mission," *Essence*, December 1991, 108.

153. Wu-Tang Clan, "C.R.E.A.M.," *Enter the Wu-Tang 36 Chambers* (BMG Music, 1993).

NOTES TO CHAPTER FOUR

1. Kevin Powell, interview by author, tape recording, Brooklyn, NY, 12 November 2001.

2. Kevin Powell, "Confessions of a Recovering Misogynist," *Ms. Magazine*, April/May 2000, 74.

3. Jeru the Damaja, "The Frustrated Nigga," *Pump Ya Fist: Hip Hop Inspired by the Black Panthers* (Polygram Records, 1995).

4. Russell A. Potter, *Spectacular Vernaculars: Hip-Hop and the Politics of Postmodernism* (Albany: State University of New York Press, 1995), 135.

5. Ice Cube, "The Nigga You Love to Hate," *AmeriKKKa's Most Wanted* (Priority Records, 1990). For more on apocalyptic visions and eschatological rhetorics as constant black nationalist themes, see chapter 5.

6. Joan Morgan, "The Nigga Ya Love to Hate," in *Rap on Rap: Straight Up Talk on Hip Hop Culture*, ed. Adam Sexton (New York: Dell, 1995), 119.

7. For a discussion on rap artists' feminization of black middle-class men, see Herman Gray, "Black Masculinity and Visual Culture" in *Black Male: Representations of Masculinity in Contemporary American Art*, ed. Thelma Golden (New York: Whitney Museum of American Art: Distributed by Harry N. Abrams (1994), 179.

8. Ice Cube, "The Bomb," *AmeriKKKa's Most Wanted*.

9. Morgan, "The Nigga Ya Love to Hate," 123.

10. Robin D. G. Kelley, *Race Rebels: Culture, Politics, and the Black Working Class* (New York: Free Press, 1994), 187.

11. Cornel West, "On Afro-American Popular Music: From Bebop to Rap," *Black Sacred Music: A Journal of Theomusicology* 6, 1 (Spring 1992): 294.

12. Nancy Kurshan, "Women and Imprisonment in the United States: History and Current Reality," *The Prison Issues Desk*; available at http://prisonactivist.org/women/women-and-imprisonment.html.

13. Ice Cube and Angela Y. Davis, "Nappy Happy," *Transition* no. 6 (1992):

182; Jungle Brothers, "Black Woman," *Done by the Forces of Nature* (Warner Brothers, 1989).

14. Jeffrey Louis Decker, "The State of Rap: Time and Place in Hip Hop Nationalism," *Social Texts* 60 (Spring 1993): 109.

15. Tricia Rose, *Black Noise: Rap Music and Culture in Contemporary America* (Hanover, NH: Wesleyan University Press, 1994), 149.

16. H. Rap Brown, *Die Nigger Die* (New York: Dial Press, 1969), 26.

17. Ice Cube, "It's a Man's World," *AmeriKKKa's Most Wanted.*

18. William Eric Perkins, "The Rap Attack: An Introduction," in *Droppin' Science: Critical Essays on Rap Music and Hip Hop Culture* (Philadelphia: Temple University Press, 1996), 28.

19. See Tommy L. Lott, "A No-Theory Theory of Contemporary Black Cinema," *Black American Literature Forum* 25, 2 (Summer 1991): 221–36.

20. Helen Koblin, "Portrait of an Ex-Pimp Philosopher, Iceberg Slim," *Los Angeles Free Press*, 25 February 1972, 4.

21. Huey Newton, "He Won't Bleed Me: A Revolutionary Analysis of Sweet Sweetback's Baadasssss Song," in *To Die for the People: The Writings of Huey P. Newton* (New York: Random House, 1972), 113.

22. Larry Neal, "Brother Pimp," in *Visions of a Liberated Future: Black Arts Movement Writings*, ed. Larry Neal and Michael Schwartz (New York: Thunder's Mouth Press, 1989), 216–17.

23. Jungle Brothers, "Black Woman"; Queen Latifah, "Ladies First," *All Hail the Queen* (Tommy Boy Music, 1989); Isis, "The Power of Myself Is Moving," *Rebel Soul* (4th & B'Way Records, 1990); Queen Latifah, "A King and Queen Creation," *All Hail the Queen* (Tommy Boy Music, 1989).

24. Sister Souljah, "360 Degrees of Power," *360 Degrees of Power* (Sony, 1992).

25. Joseph Eure and James G. Spady, eds., *Nation Conscious Rap* (Brooklyn: PC International Press, 1991), 243.

26. Decker, "The State of Rap," 68.

27. Rose, *Black Noise*, 149–50.

28. dream hampton, "Confessions of a Hip-Hop Critic," in *Step into a World: A Global Anthology of the New Black Literature*, ed. Kevin Powell (New York: Wiley, 2000), 107.

29. For further discussion on female rappers' discomfort with the term "feminist," see Tricia Rose, "Never Trust a Big Butt and a Smile," *Camera Obscura* 23 (1991): 109–31; and "Bad Sistas: Black Women Rappers and Sexual Politics in Rap Music," in *Black Noise*, 146–82.

30. See Barbara Smith, "Some Home Truths on the Contemporary Black Feminist Movement," in *Words of Fire: An Anthology of African-American Feminist Thought*, ed. Beverly Guy-Sheftall (New York: New Press, 1995), 254–67.

31. Nelson George, *Hip Hop America* (New York: Viking Penguin, 1998), 186.

32. For a discussion of how these heterosexual male anxieties are manifest in gangsta rap lyrics, see Robin Kelley, "'Pimpin' Ain't Easy': Women in the Male Gangsta Imagination," in *Race Rebels*, 214–23.

33. House Subcommittee on Commerce, Consumer Protection, and Competitiveness of the Committee on Energy and Commerce, *Music Lyrics and Commerce*, 103rd Cong., 2nd sess., 11 February 1994, 145.

34. Barbara Smith, "Some Home Truths on the Contemporary Black Feminist Movement," in *Words of Fire*, 255. Smith identified "The Black Woman Is Already Liberated" as "Myth No. 1" in this essay highlighting five major fallacies that curb the advancement of feminist thought and politics in black communities.

35. Neal, "The Black Arts Movement," in *Visions*, 76.

36. The objective of both organizations is to promote and sustain households based on the nuclear family (read: heteronormative) model. Stephney created Families Organized for Liberty and Action (FOLA) in an effort to restore "strong, healthy families in urban communities." The National Fatherhood Initiative, founded in 1994, is a multiracial, gender-inclusive organization committed to reversing what members perceive to be the "most disturbing social trend of our times": the growing number of children growing up without fathers in the United States. According to their official website, the National Fatherhood Initiative's objective is to inspire "a broad-based social movement to restore responsible fatherhood as a national priority." Available at http://www.fatherhood.org/default.asp.

37. Bill Stephney, interview by author, tape recording, New York, NY, 18 January 2002.

38. Powell, interview.

39. George, *Hip Hop America*, 187.

40. Powell, "Confessions," 75.

41. Rose, "Never Trust a Big Butt and a Smile," 115.

42. Stephney, interview.

43. Rose, *Black Noise*, 151.

44. Benj DeMott, "The Future Is Unwritten: Working-Class Youth Cultures in England and America," *Critical Texts*, 1 May 1988, 45.

45. Boogie Down Productions, "Say Gal," *Sex and Violence* (Zomba Recording Corporation, 1992).

46. Mutulu Olugbala, interview by author, tape recording, Brooklyn, NY, 16 January 2002.

47. Chuck D, telephone interview by author, 27 January 2002.

48. Powell, "Confessions," 77.

49. Decker, "The State of Rap," 71.

50. Eure and Spady, *Nation Conscious Rap*, 252.

51. Brand Nubian, "Pass the Gat," *In God We Trust* (Elektra Entertainment, 1992).

52. Farai Chideya, "Homophobia: Hip-Hop's Black Eye," in *Step into a World: A Global Anthology of the New Black Literature*, ed. Kevin Powell (New York: Wiley, 2000), 97.

53. Ice Cube, "No Vaseline," *Death Certificate* (Priority Records, 1991).

54. Grandmaster Flash and the Furious Five, "The Message."

55. Cheryl Clarke, "The Failure to Transform: Homophobia in the Black Community," in *Home Girls: A Black Feminist Anthology*, ed. Barbara Smith (New York: Kitchen Table: Woman of Color Press, 1983), 198–99.

56. Richard Harrington, "Public Enemy's Assault on the Airwaves," *Washington Post*, Sunday, 31 July 1988, Sunday Show section, G1.

57. X-Clan, "Holy Rum Swig," *Xodus* (Polygram Records, 1992).

58. Chuck D and Yusef Jah, *Fight the Power*, 9.

59. Chideya, "Homophobia," 97.

60. Ice Cube, "No Vaseline," *Death Certificate*.

61. Ibid.

62. Ibid.

63. Ice Cube, "The Predator," *The Predator* (Priority Records, 1992).

64. Michele Wallace, *Black Macho and the Myth of the Superwoman* (New York: Dial Press, 1978), 68.

65. Ice Cube, "Horny Li'l Devil," *Death Certificate*.

66. bell hooks, *Outlaw Culture: Resisting Representations* (New York: Routledge, 1994), 110.

67. In "Rappin' Black" Wise Intelligent compared his privileged position as a member of the Five Percent Nation to that of white men, whom he determined lacked the supreme wisdom, knowledge, and understanding of the Five Percent. For Wise Intelligent this spiritual ignorance marked white males as less than men—as "faggots." Poor Righteous Teachers, "Rappin' Black," *Pure Poverty* (Profile Records, 1991).

68. In their lyrics, X-Clan commonly referred to white men as "sissies" and "punks." For example, in "Grand Verbalizer, What Time Is It?" Brother J condemns what he perceives to be white men's covetous reign of power ("The damn sissies always stalk for the glory") and then issues a warning: "Sissy bomb is comin', but that's another story." X-Clan, "Grand Verbalizer, What Time Is It?" *To the East, Blackwards* (Island Records, 1990).

69. On his 1995 release *Made in America*, Nation of Islam–influenced artist Kam discussed gang tensions in South Central and suggested that instead of committing black-on-black violence, gang members should turn to the [white] instigator, "Yakub's cavey / the blue-eyed punk / playin' both sides against each

other." Kam, "Keep tha Peace," *Made in America* (Atlanta Recording Corporation, 1995).

70. Ice Cube, "Who Got the Camera," *The Predator.* The members of the Los Angeles Police Department (which has a decades-long record of responding with brutality against blacks and Latinos) were characterized as "faggots" with guns and badges by Ice Cube in "We Had to Tear This _____ Up" and in "Who Got the Camera," both produced after the 1992 Los Angeles rebellion.

71. Ice Cube, "Horny Li'l Devil," *Death Certificate.*

72. Ibid. Yo-Yo is a female rapper who, at the time, was affiliated with Ice Cube. He appeared on her first single entitled "You Can't Play with My Yo-Yo."

73. Michael Eric Dyson, *Making Malcolm: The Myth and Meaning of Malcolm X* (New York: Oxford University Press, 1995), 94.

74. Michael Eric Dyson, *Between God and Gangsta Rap: Bearing Witness to Black Culture* (New York: Oxford University Press, 1996), 186.

NOTES TO CHAPTER FIVE

1. Digable Planets, "Dial 7 (Axioms of Creamy Spies)," *Blowout Comb* (Pendulum Records, 1994).

2. James Bernard, "Rap Panther," *Mother Jones*, May/June 1991, 9.

3. Paris, "Brutal," *The Devil Made Me Do It* (Tommy Boy, 1991).

4. Joseph Eure and James G. Spady, eds., *Nation Conscious Rap* (Brooklyn, NY: PC International Press, 1991), 359.

5. Ibid., 311.

6. R. W. Connell, *Masculinities* (Berkeley: University of California Press, 1995), 214.

7. For more on Islamic religious beliefs and rap music, see Juan M. Floyd-Thomas, "A Jihad of Words: The Evolution of African American Islam and Contemporary Hip-Hop," in *Noise and Spirit: The Religious and Spiritual Sensibilities of Rap Music*, ed. Anthony B. Pinn (New York: New York University Press, 2003), 49–70.

8. Erich Auerbach, *Mimesis: The Representation of Reality in Western Literature*, trans. William R. Trask (Princeton, NJ: Princeton University Press, 1953), 14–15.

9. Theophus H. Smith, *Conjuring Culture: Biblical Formations of Black America* (New York: Oxford University Press, 1994), 58.

10. Wise Intelligent, telephone interview by author, 28 January 2002.

11. Clyde Halisi and James Mtume, eds., *The Quotable Karenga* (Los Angeles: US Organization, 1967), 28.

12. James Cone, *Black Theology and Black Power* (New York: Seabury Press, 1969), 33.

13. Boogie Down Productions, "The Real Holy Place," *Sex and Violence* (Zomba Recording Corporation, 1992). Ten years later, KRS-One changed his tune with the release of *Spiritual Minded*, on which he proclaims to be a born again "Christ-ian." For KRS-One, that meant more than just reading the Bible and attending church. To be a "Christ-ian" is to live Christlike with "Christ consciousness," he proclaims, for "He's the way, the truth AND the light / J to the E to the S to the U to the S." KRS-One, "Ain't Ready" and "Tears," *Spiritual Minded* (Koch Records, 2002). For more on KRS-One's spiritual transformation, see KRS-One, *Ruminations* (New York: Welcome Rain Publishers, 2003).

14. Claude Andrew Clegg, III, *An Original Man: The Life and Times of Elijah Muhammad* (New York: St. Martin's Press, 1997), 9.

15. Elijah Muhammad, *Supreme Wisdom: Solution to the So-Called Negroes' Problems* (Chicago: Muhammad Mosque of Islam No. 2, 1957), 28.

16. Elijah Muhammad, *Message to the Blackman in America* (Chicago: Muhammad's Temple No. 2, 1965), 53.

17. *Quotable Karenga*, 27.

18. Like many social scientists, ministers in the Nation of Islam and their rap protégés were negligent in their simplified designation of the "black church," a term used to refer to mainstream churches within black communities, in particular black Baptist and African Methodist Episcopal (A.M.E.) churches.

19. Genius/GZA, "B.I.B.L.E. (Basic Instructions Before Leaving Earth)," *Liquid Swords* (Geffen Records, 1995).

20. Public Enemy, "Rightstarter (Message to a Blackman)," *Yo! Bum Rush the Show* (Def Jam, 1987).

21. Ice Cube, "When I Get to Heaven," *Lethal Injection* (Priority Records, 1993).

22. According to historian Claude Andrew Clegg, III, Elijah Muhammad was a self-proclaimed millionaire who—while married—fathered thirteen children out of wedlock with seven women who, at one point or another, had been his personal secretaries.

23. Ice Cube, "When I Get to Heaven."

24. James H. Cone, *Martin and Malcolm and America: A Dream or a Nightmare* (Maryknoll, NY: Orbis Books, 1991), 151.

25. Grand Puba, "Soul Controller," *Reel to Reel* (Elektra Entertainment, 1992).

26. Arrested Development, "Fishin' 4 Religion," *3 Years, 5 Months and 2 Days in the Life of . . .* (Chrysalis Records, 1992).

27. Vivien Goldman, "Black Noise, Black Heat," *Spin*, November 1992, 48 and 123.

28. Audre Lorde, "Age, Race, Class, and Sex: Women Redefining Difference," in *Out There: Marginalization and Contemporary Cultures*, ed. Russell

Ferguson, Martha Gever, Trinh T. Minh-ha, and Cornel West (New York: New Museum of Contemporary Art, 1990), 287.

29. Brand Nubian, "Ain't No Mystery," *In God We Trust* (Elektra Entertainment, 1992).

30. Poor Righteous Teachers, "Each One Teach One," *Pure Poverty* (Profile Records, 1991).

31. Brand Nubian, "Meaning of the 5%," *In God We Trust.*

32. Ice Cube, "When I Get to Heaven."

33. Larry Neal, "My Lord, He Calls Me by the Thunder," in *Visions of a Liberated Future: Black Arts Movement Writings*, ed. Larry Neal and Michael Schwartz (New York: Thunder's Mouth Press, 1989), 119.

34. KRS-One, "Higher Level," *Return of the Boom Bap* (Zomba Recording Corporation, 1993).

35. Gayraud Wilmore, *Black Religion and Black Radicalism* (Garden City, NY: Anchor Press/Doubleday, 1973), 14.

36. Sterling Stuckey, *Going through the Storm: The Influence of African-American Art in History* (New York: Oxford University Press, 1994), 90.

37. Lawrence Levine, *Black Culture and Black Consciousness: Afro-American Folk Thought from Slavery to Freedom* (New York: Oxford University Press, 1977), 44.

38. Sterling Stuckey, *Slave Culture: Nationalist Theory and the Foundations of Black America* (New York: Oxford University Press, 1987), 35.

39. Stuckey, *Going Through the Storm*, 12.

40. C. L. R. James, *The Black Jacobins: Toussaint L'Ouverture and the San Domingo Revolution* (New York: Vintage Books, 1963), 87.

41. Howard Thurman, *Deep River* (New York: Harpers, 1945), 36.

42. The identity politicking of raptivists did not end at claiming an affinity with the race of Jesus. Some claimed his class identity as well. For example, Wise Intelligent in "Rappin' Black" identifies with the Son of God because he is "from poor family, just like Jesus." Poor Righteous Teachers, "Rappin' Black," *Pure Poverty*.

43. Boogie Down Productions, "The Eye Opener," *Live Hardcore Worldwide* (BMG Music, 1991).

44. Last Poets, "Opposites," *This Is Madness* (Metrotone Records, 1971).

45. Wu-Tang Clan, "C.R.E.A.M.," *Enter the Wu-Tang 36 Chambers* (BMG Music, 1993).

46. Eure and Spady, *Nation Conscious Rap*, 60.

47. *Quotable Karenga*, 13.

48. David Walker, *Appeal to the Colored Citizens of the World, but in Particular, and Very Expressly, to Those of the United States of America* (New York: Hill and Wang, 1985), 17.

49. Poor Righteous Teachers, "Freedom or Death," *Pure Poverty*.

50. Mattias Gardell, *In the Name of Elijah Muhammad: Louis Farrakhan and the Nation of Islam* (Durham, NC: Duke University Press, 1996), 151. As Farrakhan's reign as the leader of the Nation of Islam progressed, his position on "the devil" became a little less condemning. The above quote concludes by suggesting the potential for change in white behavior: "It is not the color of the white man that is the problem, it is the mind of the white man that is the problem. The mind of white supremacy has to be destroyed."

51. Ibid., 147.

52. Kam, "Keep tha Peace," *Made in America* (Atlanta Recording Corporation, 1995).

53. Brand Nubian, "Drop the Bomb," *One for All* (Elektra Entertainment, 1990).

54. Both the Nation of Islam and the Five Percent Nation of Islam assert that all black men are gods, but in the Nation of Islam there is a hierarchy among deities. Master Fard Muhammad is believed to be the manifestation of Allah in person, biblical figures like Moses and Jesus are considered "gods," and all Muslims exist as a "nation of gods." Gender further stratifies the classifications of Black Muslims. In the Five Percent Nation male members are considered "gods" and female members are regarded as "Earths," a moniker that refers to their reproductive capabilities, or as Nelson George writes, women are "the soil for their nation's growth." Nelson George, *Buppies, B-Boys, Baps, and Bohos: Notes on a Post-Soul Black Culture* (New York: HarperPerennial, 1994), 247.

55. KRS-One, "Ah Yeah," *Pump Ya Fist: Hip Hop Inspired by the Black Panthers* (Polygram Records, 1995).

56. Grand Puba, "Soul Controller," *Reel to Reel* (Elektra Entertainment, 1992).

57. Smith, *Conjuring Culture*, 147.

58. Wilson Jeremiah Moses, *The Golden Age of Black Nationalism, 1850–1925* (Hamden, CT: Archon Books, 1978), 160–61.

59. Levine, *Black Culture and Black Consciousness*, 33.

60. James H. Cone, *Spirituals and the Blues: An Interpretation* (New York: Seabury Press, 1972), 35.

61. Levine, *Black Culture and Black Consciousness*, 50–51.

62. Smith, *Conjuring Culture*, 59.

63. Ibid., 62.

64. Gardell, *In the Name of Elijah Muhammad*, 144.

65. Bishop Henry M. Turner, "God Is a Negro," in *Black Nationalism in America*, ed. John H. Bracey, Jr., August Meier, and Elliot Rudwick (New York: Bobbs-Merrill, 1970), 154.

66. Historian Wilson Jeremiah Moses defines "Egyptocentrism" as the "sometimes sentimental, at other times cynical, attempt . . . to reconstruct the

peoples of ancient Egypt in terms of traditional American racial perceptions." Wilson Jeremiah Moses, *Afrotopia: The Roots of African American Popular History* (New York: Cambridge University Press, 1998), 6.

67. Albert B. Cleage, Jr., *The Black Messiah* (New York: Sheed and Ward, 1968), 43.

68. For more on the origin of the association between the curse of Ham and "blackness" in Christian thought, see Stephen R. Haynes, *Noah's Curse: The Biblical Justification of American Slavery* (New York: Oxford University Press, 2002).

69. It is interesting to note KRS-One's anti-essentialism as he points to black fallibility—to the imperfect nature of humanity—even among Africans ("In this era black Egyptians weren't right / they enslaved black Israelites"). This possibility is often lost in most black nationalist assertions of black moral superiority.

70. Boogie Down Productions, "Why Is That?" *Ghetto Music: The Blueprint of Hip Hop* (RCA Records, 1989).

71. Eure and Spady, *Nation Conscious Rap*, 74.

72. The term "jeremiads" is derived from the Old Testament prophet and doomsayer Jeremiah. For more on the black jeremiad tradition, see David Howard-Pitney, *The Afro-American Jeremiad: Appeals for Justice in America* (Philadelphia: Temple University Press, 1993).

73. Smith, *Conjuring Culture*, 224.

74. Genius/GZA, "B.I.B.L.E. (Basic Instructions Before Leaving Earth)."

75. Levine, *Black Culture and Black Consciousness*, 34.

76. V. P. Franklin, *Black Self-Determination: A Cultural History of African-American Resistance* (Brooklyn: Lawrence Hill Books, 1992), 60.

77. Sterling Stuckey, ed., *Ideological Origins of Black Nationalism* (Boston: Beacon Press, 1972), 170.

78. Walker, *Appeal*, 15.

79. Ice Cube, "When I Get to Heaven."

80. Poor Righteous Teachers, "Each One Teach One."

81. Public Enemy, "Can't Truss It," *Apocalypse 91 . . . The Enemy Strikes Back* (Sony Music Entertainment, 1991).

82. Smith, *Conjuring Culture*, 123.

83. Ice Cube, "When Will They Shoot," *The Predator* (Priority Records, 1992).

84. Public Enemy, "Revolutionary Generation," *Fear of a Black Planet* (Def Jam, 1990).

85. Russell A. Potter, *Spectacular Vernaculars: Hip-Hop and the Politics of Postmodernism* (Albany: State University of New York Press, 1995), 108.

86. Kam, "Intro," *Made in America*.

87. Eure and Spady, *Nation Conscious Rap*, 345.

88. Goldman, "Black Noise," 123.

89. Ice Cube, *Death Certificate*. By various accounts, it appears that Ice Cube flirted with the idea of becoming a member of the Nation of Islam but was advised that he could reach a wider audience if he remained a nonmember. It is clear that Ice Cube was mentored by high-ranking members of the Nation of Islam, from Farrakhan to former N.O.I. spokesman Khallid Abdul Muhammad. For example, in an interview with writer David L. Shabazz, Muhammad recounted a conversation during which he encouraged Ice Cube to maintain a delicate stylistic balance in his lyrics. By his account, Muhammad told Ice Cube to "[k]eep his basic style and appeal" to maintain his black fan base. However, he also advised Ice Cube to "drop some science, drop some light, drop some supreme wisdom" to "attract [Black audiences] like bait" and "give them the knowledge, wisdom and understanding that we need to be elevated as a people." David L. Shabazz, *Public Enemy Number One: A Research Study of Rap Music, Culture, and Black Nationalism in America* (Clinton, SC: Awesome Records, 1999), 119–20.

90. Sister Souljah, "The Hate That Hate Produced," *360 Degrees of Power* (Sony Music Entertainment, 1992).

91. E. U. Essien-Udom, *Black Nationalism: A Search for Identity in Black America* (Chicago: University of Chicago Press, 1962), 55.

92. David Mills, "Reality in a New Rapping; Arrested Development, Drawing Raves with a Message of Maturity," *Washington Post*, Sunday, 19 July 1992, Sunday show section.

93. Neal, "My Lord, He Calls Me by the Thunder," 124.

94. Cleage, *Black Messiah*, 36.

95. Ibid., 37.

NOTES TO CHAPTER SIX

1. "On Line with Boots from The Coup: Political Activism within Hip Hop," *Davey D's Hip Hop Corner*, 6 June 1996, http://www.daveyd.com/bootstrans.html.

2. Adam Krims, *Rap Music and the Poetics of Identity* (New York: Cambridge University Press, 2000), 1.

3. Justin Driver, "The Mirth of a Nation: Black Comedy's Reactionary Hipness," *The New Republic*, 11 June 2001, 32.

4. Kevin Powell, interview by author, tape recording, Brooklyn, NY, 12 November 2001.

5. Chuck D, telephone interview by author, 27 January 2002.

6. Andrew Ross, "The Gangsta and the Diva," in *Black Male: Representations of Masculinity in Contemporary American Art*, ed. Thelma Golden (New York: Whitney Museum of American Art: Distributed by Harry N. Abrams, 1994), 163.

7. Bill Stephney, interview by author, tape recording, New York, NY, 18 January 2002.

8. Nathan Rabin, "The Coup," *The Onion*, 18 February 1999. Available from the archives at http://www.theavclub.com.

9. Adolph Reed, Jr., "Posing as Politics," *Village Voice*, 5 December 1995, 20.

10. David Jakubiak, "Conference Explores Rhymes and Reasons of Hip-Hop," *Chicago Sun-Times*, 2 October 2003.

11. Jacqueline Ostrowski, "Serious Beats," *Centerstage Chicago* (October 2003); available from http://centerstage.net/music/articles/Featured_HipHop.html.

12. The Malcolm X Grassroots Movement is a black nationalist group committed to six "principles of unity," organizing points that include the issues of human rights, reparations, self-determination, an end to genocide, political imprisonment, and sexism. For more, see www.malcolmxgrassroots.com.

13. Baye Adofo, interview by author, tape recording, Newark, NJ, 17 January 2002.

14. David Jakubiak, "Hip-Hop and Social Change Conference: Rappers, Artists, Scholars Debate the Politics of Hip-hop," *Chicago Sun-Times*, 8 October 2003.

15. Greg Braxton, "The Voices of Rap—Politics or Just Music?" *Los Angeles Times*, Sunday, 19 July 1992, Calendar section.

16. Stephney, interview.

17. Roger Catlin, "KRS-One Likes to Do More Rapping Than Talking about Racial Problems," *Hartford Courant*, 12 June 1992.

18. Chuck D and Yusef Jah, *Fight the Power: Rap, Race, and Reality* (New York: Delacorte Press, 1997), 177.

19. James T. Jones IV, "The Message from the Streets: Rappers Find Themselves Role Models," *USA Today*, 11 May 1992.

20. Alan Light, "Wisdom from the Street," *Rolling Stone*, 30 May 1991, 42.

21. Michael Small, *Break It Down: The Inside Story from the New Leaders of Rap* (Secaucus, NJ: Carol Publishing, 1992), 81.

22. Chuck D and Yusef Jah, *Fight the Power*, 180.

23. Jeff Chang, "'Stakes Is High': Conscious Rap, Neosoul, and the Hip-Hop Generation," *The Nation*, 13/20 January 2003, 17.

24. David L. Shabazz, *Public Enemy Number One: A Research Study of Rap Music, Culture, and Black Nationalism in America* (Clinton, SC: Awesome Records, 1999), 43.

25. See Todd Boyd, "Who We Be: Introducin' the New H.N.I.C.," introduction in *The New H.N.I.C.: The Death of Civil Rights and the Reign of HipHop* (New York: New York University Press, 2002).

26. Mary A. Johnson, "Arrested Development Gives Pep Talk to Inner-City Kids," *Chicago Sun-Times*, 5 July 1993, Late Sports Final. Taree acknowledged

that there were ways her group could take care of business and demonstrate their commitment to social justice: "[I]n each community we go to there are successful organizations, and we come to support them."

27. Rosa Clemente, telephone interview by author, 9 January 2002.

28. Mutulu Olugbala, interview by author, tape recording, Brooklyn, NY, 16 January 2002. The International People's Democratic Uhuru Movement, an offshoot of the Black Panther–influenced Afrikan People's Socialist Party, is a nationalist organization committed to gaining democratic rights for and self-determination in black communities. For more information, see www.inpdum.com.

29. Chuck D, interview.

30. Richard Harrington, "Public Enemy's Assault on the Airwaves," *Washington Post*, Sunday, 31 July 1988, Sunday Show section, G1.

31. Nelson George, *Hip Hop America* (New York: Viking Penguin, 1998), 154.

32. Powell, interview.

33. Clemente, interview.

34. Toni Blackman made this remark on 3 October 2003 during the "Political Present" panel at the Field Museum's Hip Hop and Social Change conference. Blackman was named "U.S. Hip Hop Ambassador" by the U.S. Department of State, in part because of her work as the founder and executive director of the Freestyle Union, a hip-hop organization that focuses on artist development to promote collective responsibility and community service among urban youth.

35. M-1 made this statement on 3 October 2003 during the "Political Present" panel at the Field Museum's Hip Hop and Social Change conference.

36. Ras Baraka, telephone interview by author, 10 January 2002.

37. Powell, interview.

38. Adofo, interview.

39. Ibid.

40. Powell, interview.

41. Adofo, interview.

42. Baraka, interview.

43. Fred Hampton, Jr., interview by author, tape recording, Chicago, IL, 3 October 2003.

44. Talib Kweli, interview by author, tape recording, Brooklyn, NY, 16 January 2002.

45. In the early 1980s Nehanda Abiodun was charged with violating the RICO Conspiracy Act for her alleged involvement in the escape of former Black Liberation Army member Assata Shakur.

46. Adofo, interview.

47. Kweli, interview.

48. Adofo, interview.

49. Kweli, interview.

50. Adofo, interview.

51. Ibid.

52. Baraka, interview.

53. Stephney, interview.

54. Chang, "'Stakes Is High,'" 20.

55. George Lipsitz, *Dangerous Crossroads* (New York: Verso, 1994), 137.

56. Ibid., 33.

57. Nathan Rabin, "KRS-One," *The Onion*, 25 April 2001. Available from the archives at http://www.theonionavclub.com.

58. Clarence Lusane, "Rap, Race, and Politics" *Race and Class* (Great Britain) 35, 1 (1993): 54.

59. Toni Blackman, Hip Hop and Social Change conference.

60. Clemente, interview.

61. See Charles Payne, "'Men Led, but Women Organized': Movement Participation of Women in the Mississippi Delta," in *Women in the Civil Rights Movement: Trailblazers and Torchbearers, 1941–1965*, ed. Vicki L. Crawford, Jacqueline Anne Rouse, and Barbara Woods (Bloomington: Indiana University Press, 1990), 1–12.

62. Baraka, interview.

63. Clemente, interview.

64. Kevin Powell, "The New Nationalists," *Essence*, December 1991, 104.

65. Clemente, interview.

66. "Hip-Hop Ambassador: Meet Toni Blackman"; available from http://www.echoinggreen.org/index.cfm?fuseaction=Page.viewPage&pageId=10 5.

67. For more on Sista II Sista, see http://www.sistaiisista.org/.

68. Hazel Carby, *Race Men* (Cambridge, MA: Harvard University Press, 1998), 5.

69. Ibid., 10.

70. Anne McClintock, "'No Longer in a Future Heaven': Gender, Race and Nationalism," in *Dangerous Liaisons: Gender, Nation, and Postcolonial Perspectives*, ed. Anne McClintock, Aamir Mufti, and Ella Shohat (Minneapolis: University of Minnesota Press, 1997), 89.

71. The feud between these two groups, which, according to the source referenced, began either because of ideological differences or because of recruitment from rival gangs, turned fatal on January 17, 1969. On that date two Panthers, John Huggins and Alprentice "Bunchy" Carter, were shot to death by US members at a UCLA Black Student Union meeting. The war of words that ensued was riddled with gendered and sexual language—in fact, this conflict was one of the reasons Black Panther leaders were forced to, at least publicly, address issues of sexism and the sexual division of labor within their organization. After making public statements against the US Organization's "male chauvinism," leaders like

Fred Hampton and Bobby Seale could not continue to condone such behavior within their own ranks. For more on the conflict between the Black Panther Party and the US Organization, see Scot Brown, *Fighting for US: Maulana Karenga, the US Organization, and Black Cultural Nationalism* (New York: New York University Press, 2003).

72. bell hooks, *Outlaw Culture: Resisting Representations* (New York: Routledge, 1994), 109–13.

73. Toni Cade Bambara, "On the Issue of Roles," in *The Black Woman: An Anthology*, ed. Toni Cade Bambara (New York: Penguin Books USA, 1970), 103.

74. Dean E. Robinson, *Black Nationalism in American Politics and Thought* (New York: Cambridge University Press, 2001), 134.

75. Sarah Jones's "Your Revolution" appears on DJ Vadim's *U.S.S.R.: Life from the Other Side* (Montreal: Ninja Tune, 1999).

Selected Bibliography

Books and Articles

Anderson, Benedict. *Imagined Communities: Reflections on the Origin and Spread of Nationalism*. Thetford, Norfolk: Thetford Press, 1983.

Bambara, Toni Cade. *The Black Woman: An Anthology*. New York: Penguin Books USA, 1970.

Baraka, Imamu Amiri. *Raise, Race, Rays, Raze: Essays since 1965*. New York: Random House, 1971.

———. *Selected Poetry of Amiri Baraka/LeRoi Jones*. New York: Morrow, 1979.

———. *The Autobiography of LeRoi Jones/Amiri Baraka*. New York: Freundlich Books, 1984.

Bederman, Gail. *Manliness and Civilization: A Cultural History of Gender and Race in the United States, 1880–1917*. Chicago: University of Chicago Press, 1995.

Boyd, Todd. *The New H.N.I.C.: The Death of Civil Rights and the Reign of HipHop*. New York: New York University Press, 2002.

Bracey, John H., Jr., August Meier, and Elliot Rudwick, eds. *Black Nationalism in America*. New York: Bobbs-Merrill, 1970.

Breitman, George, ed. *Malcolm X Speaks: Selected Speeches and Statements*. New York: Grove, 1965.

Brown, Elaine. *A Taste of Power: A Black Woman's Story*. New York: Pantheon Books, 1992.

Brown, H. Rap. *Die Nigger Die*. New York: Dial Press, 1969.

Bush, Rod. *We Are Not What We Seem: Black Nationalism and Class Struggle in the American Century*. New York: New York University Press, 1999.

Carby, Hazel. *Race Men*. Cambridge, MA: Harvard University Press, 1998.

Chang, Jeff. "'Stakes Is High': Conscious Rap, Neosoul, and the Hip-Hop Generation." *Nation*, 13/20 January 2003, 17–21.

Cleage, Albert B., Jr. *The Black Messiah*. New York: Sheed and Ward, 1968.

Cleaver, Eldridge. *Soul on Ice*. New York: Dell, 1968.

Clegg, Claude Andrew III. *An Original Man: The Life and Times of Elijah Muhammad*. New York: St. Martin's Press, 1997.

Cone, James H. *Black Theology and Black Power*. New York: Seabury Press, 1969.

———. *Spirituals and the Blues: An Interpretation*. New York: Seabury Press, 1972.

Connell, R. W. *Masculinities*. Berkeley: University of California Press, 1995.

Cooper, Anna Julia. *A Voice from the South*. New York: Oxford University Press, 1988.

Crummell, Alexander. *Destiny and Race: Selected Writings, 1840–1898*. Wilson Jeremiah Moses, ed. Amherst: University of Massachusetts Press, 1992.

Cube, Ice, and Angela Y. Davis. "Nappy Happy." *Transition*, no. 6 (1992): 174–92.

D, Chuck, and Yusef Jah. *Fight the Power: Rap, Race, and Reality*. New York: Delacorte Press, 1997.

Decker, Jeffrey Louis. "The State of Rap: Time and Place in Hip Hop Nationalism." *Social Texts* 60 (Spring 1993): 53–84.

DeMott, Benj. "The Future Is Unwritten: Working-Class Youth Cultures in England and America." *Critical Texts*, 1 May 1988, 42–56.

Dent, Gina, ed. *Black Popular Culture*. Seattle, WA: Bay Press, 1992.

Draper, Theodore. *The Rediscovery of Black Nationalism*. New York: Viking Press, 1969.

Dyson, Michael Eric. *Making Malcolm: The Myth and Meaning of Malcolm X*. New York: Oxford University Press, 1995.

———. *Between God and Gangsta Rap: Bearing Witness to Black Culture*. New York: Oxford University Press, 1996.

Essien-Udom, E. U. *Black Nationalism: A Search for Identity in Black America*. Chicago: University of Chicago Press, 1962.

Eure, Joseph, and James G. Spady, eds. *Nation Conscious Rap*. Brooklyn, NY: PC International Press, 1991.

Flowers, Sandra Hollin. *African American Nationalist Literature of the 1960s: Pens of Fire*. New York: Garland, 1996.

Foner, Philip S. *The Black Panthers Speak*. Philadelphia: Lippincott, 1970.

Franklin, V. P. *Living Our Stories, Telling Our Truths: Autobiography and the Making of the African-American Intellectual Tradition*. New York: Scribners, 1995.

Gardell, Mattias. *In the Name of Elijah Muhammad: Louis Farrakhan and the Nation of Islam*. Durham, NC: Duke University Press, 1996.

Genovese, Eugene D. "The Legacy of Slavery and the Roots of Black Nationalism." In *For a New America: Essays in History and Politics from Studies on the Left, 1959–1967*, James Weinstein and David W. Eakins, eds., 394–420. New York: Random House, 1970.

George, Nelson. *Buppies, B-Boys, Baps, and Bohos: Notes on a Post-Soul Black Culture*. New York: HarperPerennial, 1994.

————. *Hip Hop America*. New York: Viking Penguin, 1998.

Gilroy, Paul. *The Black Atlantic: Modernity and Double Consciousness*. Cambridge, MA: Harvard University Press, 1993.

Giovanni, Nikki. *Black Feeling/Black Talk/Black Judgment*. New York: Morrow Quill Paperbacks, 1979.

Glaude, Eddie S., Jr., ed. *Is It Nation Time? Contemporary Essays on Black Power and Black Nationalism*. Chicago: University of Chicago Press, 2002.

Golden, Thelma, ed. *Black Male: Representations of Masculinity in Contemporary American Art*. New York: Whitney Museum of American Art: Distributed by Harry N. Abrams, 1994.

Guy-Sheftall, Beverly, ed. *Words of Fire: An Anthology of African-American Feminist Thought*. New York: New Press, 1995.

Halisi, Clyde, and James Mtume, eds. *The Quotable Karenga*. Los Angeles: US Organization, 1967.

Harper, Phillip Brian. *"Are We Not Men": Masculine Anxiety and the Problem of African-American Identity*. New York: Oxford University Press, 1996.

Hebdige, Dick. *Subculture: The Meaning of Style*. London: Methuen, 1982.

Heim, Chris. "Boogie Down Productions' Rap Is Educational." *Chicago Tribune*, 28 September 1990.

hooks, bell. *Ain't I a Woman: Black Women and Feminism*. Boston: South End Press, 1981.

————. *Outlaw Culture: Resisting Representations*. New York: Routledge, 1994.

"In Defense of Self-Defense: An Exclusive Interview with Minister of Defense, Huey P. Newton." *Black Panther*, 16 March 1968.

Jones, LeRoi. *Blues People: The Negro Experience in White America and the Music That Developed from It*. New York: Morrow Quill Paperbacks, 1963.

————. *Home: Social Essays*. New York: Morrow, 1966.

Jones, LeRoi, and Larry Neal, eds. *Black Fire: An Anthology of Afro-American Writing*. New York: Morrow, 1968.

Kelley, Robin D. G. *Race Rebels: Culture, Politics, and the Black Working Class*. New York: Free Press, 1994.

Krims, Adam. *Rap Music and the Poetics of Identity*. New York: Cambridge University Press, 2000.

Lester, Julius. *Look Out, Whitey! Black Power's Gon' Get Your Mamma*. New York: Dial Press, 1968.

Levine, Lawrence. *Black Culture and Black Consciousness: Afro-American Folk Thought from Slavery to Freedom*. New York: Oxford University Press, 1977.

Lipsitz, George. *Dangerous Crossroads*. New York: Verso, 1994.

Lubiano, Wahneema, ed. *The House That Race Built: Black Americans, U.S. Terrain*. New York: Pantheon Books, 1997.

Lusane, Clarence. "Rap, Race, and Politics." *Race and Class* (Great Britain) 35, no. 1 (1993): 41–56.

McClintock, Anne, Aamir Mufti, and Ella Shohat. *Dangerous Liaisons: Gender, Nation, and Postcolonial Perspectives*. Minneapolis: University of Minnesota Press, 1997.

Mercer, Kobena. "Fear of a Black Penis." *Artforum International* 32, no. 8 (April 1994): 80–81, 122.

Moses, Wilson Jeremiah. *The Golden Age of Black Nationalism, 1850–1925*. Hamden, CT: Archon Books, 1978.

———. *Afrotopia: The Roots of African American Popular History*. New York: Cambridge University Press, 1998.

———, ed. *Classical Black Nationalism: From the American Revolution to Marcus Garvey*. New York: New York University Press, 1996.

Muhammad, Elijah. *Message to the Blackman in America*. Chicago: Muhammad's Temple No. 2, 1965.

Mumininas of Committee for Unified NewArk. *Mwanamke Mwananchi (The Nationalist Woman)*. Newark, NJ: Jihad Productions, 1971.

Neal, Larry, and Michael Schwartz, eds. *Visions of a Liberated Future: Black Arts Movement Writings*. New York: Thunder's Mouth Press, 1989.

Newton, Huey P. *To Die for the People: The Writings of Huey P. Newton*. New York: Random House, 1972.

Office of Policy Planning and Research, United States Department of Labor. *The Negro Family: The Case for National Action*. Washington, DC: GPO, 1965.

Perkins, William Eric, ed. *Droppin' Science: Critical Essays on Rap Music and Hip Hop Culture*. Philadelphia: Temple University Press, 1996.

Potter, Russell A. *Spectacular Vernaculars: Hip-Hop and the Politics of Postmodernism*. Albany: State University of New York Press, 1995.

Powell, Kevin. "Confessions of a Recovering Misogynist." *Ms. Magazine*, April/May 2000, 72–77.

———, ed. *Step into a World: A Global Anthology of the New Black Literature*. New York: Wiley, 2000.

Ransby, Barbara, and Tracye Matthews. "Black Popular Culture and the Transcendance of Patriarchal Illusions." *Race & Class* 35, no. 1 (July–September 1993): 57–68.

Reed, Adolph L., Jr. *Class Notes: Posing as Politics and Other Thoughts on the American Scene*. New York: New Press, 2000.

Rhodes, Jane. *Mary Ann Shadd Cary: The Black Press and Protest in the Nineteenth Century*. Bloomington: Indiana University Press, 1998.

Robinson, Dean E. *Black Nationalism in American Politics and Thought*. New York: Cambridge University Press, 2001.

Rose, Tricia. "Never Trust a Big Butt and a Smile." *Camera Obscura* 23 (1991): 109–31.

————. *Black Noise: Rap Music and Black Culture in Contemporary America.* Hanover, NH: Wesleyan University Press, 1994.

Rule, Sheila. "Generation Rap." *New York Times,* 3 April 1994.

Sales, William W., Jr. *From Civil Rights to Black Liberation: Malcolm X and the Organization of Afro-American Unity.* Boston: South End Press, 1994.

Scheer, Robert, ed. *Eldridge Cleaver: Post-Prison Writings and Speeches.* New York: Random House, 1969.

Scott, James C. *Domination and the Arts of Resistance: Hidden Transcripts.* New Haven, CT: Yale University Press, 1990.

Seale, Bobby. *Seize the Time: The Story of the Black Panther Party and Huey P. Newton.* New York: Random House, 1970.

Sexton, Adam, ed. *Rap on Rap: Straight Up Talk on Hip Hop Culture.* New York: Dell Publishing, 1995.

Small, Michael. *Break It Down: The Inside Story from the New Leaders of Rap.* Secaucus, NJ: Carol Publishing, 1992.

Smith, Barbara, ed. *Home Girls: A Black Feminist Anthology.* New York: Kitchen Table: Woman of Color Press, 1983.

Smith, Theophus H. *Conjuring Culture: Biblical Formations of Black America.* New York: Oxford University Press, 1994.

Spencer, Jon Michael, ed. *The Emergency of Black and the Emergence of Rap.* Special Issue of *Black Sacred Music: A Journal of Theomusicology* 5, no. 1 (Spring 1991).

Stuckey, Sterling. *Slave Culture: Nationalist Theory and the Foundations of Black America.* New York: Oxford University Press, 1987.

————. *Going through the Storm: The Influence of African-American Art in History.* New York: Oxford University Press, 1994.

————, ed. *The Ideological Origins of Black Nationalism.* Boston: Beacon Press, 1972.

Tate, Gregory. *Flyboy in the Buttermilk: Essays on Contemporary America.* New York: Simon & Schuster, 1992.

Ullman, Victor. *Martin R. Delany: The Beginnings of Black Nationalism.* Boston: Beacon Press, 1971.

United States House Subcommittee on Commerce, Consumer Protection, and Competitiveness of the Committee on Energy and Commerce. *Music Lyrics and Commerce.* 103rd Cong., 2nd sess., 1994.

Van Deburg, William L. *New Day in Babylon: The Black Power Movement and American Culture, 1965–1975.* Chicago: University of Chicago Press, 1992.

————. *Modern Black Nationalism: From Marcus Garvey to Louis Farrakhan.* New York: New York University Press, 1997.

Walker, David. *Appeal to the Colored Citizens of the World, but in Particular, and Very Expressly, to Those of the United States of America.* New York: Hill and Wang, 1965.

Wallace, Michele. *Black Macho and the Myth of the Superwoman*. New York: Dial Press, 1978.

West, Cornel. "On Afro-American Popular Music: From Bebop to Rap." *Sacred Music of the Secular City*. Special Issue of *Black Sacred Music: A Journal of Theomusicology* 6, no. 1 (Spring 1992): 282–94.

Wilmore, Gayraud. *Black Religion and Black Radicalism*. Garden City, NY: Anchor Press/Doubleday, 1973.

Woodard, Komozi. *A Nation within a Nation: Amiri Baraka (LeRoi Jones) and Black Power Politics*. Chapel Hill: University of North Carolina Press, 1999.

Discography

Arrested Development. *3 Years, 5 Months, and 2 Days in the Life of . . .* Chrysalis Records, 1992.

Boogie Down Productions. *By All Means Necessary*. RCA Records, 1988.

———. *Edutainment*. Jive Records, 1990.

———. *Ghetto Music: The Blueprint of Hip Hop*. RCA Records, 1989.

———. *Live Hardcore Worldwide*. BMG Music, 1991.

———. *Sex and Violence*. Zomba Recording Corporation, 1992.

Brand Nubian. *In God We Trust*. Elektra Entertainment, 1992.

———. *One for All*. Elektra Entertainment, 1990.

dead prez. *Let's Get Free*. Relativity Records, 2000.

Digable Planets. *Blowout Comb*. Pendulum Records, 1994.

Freestyle Fellowship. *Innercity Griots*. Island Records, 1993.

Genius/Gza. *Liquid Swords*. Geffen Records, 1995.

Grand Puba. *Reel to Reel*. Elektra Entertainment, 1992.

Ice Cube. *AmeriKKKa's Most Wanted*. Priority Records, 1990.

———. *Death Certificate*. Priority Records, 1991.

———. *Lethal Injection*. Priority Records, 1993.

———. *The Predator*. Priority Records, 1992.

Isis. *Rebel Soul*. 4th & B'Way Records, 1990.

Jeru the Damaja. *The Sun Rises in the East*. Payday, 1994.

Jungle Brothers. *Done by the Forces of Nature*. Warner Brothers, 1989.

Kam. *Made in America*. Atlanta Recording Corporation, 1995.

KRS-One. *KRS-One*. Jive Records, 1995.

———. *Return of the Boom Bap*. Zomba Recording Corporation, 1993.

———. *Spiritual Minded*. Koch Records, 2002.

Last Poets, The. *This Is Madness*. Metrotone Records, 1971.

Paris. *Guerrilla Funk*. Priority Records, 1994.

———. *Sleeping with the Enemy*. Scarface Records, 1992.

Poor Righteous Teachers. *Pure Poverty*. Profile Records, 1991.

Public Enemy. *Apocalypse 91 . . . The Enemy Strikes Back*. Sony Music Entertainment, 1991.

———. *Fear of a Black Planet*. Def Jam, 1990.

————. *It Takes a Nation of Millions to Hold Us Back*. CBS Records, 1988.

————. *Yo! Bum Rush the Show*. Def Jam, 1987.

Pump Ya Fist: Hip Hop Inspired by the Black Panthers. Polygram Records, 1995.

Queen Latifah. *All Hail the Queen*. Tommy Boy Music, 1989.

Sister Souljah. *360 Degrees of Power*. Sony Music Entertainment, 1992.

Wu-Tang Clan. *Enter the Wu-Tang 36 Chambers*. BMG Music, 1993.

X-Clan. *To the East, Blackwards*. Island Records, 1990.

————. *Xodus*. Polygram Records, 1992.

Index

About the Author

Charise Cheney is Associate Professor of Ethnic Studies at California Polytechnic State University.